APPOINTED

DAVID W. BUSCH

The Biblical Fall Feasts and the Return of the Lord Jesus Christ

APPOINTED

"He shall come to us as the rain,
as the latter and former rain unto the earth."
Hosea 6:3

ACW Press
Eugene, Oregon 97405

Scripture quotations are taken from the King James Version of the Bible.

Appointed
Copyright ©2003 David W. Busch
All rights reserved

Cover Design by Alpha Advertising
Interior Design by Pine Hill Graphics

Packaged by ACW Press
85334 Lorane Hwy
Eugene, Oregon 97405
www.acwpress.com
The views expressed or implied in this work do not necessarily reflect those of ACW Press.
Ultimate design, content, and editorial accuracy of this work is the responsibility of the
author(s).

Library of Congress Cataloging-in-Publication Data
(Provided by Cassidy Cataloguing Services, Inc.)

Busch, David W.

   Appointed : the Biblical fall feasts and the return of the Lord Jesus Christ /
   David W. Busch. -- 1st ed. -- Eugene, Ore. : ACW Press, 2003.

   p. ; cm.

   ISBN: 1-932124-17-9

      1. Second Advent. 2. Eschatology. 3. Jesus Christ--Apparitions and
   miracles. 4. Jesus Christ--Messiahship. 5. Fasts and feasts in the Bible.
   6. Bible--Theology. I. Title. II. Biblical fall feasts and the return of the
   Lord Jesus Christ.

BT886.3
236--dc22   0311

Printed in the United States of America.

— Acknowledgments —

I would like to take this opportunity to thank my mother and father for the strong support and help they have given me through this whole process. I would also like to thank the many brothers and sisters in Christ with whom I have fellowship, who have enthusiastically urged me on in this endeavor. Without their encouragement and provocations this book may not have come to fruition. *"That is, that I may be comforted together with you by the mutual faith both of you and me."* (Rom 1:12) Above all, I wish to give glory to the great God, and our Savior, Jesus Christ. He is the one who has brought all of these wonderful people into my life in the first place. It is by Him, and for Him, and through Him that all of this is accomplished. I give Him thanks for giving me the privilege of proclaiming His Word and I pray that this work contributes to your *"…godly edifying which is in faith."* (I Tim 1:4)

— Table of Contents —

— To the Reader —

This book is written with the advanced and serious student of Scripture in mind. It is my sincere hope that you will not only closely examine the scriptures excerpted here but that you will go to the Bible itself and study the full context of the passages, even if you may be familiar with them. I realize, however, that there will be a wide array of people who will read this book. Not everyone will be as far along the edification process as others and, indeed, some will not even be believers at all. If you are fairly familiar with the basic subjects of biblical prophecy as it relates to eschatology or end-time events, then you should have an easier time grasping what is discussed in this book, even though I suspect there may be much that you have yet to be introduced to. If you are not knowledgeable on this subject, or perhaps are completely in the dark about it, then quite obviously it may take more effort to fully digest the material.

I have tried to address this diversity of readership and anticipate where some foundational groundwork may need to be laid. Some points may seem redundant but are really crucial to understand and have a great deal of doctrinal importance. Much of Bible exposition consists of making connections, comparing spiritual things with spiritual things. Therefore, it may be necessary to reiterate certain issues in order to further understanding and comprehension where it may be lacking. Yet, there is far too much that probably needs to be said on various topics that simply can't be addressed fully in this book, as well as doctrines that the reader still feels left in the dark about and so I will apologize for that in advance.

You will also find that there is a great deal of scripture that is not only cited but quoted, and extensively at that. For that I make no apologies. "*I will worship toward thy holy temple, and praise thy name for thy lovingkindness and for **thy truth**: for thou hast **magnified** thy word **above** all thy name*" (Psalm 138:2). When you understand what God says about His name you appreciate what an awesome declaration that is. It is my endeavor to help you better understand what it is He has to say on the matter, as that is what is important, not what I might say or think. Therefore, please read these scriptures carefully. There are words that are pregnant with meaning and many concepts will be missed if verses are just glanced over. Don't make the mistake of thinking you have the basic gist of it and then move on. That has been done out of necessity too often in this work. What is included, therefore, is essential for a firm understanding of the subjects in discussion. Again, it is from *His* words that I will be putting a picture together so it is extremely important that you pay close attention to what He says.

If your objection to anything set forth in this work is based upon a different understanding of what you believe the Scriptures teach, that is fine. Actually, it is quite valid and healthy. "*These were more noble than those in Thessalonica, in that they received the word with all readiness of mind, and searched the scriptures daily, whether those things were so*" (Acts 17:11). This is my meager attempt to aid you in your study of Scripture. It is your job to trust God and not man. It is your job to put it to the test and see if it really is what God says on the matter. It is incumbent upon you to take the truths you discover in His Word and appreciate the implications they have for both your daily life and your eternal future.

The goal is that the more you know of what God has to say, the more you will know about Him and, ultimately the more you will know *Him*. That is what He seeks from you, intimacy. But it is very difficult to commune with, and put your trust in, someone of whom you know nothing, especially if you don't have an appreciation for why they are to be trusted. God does not want blind faith. He requires much more than that from you. He requires real faith that comes from knowing who He is and that He is able to perform that which He has spoken. He declares blind faith to be dangerous and deceptive as there are many powerful forces that want you to trust your future to them. He has gone out of His way to dispel the darkness and remove the blindness. He claims to be *the Truth* and He claims to prove it. "*Now faith is **the substance** of things hoped for, **the evidence** of things not seen*" (Hebrews 11:1).

If, however, your objection to what is set forth is that "better" manuscripts say, or "I prefer it to be translated as..." then that is quite another matter. When you find what you *think* was *probably* the Word of God at one time or another, let me know. In the meantime, we are about to study the Bible, God's preserved words, the Scriptures, the very words of life. I do hope that you have that most precious and holy of books in front of you right now. If not, then good luck. I am sure you will stumble upon the truth at some point.

The battle from the very beginning has been over what God has said versus the particular tactics of the deceiver. What we need are words with knowledge.

"*Now the serpent was more **subtil**...And he said unto the woman, Yea, **hath God said**, Ye shall not eat of **every** tree of the garden...And the serpent said unto the woman, Ye shall **not** surely die*" (Genesis 3:1,4).

Who will you believe?

"*Ye shall not **add** unto the word which I commanded you neither shall ye **diminish** ought from it*" (Deuteronomy 4:2).

"*What thing soever I command you, observe to do it: thou shalt not **add** thereto, nor **diminish** from it*" (Deuteronomy 12:32).

"*Oh that my words were now **written**! Oh that they were printed **in a book**! That they were engraven with an iron pen and lead in the rock **for ever***" (Job 19:23,24). That Book is still around and it's not going to disappear any time soon, though there have been those who would like to make it do just that.

"*Then the LORD answered Job out of the whirlwind, and said, Who is this that **darkeneth** counsel by **words without knowledge**?*

Gird up now thy loins like a man; for I will demand of thee, and answer thou me" (Job 38:1-3).

"Every word of God is pure: he is a shield unto them that put their trust in him. Add thou not unto his words, lest he reprove thee, and thou be found a liar" (Proverbs 30:5,6).

"Thus saith the LORD; *Stand in the court of the* LORD's *house, and speak unto all the cities of Judah, which come to worship in the* LORD's *house, all the words that I command thee to speak unto them; diminish not a word: If so be they will hearken, and turn every man from his evil way, that I may repent me of the evil, which I purpose to do unto them because of the evil of their doings"* (Jeremiah 26:2,3).

"And it came to pass, that when Jehudi had read three or four leaves, he cut it with a penknife, and cast it into the fire that was on the hearth, until all the roll was consumed in the fire that was on the hearth…Then the word of the LORD *came to Jeremiah, after that the king had burned the roll, and the words which Baruch wrote at the mouth of Jeremiah, saying, take thee again another roll, and write in it all the former words that were in the first roll, which Jehoiakim the king of Judah hath burned."* (Jeremiah 36:23,27,28)

God has never cared about "the originals." He is in the business of making copies.

"Heaven and earth shall pass away, but my words shall not pass away" (Matthew 24:35). Those words are still around. In fact, you just read them.

"And Jesus answered him, saying, It is written, That man shall not live by bread alone, but by every word that proceedeth out of the mouth of God" (Matthew 4:4).

"For the word of God is quick, and powerful, and sharper than any twoedged sword, piercing even to the dividing asunder of soul and spirit, and joints and marrow, and is a discerner of the thoughts and intents of the heart" (Hebrews 4:12).

"We have also a more sure word of prophecy; whereunto ye do well that ye take heed, as unto a light that shineth in a dark place, until the day dawn, and the day star arise in your hearts: knowing

this first, that no prophecy is of any private interpretation. For the prophecy came not in old time by the will of man: but holy men of God spake as they were moved by the Holy Ghost...But there were false prophets also among the people, even as there shall be false teachers among you, who privily shall bring in damnable heresies, even denying the Lord that bought them..." (2 Peter 1:19–2:1).

*"If we receive the witness of men, **the witness** of God is greater: for this is **the witness** of God which **he hath testified** of his Son. He that believeth on the Son of God hath **the witness** in himself: he that believeth not God hath made him a liar; because he believeth not **the record** that God gave of his Son. And this is **the record**, that God hath given to us eternal life, and this life is in his Son"* (1 John 5:9-11).

*"For the former things are passed away. And he that sat upon the throne said, Behold, I make all things new. And he said unto me, Write: for **these words** are **true** and **faithful**"* (Revelation 21:4,5).

*"For I testify unto every man that heareth the words of the prophecy of this book, If any man shall **add** unto these things, God shall add unto him the plagues that are written in this book: And if any man shall **take away** from the words of the book of this prophecy, God shall take away his part out of the book of life, and out of the holy city, and from the things which are written in this book"* (Revelation 22:18,19).

— An Introductory Note —

This will by no means be an exhaustive study of the feasts of Israel. There already exists a tremendous body of information and numerous works that give an in-depth examination of the feasts themselves, their significance and meaning. It is my desire to deal with some particular aspects of them that I feel have not been properly appreciated thus far by those many devout and careful students of the Scriptures who have contributed to this very important subject. That particular aspect is the timing of the feasts in relation to their fulfillment—specifically, the fall feasts. We will touch upon many subjects in our exploration as that is inescapable in these matters, but the fall feasts will be our main pursuit.

Through this study I hope you gain a better understanding and appreciation of God as the Alpha and Omega, the beginning and the end. The events that will transpire on this earth in the time to come happen for a reason. They are not random events, but fit carefully into the plans and purposes of God, and are inextricably linked to the events that have occurred in the past going all the way back to the very beginning of creation. Man's long history is the recording of the journey between those two points, the beginning and the end, Genesis and Revelation. Let us now survey the landscape and see what God has to say on the matter.

Chapter One

HaShem: His Name Is Jehovah

Eternity, God's Grace
and
Israel's Future

To man history may seem like ages, but to the One who dwells in eternity, *"One day is with the Lord as a thousand years, and a thousand years as one day"* (2 Peter 3:8). The Lord does not grow forgetful with the passage of time as we often do. When He makes a promise to accomplish something, though hundreds of years may pass, He is as anxious to fulfill His word as the first day He spoke it. If significant time passes, it is because He is working something out in the accomplishment of those purposes.

"And he said unto Abram, Know of a surety that thy seed shall be a stranger in a land that is not theirs, and shall serve them; and they shall afflict them four hundred years...But in the fourth generation they shall come hither again: for the iniquity of the Amorites is not yet full" (Genesis 15:13,16).

God created an entirely new nation for Himself from Abraham, Isaac and Jacob. This too was not random. He made it clear to them that they were to be instrumental in the unfolding and outworking of His plans and purposes for planet Earth. This nation would be His focus and center of activity and it would be through this nation that God would reveal Himself. The true knowledge of the true God would be deposited with this people in the midst of the blindness, darkness and deception that prevailed over the nations of the world. With every man going after his own way and continuing the rebellion against the Creator, civilization would continue to follow its preferred leader, the god of this world, the father of rebellion and deception—Satan.

"Wherein in time past ye walked according to the course of this world, according to the prince of the power of the air, the spirit that now worketh in the children of disobedience" (Ephesians 2:2).

The pure knowledge and testimony of God would be maintained in this mess and atmosphere of confusion. It would be through this nation that the promised seed of the woman would come (see Genesis 3:15). God was going to contend with that old serpent and in the end He would repossess this earth and reconcile it back to Himself. Man would once again fulfill the role that God had intended for him and through that seed of the woman, the Messiah, the Lord would destroy the works of the devil and dwell in the midst of His creation as He had always intended.

"Therefore the Lord himself shall give you a sign; Behold, a virgin shall conceive, and bear a son, and shall call his name Immanuel…For unto us a child is born, unto us a son is given: and the government shall be upon his shoulder: and his name shall be called Wonderful, Counsellor, The mighty God, The everlasting Father, The Prince of Peace. Of the increase of his government and peace there shall be no end, upon the throne of David, and upon his kingdom, to order it, and to establish it with judgement and with justice from henceforth even for ever. The zeal of the LORD of hosts will perform this" (Isaiah 7:14; 9:6,7).

However, the nation which He called would also have to learn some lessons. He did not choose them because they were worthier than others, because they deserved this above other people. They were simply chosen. He would do this for His holy name's sake. God had made promises to their father Abraham and they would have the unique privilege of being utilized by Him in the out-working and fulfillment of His grand designs.

"Now therefore, I pray thee, if I have found grace in thy sight, shew me now thy way, that I may know thee, that I may find grace in thy sight: and consider that this nation is thy people" (Exodus 33:13).

But, as is apt to occur in those who have a knowledge of God and enjoy a relationship with Him, many became puffed up. They forgot that though they were children of Abraham, they were also children of Adam. They still suffered from that spiritual disease passed on from the first couple and were not naturally righteous or spiritually fit to be utilized by God. When this is understood, one will not make the mistake of presumptuously declaring, "All that the Lord has said we will do." This is what the Law was all about, and in connection with God bringing the children of Israel out of Egypt He gave them something very special and significant.

"And Moses said unto God, Behold, when I come unto the chil-dren of Israel, and shall say unto them, The God of your fathers hath sent me unto you; and they shall say to me, What is his name? what shall I say unto them? And God said unto Moses, I AM THAT I AM: and he said, Thus shalt thou say unto the children of Israel, I AM hath sent me unto you. And God said moreover unto Moses, Thus shalt thou say unto the children of Israel, The LORD God of your fathers, the God of Abraham, the God of Isaac, and the God of Jacob, hath sent me unto you: this is my name for ever, and this is my memorial unto all generations" (Exodus 3:13-15).

God revealed to Israel the name by which they would know Him, Jehovah. He demonstrated His full name and eternality as He brought them out of Egypt just as He had declared to Abraham that He would (Genesis 15:14). But in the very same verse He abbreviates His name, I AM_____. Why? It calls for comple-tion. I AM what? He has already demonstrated His eternality in fulfilling His promises in His *full* name. Here, however, I believe He looks forward to what it is He will fulfill as that eternal One.

All throughout the Scriptures Israel will be exhorted to think upon and trust in the name of Jehovah. God Himself will fill in those blanks for Israel. Being Adam's children, they need God to be some things for them and accomplish particular acts on their behalf. They cannot meet the righteous demands of His holy law and will, therefore, have to rely on His grace if they are ever to be dealt with by Him and survive. This is what they needed to acknowledge and trust in.

It would be by God's grace and mercy that Israel would enter into the promises to which they had been called. God would deliver on His promises and fulfill everything that He had declared. He would be everything they needed Him to be. He would personally put His name into effect and at the appointed times Israel would see their God as He manifested His mercy and grace and laid bare His holy arm before the people. It is during the feasts that Jehovah would perform for His people and they would see just what His name meant.

"And he said, I beseech thee, shew me thy glory. And he said, I will make all my goodness pass before thee, and I will proclaim the name of the LORD before thee; and will be gracious to whom I will be gracious, and will shew mercy on whom I will shew mercy... And the LORD descended in the cloud, and stood with him there, and proclaimed the name of the LORD. And the LORD passed by before him, and proclaimed, The LORD, The LORD God, merciful and gracious, longsuffering, and abundant in goodness and truth" (Exodus 33:18,19; 34:5,6).

TRUSTING IN HIS NAME
JEHOVAH-THE LORD

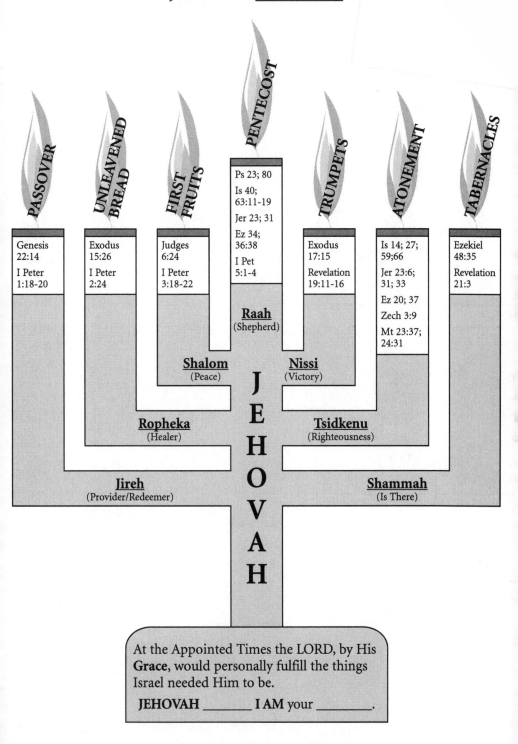

PASSOVER

UNLEAVENED BREAD

FIRST FRUITS

PENTECOST

TRUMPETS

ATONEMENT

TABERNACLES

Genesis 22:14	Exodus 15:26	Judges 6:24	Ps 23; 80	Exodus 17:15	Is 14; 27; 59;66	Ezekiel 48:35
I Peter 1:18-20	I Peter 2:24	I Peter 3:18-22	Is 40; 63:11-19	Revelation 19:11-16	Jer 23:6; 31; 33	Revelation 21:3

Ps 23; 80
Is 40;
63:11-19
Jer 23; 31
Ez 34;
36:38
I Pet
5:1-4

Is 14; 27;
59;66
Jer 23:6;
31; 33
Ez 20; 37
Zech 3:9
Mt 23:37;
24:31

Raah
(Shepherd)

Shalom
(Peace)

Nissi
(Victory)

Ropheka
(Healer)

Tsidkenu
(Righteousness)

Jireh
(Provider/Redeemer)

Shammah
(Is There)

J
E
H
O
V
A
H

At the Appointed Times the LORD, by His **Grace**, would personally fulfill the things Israel needed Him to be.

JEHOVAH _____ **I AM** your _____.

Chapter Two

The Five Courses of Punishment

Leviticus 26

&

Israel's History

Before we move on, it is necessary to lay the foundation for a most essential and fundamental concept. This doctrine will need to be understood as it sets the framework for the information contained in this book. God is a God of order and He has revealed in advance what the outworking of His plans will look like and the course those events will follow. This is part of His substantiation that He is indeed the eternal One who knows the end from the beginning and has proven Himself trustworthy. It is, therefore, possible to know Him more intimately, know who you are in His plans and purposes, know what is going to happen in the future, and prepare accordingly. The particular concept is shown in Leviticus chapter 26 where God presents in advance Israel's entire history.

In light of the covenant made at Sinai, God set before Israel the blessings and the curses. It was an if/then contract which held out righteousness and the blessings of the kingdom if they complied. If they failed to meet the righteous requirements of the Law contract, however, then a series of curses would come upon the nation. They had failed to keep God's commands before they ever got to Sinai, and still didn't see their need to be dealt with by God according to His grace. Moses made it abundantly clear to them that they were indeed going to break the contract and, therefore, according to that contract, five courses of punishment would come upon the nation.

When Moses spoke to them of the coming curses, he did so as if it were a foregone conclusion. There was no question as to *whether* the nation would experience these curses. Moses understood the failure of the people and, therefore, the destiny of the nation. He also understood, however, the determination of God to bring them into the promises, but all in due time. We don't have the time to go through Leviticus 26 in detail, as it is a lengthy passage, but I highly encourage you to examine it on your own.

Briefly stated, the passage is divided naturally by the text into five sections, each beginning with the phrase, "*And if ye will not yet for all this hearken unto me, then I will punish you seven times more for your sins.*"

The sections are divided as follows:

<u>First Course</u>—Leviticus 26:16,17
<u>Second Course</u>—Leviticus 26:18-20
<u>Third Course</u>—Leviticus 26:21,22
<u>Fourth Course</u>—Leviticus 26:23-26
<u>Fifth Course</u>—Leviticus 26:27-46

This would be the history of the nation as God unfolded His plan for earth and continued to work towards its fulfillment. This is what is recorded on the pages of His Word as you go from the birth of the nation to its rebirth and the consummation of God's purposes for earth. This is the prophetic program and constitutes the better portion of His written Word, the Bible. For a better appreciation of this concept, I would direct you to the chart at the end of this chapter.

The Scriptures record the times when the nation is warned that they are ripe for the next course of punishment, and then the subsequent arrival of those prophesied curses. They manifested time and again that God was fulfilling His responsibilities under the contract. When the kingdom was divided and the prophet Elijah was raised up and stopped the rain and caused the famine, the nation should have recognized that the Second Course had arrived, as outlined in Leviticus 26:19. Then when the prophet Elisha was raised up and the two she bears came out and killed the mocking youngsters, the nation should have recognized that the Third Course had arrived as outlined in Leviticus 26:22.

It is apparent just by glancing at Leviticus 26 that the Fifth Course is by far the one about which the most is said. Later on in the Scriptures, especially Daniel, you are told that this Fifth and last Course would be composed of five installments, beginning as Leviticus 26 describes with God walking contrary to the nation in fury, destroying the prized cities and sanctuaries and scattering the people among the heathen. Interestingly, you are told in the prophets that the Fifth Course will end as it began and, therefore, special attention needs to be paid when reading Isaiah through Malachi.

Those books are not simply filled with historical footnotes. There is a reason why specific events were recorded, just as there is a reason why David records his experiences in the Psalms as do other prophets in their books. Simply stated, David is a type of the remnant and just as God had done before, He gave Israel a fore-taste and type of what would come. There are things which were not fulfilled back in the first installment and are not meant to be understood that way when read. Saying this passage uses strong language to describe foreign armies, etc., simply doesn't do justice to the text or God. Babylon, for instance, has never been destroyed the way God says it will be. That is because it is a player in the last installment and is appointed to be destroyed at that time. When you appreciate the structure of God's Word, there is much to be gleaned that has too often been overlooked.

Beginning in Isaiah, you are given a view that looks out across the landscape of the Fifth Course of Punishment starting in the First installment and running all the way to the consummation in the 5th installment and the kingdom that follows. There would come a time in the 5th Course when Israel would be formally confronted with the issue of a *national* repentance (see Leviticus 26:40,41). Looking ahead, we will simply note that it would occur during the 4th installment of that 5th course of punishment with the ministry of John the Baptist and the days of the Messiah with Christ in their midst.

Christ came as the latter rain to Israel in His earthly ministry and during the spring feasts He functioned as the Redeemer and accomplished all that He legally needed to in order to be able to have His Day of Wrath and provide for His people in light of the remaining feasts. And so, after His glorious resurrection when He had successfully accomplished the redemptive work, He declared, "*All power is given unto me in heaven and in earth*" (Matthew 28:18).

All things were now ready, and in accordance with the Scriptures He would return to heaven and sit at the Father's right hand (Psalm 110). Repentance would then be given to Israel and the rebellious nation would be given the opportunity to respond to the sign of Jonah (the resurrection) and the witness of the Holy Spirit. This opportunity would come to an end, however, and Christ would arise to have His Day of Wrath—the fifth and last installment in Israel's five courses of punishment. It is the prophesied Lord's Day in which God will fulfill all that He has declared throughout the Scriptures concerning the repossession of this planet and the hallowing of His name in all the earth. It is at that coming time that God will bring to a close man's history *as we know it*. He will then begin a whole new history however and one which He is quite anxious and zealous to get underway. It is with this understanding and picture in view that we now turn to the remaining fall feasts of Israel on God's calendar.

Concerning the dispensational chart, in my understanding the 4th and 5th installments of the 5th Course of Punishment could be broken down a bit differently. Nevertheless, for the sake of increasing understanding and comprehension concerning the basic concepts involved, all references in this book to the installments are consistent with this dispensational chart. If you desire to further explore many of the issues discussed in this book then I highly encourage you to contact Enjoy the Bible ministries and request the many materials by Keith Blades that they produce.

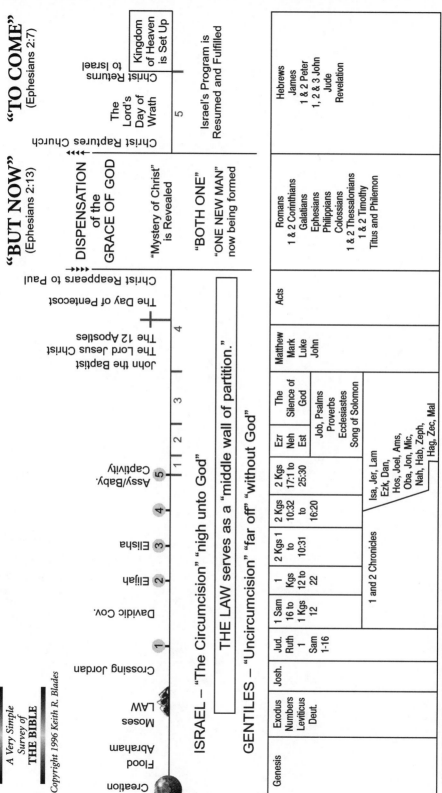

A Very Simple Survey of **THE BIBLE**

Copyright 1996 Keith R. Blades

"TO COME" (Ephesians 2:7)

"BUT NOW" (Ephesians 2:13)

DISPENSATION of the GRACE OF GOD

"Mystery of Christ" is Revealed

"BOTH ONE"

"ONE NEW MAN" now being formed

Kingdom of Heaven is Set Up

Christ Returns to Israel

The Lord's Day of Wrath

Israel's Program is Resumed and Fulfilled

Christ Raptures Church

Christ Reappears to Paul

The Day of Pentecost

The Lord Jesus Christ
The 12 Apostles

John the Baptist

ISRAEL – "The Circumcision" "nigh unto God"

THE LAW serves as a "middle wall of partition."

GENTILES – "Uncircumcision" "far off" "without God"

Assy/Baby. Captivity

Elisha

Elijah

Davidic Cov.

Crossing Jordan

LAW
Moses

Abraham
Flood
Creation

Genesis	Exodus Numbers Leviticus Deut.	Josh.	Jud. Ruth 1 Sam 1-16	1 Sam 16 to 1 Kgs 12	1 Kgs 12 to 22	2 Kgs 1 to 10:31	2 Kgs 10:32 to 16:20	2 Kgs 17:1 to 25:30	Ezr Neh Est	The Silence of God	Matthew Mark Luke John	Acts	Romans 1 & 2 Corinthians Galatians Ephesians Philippians Colossians 1 & 2 Thessalonians 1 & 2 Timothy Titus and Philemon	Hebrews James 1 & 2 Peter 1, 2 & 3 John Jude Revelation
				1 and 2 Chronicles					Job, Psalms Proverbs Ecclesiastes Song of Solomon					

Isa, Jer, Lam
Ezk, Dan,
Hos, Joel, Ams,
Oba, Jon, Mic,
Nah, Hab, Zeph,
Hag, Zec, Mal

Chapter Three

Keeping Appointments

The Days of the Messiah,
The Fall Feasts of Israel
&

The Return of the Lord Jesus Christ

I t is often understood that the fall feasts are connected with the second coming of Christ just as the spring feasts were connected with the first coming of Christ. On this score it is most often put forth that Rosh HaShanah with its blowing of trumpets represents the rapture of the church, followed by the Days of Awe or the seven years of tribulation, concluding with Yom Kippur representing the bodily return of the Lord Jesus Christ to earth and finally Succot (Feast of Tabernacles) representing the 1000-year kingdom age. It is even suggested by some that the rapture will actually take place on Rosh HaShanah for this reason.

That might strike your curiosity as conflicting with the warnings of date setting that have been proclaimed loudly throughout Christendom and the doctrine of the imminence of our "catching away" to be with the Lord. Then again, there are students of Scripture who would say that there is no such doctrine and have rather elaborate arguments to demonstrate such. I personally am in agreement with all of them to some extent, but not when it comes to many of their justifications and understanding of various scriptures.

With respect to the Rosh HaShanah position, it should be stated that the justification for making it the literal date of the rapture and still being consistent with "not knowing the day or the hour" of the Lord's return is that Rosh HaShanah has also been known as the "hidden day" or the unknown day and that is what is being referred to in the various passages. You may perceive problems with that position—and I myself do not share it—but at least it is consistent. It is that issue of consistency that I wish here to address and expand upon.

The idea that Rosh HaShanah merely "represents" the tribulation period—or anything else for that matter—simply does not do justice to what God has revealed about these feasts in His word and the precedent that He has set in that which has already been fulfilled: namely, that Passover did not simply "represent" the crucifixion and death of the Lord Jesus Christ. The spring feasts were fulfilled to the very day, to the very hour.

Scripture repeatedly declares that though the people sought to lay hands on Him throughout His earthly ministry they were unable to because His "hour" had not yet come (John 7:30; 8:20). Then at His triumphal entry into Jerusalem, which was really a rehearsal for the true triumphal entry yet to come at His return, the Lord declares, "*The hour is come, that the Son of Man should be glorified...Now is my soul troubled; and what shall I say? Father, save me from this hour: but for this cause came I unto this hour*" (John 12:23,27).

As that Passover Lamb, Jesus was officially presented to the nation on Palm Sunday, the tenth of Nisan as demanded in the Law (Exodus 10:3). He was then put up for examination for four days in accordance with the Law to show beyond a shadow of a doubt that He truly was the Lamb of God, without spot or blemish. He was examined during that time in the temple by the three major groups of leadership in the nation—the Herodians, the Sadducees and the Pharisees. Each one in turn come to Him and are given their chance to launch the best that they can throw at Him. And each one leaves speechless and marveled, with the end of it all being, "*And no man was able to answer him a word, neither durst any man from that day forth ask him any more questions*" (Matthew 22:46).

Here indeed was the One that John the Baptist had told the nation to behold—"*the Lamb of God, which taketh away the sin of the world*" (John 1:29). Here indeed was that Lamb that had been promised to Abraham. When Isaac asked his father Abraham where the sacrifice was, Abraham answered, "*My son, God will provide himself a lamb for a burnt offering*" (Genesis 22:8). God would provide the lamb. God would provide *himself* the lamb. And this provision would be in connection with the sacrifice of the only son of the father.

So much could be said about these precious verses but space does not allow. For our purposes, the Lord Jesus Christ, as the Son of the living God and only begotten of the Father, was that promised and long awaited Lamb. Abraham did not see that promised provisional lamb. He only saw a *ram* caught in the thicket (Genesis 22:13). Yet just as he had declared, it was about to be seen in the mount of the Lord (Genesis 22:14). It was here that the Lord personally would actually fulfill His name Jehovah-jireh (the LORD is my provider). "*Your father Abraham rejoiced to see my day: and he saw it, and was glad*" (John 8:58).

So, as he nears the fourteenth of Nisan, the Lord prepares to be killed by the whole assembly of the congregation of Israel as required of the Lamb (Exodus 12:6). In accordance with that the Scriptures state, "*And one of them, named Caiaphas, being the high priest that same year, said unto them, Ye know nothing at all, Nor consider that it is expedient for us, that one man should die for the people, and that the whole nation perish not. And this spake he not of himself: but being high priest that same year, he prophesied that Jesus should die for that nation…then from that day forth they took counsel together for to put him to death*" (John 11:49-54).

As high priest Caiaphas officially chose the sacrifice. Again, "*Then the band and the captain and the officers of the Jews took*

Jesus, and bound him, And led him away to Annas first; for he was father in law to Caiaphas, which was the high priest that same year. Now Caiaphas was he which gave counsel to the Jews, that it was expedient that one man should die for the people" (John 18:12-14).

It sure seems that the Holy Spirit is concerned about that particular issue, especially as it relates to Caiaphas' official position in the nation and that the decree he made was actually by the Spirit. Christ had to fulfill the law perfectly—and he did. The very language of being bound and led away is that of the lamb being led to the slaughter.

And as that lamb being led to the slaughter, He is silent. *"He was oppressed, and he was afflicted, yet he opened not his mouth: he is brought as a lamb to the slaughter, and as a sheep before her shearers is dumb, so he openeth not his mouth"* (Isaiah 53:7). *"And the high priest stood up in the midst, and asked Jesus, saying, Answerest thou nothing? What is it which these witness against thee? But he held his peace, and answered nothing"* (Mark 14:60,61). *"Then he questioned with him in many words; but he answered him nothing"* (Luke 23:9). The only time Christ will utter a word is when the high priest adjures him by the living God as required by the Law (Matthew 26:63,64; Leviticus 5:1).

Even when the rulers are breaking the Law left and right during His trials, Christ shows Himself to be spotless and the perfect fulfiller of the Law in every detail. He is fully shown by all to be without spot or blemish as required of the Passover lamb and is, therefore, a worthy sacrifice.

"Then said Pilate to the chief priests and to the people, I find no fault in this man...And Pilate, when he had called together the chief priests and the rulers and the people, Said unto them, Ye have brought this man unto me, as one that perverteth the people: and, behold, I, having examined him before you, have found no fault in this man touching those things whereof ye accuse him: No, nor yet Herod: for I sent you to him; and lo, nothing worthy of death is done unto him...But they cried, saying, Crucify him, crucify him. And he said unto them the third time, Why, what evil hath he done? I have

found no cause of death in him: I will therefore chastise him and let him go. And they were instant with loud voices, requiring that he might be crucified. And the voices of them and of the chief priests prevailed. And Pilate gave sentence that it should be as they required" (Luke 23:13,14,21,22-24).

"Pilate saith unto him, What is truth? And when he had said this, he went out again unto the Jews, and saith unto them, I find no fault at all" (John 18:38). *"Again the high priest asked him, and said unto him, Art thou the Christ, the Son of the Blessed? And Jesus said, I am: and ye shall see the Son of man sitting on the right hand of power, and coming in the clouds of heaven. Then the high priest rent his clothes, and saith, What need we any further witnesses? Ye have heard the blasphemy: what think ye? And they all condemned him to be **guilty of death**. And some began to spit on him, and to cover his face, and to buffet him"* (Mark 14:61-65).

The high priest rends his clothes, which is forbidden by the Law, and he is therefore unfit to actually offer up any sacrifices to the Lord (Exodus 28:32; 39:22; Leviticus 10:6; 21:10). No matter, he has already served his purpose in officially choosing the sacrifice and declaring it to be guilty (worthy) of death. He of course did not realize that he was prophesying, just as he did not realize before that the Lord was using him in his official capacity. But now he is legally unclean and unfit to continue in that capacity. God has His own sacrifice for the people. The high priest's act is a demonstration of the wrath that awaits the unrepentant nation. Now is the time for the perfect and spotless Lamb of God to offer up *Himself* as a sacrifice. It truly was His love for you and me that held him to that cross, not the nails.

*"Then said he, Lo, I come to do thy will, O God. He taketh away the first, that he may establish the second. By the which will we are sanctified through the offering of the body of Jesus Christ once for all. And every priest standeth daily ministering and offering oftentimes the same sacrifices, which can never take away sins: But this man, after **he had offered** one sacrifice for sins for ever, sat down on the right hand of God; From henceforth expecting till his enemies be*

made his footstool. For by one offering he hath perfected for ever them that are sanctified" (Hebrews 10:9-14).

That brings us to the crucifixion itself on the fourteenth of Nisan. I realize there is disagreement among many as to whether it was the fourteenth or fifteenth, but for our purposes, regardless of the position you take, it is recognized by all that whatever is being fulfilled as to the Passover seder or crucifixion, it is being fulfilled to the day. Likewise, the feast of firstfruits does not just *represent* the resurrection of the Messiah, but Christ literally arose from the dead on the actual day of firstfruits in fulfillment of that feast.

Finally, fifty days later came the feast of Shavuot or Pentecost. It was when the day of Pentecost had *fully* come that the Lord sent the promise of the Father, the Holy Spirit. It was not just any Pentecost, it was not just *represented* by Pentecost, but its literal fulfillment when the day actually had fully come. So what's the point? The point is why do we—with a full understanding of these matters—come along and say that Rosh HaShanah "represents" the tribulation? Whatever the fall feasts speak to, they must find their fulfillment literally and to the day.

Undoubtedly this will ruffle some doctrinal and theological feathers, but in reality it need not. Even if accepted, its implications may be understood and assimilated in a variety of ways by those holding differing eschatological views—up to a point anyway. It does not in itself really address many issues, especially those that relate directly to the Body of Christ; i.e., the rapture. Nevertheless, there will be those who think it does and align it with the particular teaching they espouse. I feel that the key to understanding that issue is inextricably tied to truly comprehending the nature of the Body of Christ and what God is and is not doing today. But the main point of this work is to simply lay a starting point for the timing of the feast's fulfillment and demonstrate what my current understanding of its implications are.

One thing that must be understood is that the feasts deal with God's program with Israel and this earth. What God is doing with you and me today is part of the mystery, something He had never revealed in ages and generations past before He raised up Paul as a totally new apostle and revealed it to him. Regardless of when you believe the Body of Christ began, that much is evident from the Scriptures. It is also for a specific purpose that God is doing what He is doing today. One of the main characteristics of this period in which we live is that God is holding off His infamous Day of Wrath, the Day of the Lord, the Lord's Day. During this period in which we live God has suspended temporarily His program with Israel and they consequently do not see the fulfillment of that program with them.

As long as God continues doing what He is currently doing today, that prophetic Day of His Wrath will not come. This is why Paul tells us in connection with our catching away to be with the Lord that we have been delivered from the wrath to come. The rapture of which Paul tells us is in keeping with the nature of this dispensation; namely, it was a mystery. The rapture of the Body of Christ is part of that mystery naturally enough and Paul was the one uniquely commissioned to minister to it by the risen, ascended and exalted Christ.

During the Lord's earthly ministry, however, the program going on today was not in view. As Paul declares, "*Now I say that Jesus Christ was a minister of the circumcision for the truth of God, to confirm the promises made unto the fathers*" (Romans 15:8). Not understanding the need to "rightly divide the word of truth," as necessitated by the different programs of God and Paul's unique apostleship, it is no surprise that many honest and careful students of the Scriptures reject a pre-tribulation rapture. The fact is, in Israel's program there is no rapture of believers, be it pre-tribulational, pre-wrath or otherwise. During the period of the Gospels and opening chapters of Acts, Israel is in the climactic stage of her program. The time schedule was almost complete, Messiah was in their midst and the kingdom of heaven was being preached as "at hand."

Once the Lord departed from them and went back to the Father, there would be only one thing left according to the program—the

Lord's Day of Wrath. While on earth, Christ prepared His little flock to go through that period of time. They would see come to a climax all that the Scriptures had spoken about that time, the policy of evil that existed since the Fall and the consummation of God's promises with the nation in the repossession of planet Earth. He specifically taught and counseled them on being able to endure through that period that was coming. They were even going to receive special miraculous powers when He baptized them with the Holy Spirit for the express purpose of being able to endure the conditions of that time and combat the evil of the day. In connection with preaching the gospel of the kingdom, they will be able to take up serpents and drink any deadly thing and it will not hurt them (Mark 16:18).

As an aside, this gospel is not the gospel of the grace of God committed unto the apostle Paul. It is the same gospel they had been preaching all along, the same gospel that the Lord told them they would continue preaching when He was gone. Even a cursory reading of the Gospels shows that the gospel they preached didn't include the death, burial and resurrection of Christ. It is the gospel of the circumcision, the good news about God's program with Israel and the fact that the God of heaven is going to set up His kingdom on earth (Daniel 2:44).

They will need those particular miraculous powers because specifically during that time of the 5th and final installment of the 5th course of punishment, God will send poisonous serpents and beasts of the earth to bite those on earth as called for by Deuteronomy 32:24, Jeremiah 8:17, and Revelation 6:8, among others. The water will also be poisoned during that time and many men will die because of it (Revelation 8:10). Much more could be said but suffice it to say the Lord's Day of Wrath plays a huge role in God's program with Israel, and in light of the Lord's departure that is what is in view for the believers He leaves behind.

Not only does the Lord prepare His followers to go through that time, but He emphatically teaches them that He will not return until that period of time is over. In fact, once they have fled

Jerusalem and are in the position of being "hidden" when they hear rumors that the Lord has returned, under no circumstances are they to believe them (Matthew 24:23-27). These messages are from false prophets and liars who simply want to get the remnant to come out of their hiding places so they can exterminate them. The Lord will assuredly by no means return according to the prophetic program before that prophesied *determined* time is over.

It is only at the end of that time that the remnant, the seed called out of Jacob, can expect Him and not before. We don't have the space here to fully address this issue but I will simply say that they will have to endure the time of wrath. If they are among the wise ones in Israel they will be protected from the deception and temptations of that time. There is the opportunity for the faithful to be hidden but not by a rapture. The idea of making a difference between the wrath of God versus the wrath of man is really irrelevant as they are expressly promised the ability to be hidden from *man's* wrath during that time (Luke 21:36). Much, much more could be said concerning that, especially as it relates to the various positions about a pre-wrath rapture, but we must go on.

There is, in light of all that heaviness and prophecy, a wonderful and gracious event which occurs. Amazingly, that prophesied Day of His Wrath did not come, and has not come. Not yet. Why? Well, read Paul's epistles and find out. God had a secret purpose that He had kept hidden in Himself in ages and generations past. He didn't tell anyone about it. But in His wisdom, and by keeping that secret, He took the wise one in his own craftiness. In the cross of the Lord Jesus Christ, God was accomplishing something that if Satan and his cohorts had known, they would never have crucified the Lord of Glory. That something was nothing less than the complete and utter destruction of the entire satanic plan of evil. Not only would God reconcile the earth and all its governmental authority back unto Himself, but He planned that in Christ Jesus He would gather all things, including those principalities, powers, mights and dominion in the heavenly places (Ephesians 1:21; Colossians 1:16).

Today, God is putting on display the matchless riches of His grace in dealing with the Gentiles in a way that He had never spoken. There was no mystery about Gentile salvation. They are to be dealt with very specifically according to the prophetic program and will yet be, as I shall discuss later. Indeed, it is at the very heart of God's program with Israel, in relation to His purposes with the earth, the gospel of the kingdom and the fulfillment of the Abrahamic Covenant that Israel is finally the world blessing she is called to be. Today, however, God is putting that on hold while He forms a new creature, the Body of Christ, where there is neither Jew nor Greek. This one new man will be made fit for the heavenly places where its vocation is and thereby God will "*gather in one all things in Christ, both which are in heaven, and which are on earth; even in him*" (Ephesians 1:10).

God's dealings with those in the world today necessarily preclude Him working in His program with Israel. However, the situation that exists at the present is an unnatural one. These are wild branches that have been grafted in. Israel is not today enjoying a unique position with respect to God's dealings, but she most assuredly will as has been promised her, in accord with God's purposes for the earth which include geographical boundaries, nations and so on. The time will come when God will break off the unnatural branches, end His current program with the Body of Christ and rescind the special message of His grace that now goes to the Gentiles apart from Israel's program. With that He will graft back in the natural branches, resume the prophetic program with Israel and this earth and thus mark the arrival of the only thing which yet awaits fulfillment, namely the Day of the Lord.

Believers will be on this earth during that time of wrath as was expected. The "church" will be on this earth as was also expected. (I speak of the true church and not just the professing one.) No, this is not a partial rapture. The remnant of Israel was to be the seed called out of Jacob. If a member of Israel wanted to be saved and survive the coming time, they had to become part of the Lord's little flock and separate themselves from the apostate nation. This would be the righteous nation prophesied about in the scriptures. They were the Lord's called out and would make up His congregation. There was a church in the Old Testament, however. And there was a church before Pentecost—it was *added* to then. The church is the distinct object of the Lord and can rightly be called His people. Most would not say that those in the wilderness were part of the Body of Christ, but they were part of the Lord's church.

I think there has been much misunderstanding of just what the church is. The church is the Lord's called out and that much is understood by everyone. But that doesn't mean that those who are called out—especially at different times—are being called out or used for the same things or according to the same terms or program. The difference is that it is the Lord's assembly versus the hosts of others. The church, however, does not necessarily identify a particular group of God's people or a particular dispensation or program of God. The term "church" is simply the New Testament word for what had always been spoken of by the Hebrew prophets as the "assembly," "congregation" and other such terms.

The church was not a mystery. As far as the prophetic program was concerned, it was well prophesied as the remnant that would go through the time of trouble as they carried the testimony of Jesus Christ and suffered persecution from the nation because of it. The Body of Christ was indeed a mystery, and we are indeed members of the church. But the two are not synonymous. We are part of a program that was a mystery. We are not being used by God according to His program with Israel. That is why we are the church, *which is His body*. We are part of the one new man. The church in the wilderness was not His body, nor were those that were being called out during the early chapters of Acts. They were indeed the church, but also the remnant of Israel in accordance with God's program with Israel.

So, while the church will be here during the time of Jacob's trouble, the Body of Christ,—the one new man—will have been taken away ending the current dispensation of the grace of God to the Gentiles. I realize many will differ on this point. That's fine. As long as you diligently search the Scriptures and are convinced that is what *they* teach, then please, obey the Holy Spirit.

Understanding our identity as members of the Body of Christ is extremely beneficial in understanding our relationship to Israel's program and the remaining feasts. We know that "*All scripture is given by inspiration of God, and is profitable for doctrine, for reproof, for correction, for instruction in righteousness*" (2 Timothy 3:16).

When studying the Bible to show ourselves approved unto God for the accomplishment of the goals listed above, it is of utmost importance that we rightly divide the word of truth (2 Timothy 2:15). This need to rightly divide the Bible is in light of the revelation of the mystery and the change in program that has occurred and is revealed through the distinctive ministry and apostleship of Paul and his epistles. The whole point is that God is doing something different. We are told that, "*For whatsoever things were written aforetime were written for our learning, that we through patience and comfort of the scriptures might have hope*" (Romans 15:4).

These things were written for our learning, not obedience. Paul's epistles are written to you as a member of the Body of Christ for your obedience in accordance with the mystery program God is conducting today. The fact of the matter is that it is no longer a mystery but has been revealed through Paul's distinctive ministry, and we are to be filled with understanding concerning all the wisdom and knowledge of God. That was constantly Paul's burden and prayer for believers. Unfortunately, for far too many believers it is still a mystery. It must be remembered that while all Scripture is indeed *for* us, it is not all *to* or *about* us.

In accordance with the character of this present dispensation, the apostle Paul tells us that while those things were written for our learning, "*Let no man therefore judge you in meat, or in drink, or in respect of an holy day, or of the new moon, or of the sabbath days. Which are a shadow of things to come; but the body is of Christ*" (Colossians 2:16,17). Again, to the Galatians Paul declared, "*Ye observe days, and months, and times, and years. I am afraid of you, lest I have bestowed labor in vain"* (Galatians 4:10,11).

Returning to Colossians, these various ordinances deal with things to come. Many would like to translate this as though it said *were* a shadow of things to come. But the fact is, as the Scripture declares, they *are* a shadow of things *to come,* and will see their fulfillment when God resumes Israel's program and the kingdom of heaven on earth is established.

"Who are Israelites; to whom **pertaineth** *the adoption, and the glory, and the covenants, and the giving of the law, and the service of God, and the promises; whose are the fathers, and of whom as concerning the flesh Christ came, who is over all, God blessed for ever. Amen"* (Romans 9:3-5).

"As concerning the gospel, they are enemies for your sakes: but as touching the election, they are beloved for the father's sakes. For the gifts and calling of God are without repentance" (Romans 11:28,29).

So let us now turn to an examination of some of those shadows to help us better understand and appreciate the "things to come."

The course of events according to the prophetic program
Without the revelation of the Mystery.
From Evening to Evening—6 PM to 6 PM

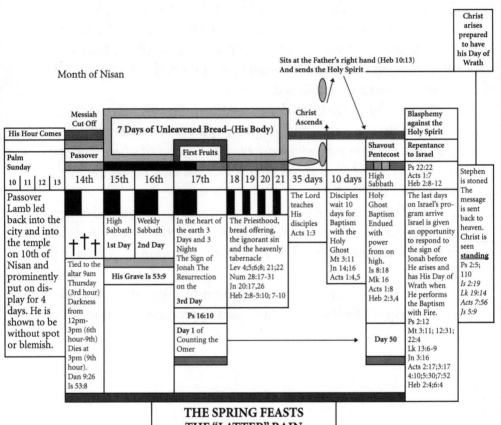

THE SPRING FEASTS
THE "LATTER" RAIN
Days of The Messiah Part I

THE LORD'S DAY
(Rev. 1:10)
The Day of the LORD

Messiah returns by His name JAH
Riding upon the Heavens

Daniel's 70th Week (7 Years)

Last Stage of the Times of the Gentiles

Month of Elul Immed-iately after tribulation of those days Mt 24:29

The **Seventh** Month-Tishrei
Beginning of the "New" Year
The Government rests on His Shoulders

Jehovah Nissi The LORD Our "Victory"	Jehovah Tsidkenu The LORD Our "Righteousness"	Jehovah Shammah The LORD "Is There"

1290 Days (Dan 12:11)

3½ years ——→ Great Tribulation

Beginning of Sorrows Wars and Rumors of Wars Dan 11:5-20 Mt 24:4-8	Works deceitfully Ps 10:7;55:21 Pr 12:6; SOS; Is 8:9-12; 30:10 Jer 9:8; 29:8 Dan 11:23-30	Mid point 1 month 30 days Abomination of Desolation Is 33:8; Dan 9:26; 11:31-39: Ob 13	3½ years ——→ 42 months 1260 days The Determined Time Dan 7:25; 9:27; 11:39; Mt 24:21,22

Rosh HaShanah Blowing of Trumpets The Days of Awe Rev 14:20

Yom Kippur Day of Atonement "Great" Trumpet blown Is 27:13 Mt 24:31

Succot The Feast of Tabernacles The Marriage Supper Of the Lamb Mt 22:1-14; Rev19:9

King of the North #6	King of the North #7	Final King of the North #8 makes league and confirms The covenant for 7 years. Dan 11:21-23 Rev 17:11	- Covenant is broken and Jerusalem is trodden down - Antichrist divides the land and the spoil and goes to his golden city Babylon. - Jews who refuse to worship his image are exterminated or taken into captivity and sold as slaves.	30 days	1st S A B B A T H	2 3 4 5 6 7 8 9	10th Day Sabbath	11-14	15th Day Sabbath	16-21	22nd S A B B A T H
The Assyrian Dan 11:5-20 Rev 17:10				- Darkness, Sun dark-ened and Moon turned to blood.			Afflict souls for "Entire" congrega-tion. All Israel saved. National Rebirth. The Jubilee Year Is 40; 62:4; 66:8 Ez 16; 36;37 Hos 2:19,20; 14:4 Zech 3:9 Jn 3:7 Rev 19:7	Royal Prepa-ration for the king-dom. The giving of rewards. Is 40:10 Mt 5:12; 6:4,18 10:41; 16:27; 25:14,31 Rev 22:12	Daniel's 45th Day The Royal 7 Day Celebration Time for rejoicing and singing Ps 98:4		

The 10 Nation Confederacy

Ps 83 Dan 11:23 Rev 17:10

Midst of the week– Space of half an hour Rev 8:1

ONE HOUR

- The faithful remnant having fled is hidden and miraculously pro-vided for in the wilderness. - The two witnesses begin their ministry. Mal 4:1-5; Lk 9:28-30 - The 7 angels blow their trumpets

Ps 79 Is 10:23 Joel 3:1-6 Lk 21:24 Rev 11:2,3

- Armies of the kings of the earth gathered to Arma-geddon. - Won't know the day or hour Joel 3:9-15 Zech 14:7 Mt 24:29, 32-36 Rev 16:10, 12-16

The **"Great & Terrible"** Day of the LORD Christ bursts on the scene as lightning. The Lion of Judah roars and utters His awesome voice as He goes forth as the Mighty Man of War to do battle. Ps 18:7-14;45;68:4; 97 Is 30:27-28;24:20,21; 42:13;63;64;Ez 38:19-23 Joel 2:11;Hab 3 Zech 14:3; Mal 4:2,5 Mt 24:27; Rev 19:11-21

2nd Sabbath after the 1st II Chron 5:3 Ps 46:4; 104:13 Is 12;55; Lk 6:1; Jn 7:37; Rev 22:1

Season of Teshuvah (Repentance) 40 Days Elul 1-Tishrei 10

Daniel's Extra 45 Days ——————————→ Day 1,335

The First Resurrection Day 1,335

THE FALL FEASTS
THE "EARLY" RAIN
Days of The Messiah Part II

Chapter Four

The Season of Repentance

Darkness,
The Day and the Hour
&
Daniel's Extra 45 Days

I f you have followed and understood the argument presented thus far, you may be a bit perplexed and have some questions. Quite obviously, if my understanding is correct, then the passages in the Gospels that refer to one being taken and one being left do not refer to the rapture. Those verses build upon some particular events that will transpire during the Day of the Lord in Israel's program. It is not even a rapture in Israel's program as the Lord has explicitly told His followers not to expect Him until the end of that period. Even standing on its own, that issue is generally recognized as referring to being taken in judgement not glory or escape.

While there is disagreement as to the timing of these particular events as outlined in Zechariah 14, it is my belief that it takes place at the midpoint of Daniel's seventieth week. This is when the prophesied abomination of desolation will take place in the temple, and an ensuing captivity takes place for the nation of Israel for the determined period of 42 months, or 3-1/2 years, until the times of the Gentiles is fulfilled. This event is manifestly declared in Zechariah where the Lord says, "*For I will gather all nations against Jerusalem to battle; and the city shall be taken, and the houses rifled, and the women ravished; and half of the city shall go forth into captivity, and the residue of the people shall not be cut off from the city*" (Zechariah 14:2).

If one is taken and one is left, that sounds an awful lot like half. It was this event that the Lord warned His followers about in Matthew 24, Luke 21 and other passages. The nations gather at the end but they do so because of some things that have taken place at the midpoint 3-1/2 years earlier. It is uniquely tied to the *spoil* that was divided in connection with the sacking of the city as mentioned in the preceding verse: "*Behold, the day of the Lord cometh, and thy spoil shall be divided in the midst of thee*" (Zechariah 14:1).

But what about the verses in the Gospels that declare, "*But of that day and hour knoweth no man, no not the angels of heaven, but of my Father only…Watch therefore: for ye know not what hour your Lord doth come*" (Matthew 24:36,42). These warnings need to be understood in the totality of all that He has taught thus far about this subject. He, along with the entire Old Testament writers, has prepared the remnant that would go through the prophesied Day of the Lord to know what to expect and endure that time. In the immediate context He has already told them, "*So likewise ye, when ye shall see all these things, know that it is near, even at the doors*" (Matthew 24:33).

"*And when these things begin to come to pass, then look up, and lift up your heads; for your redemption draweth nigh…So likewise ye, when ye see these things come to pass, know ye that the kingdom of God is nigh at hand*" (Luke 21:28).

The Lord has just given them a detailed exposition of Daniel chapter 11 and has told them to read it so they would understand that the end result is going to be the return of the rejected stone that is going to hit the feet of Nebuchadnezzar's image, destroy all the kingdoms of man ending the times of the Gentile's dominion over Israel and set up the glorious long-awaited kingdom of heaven on earth. This is why the Scripture prophetically declares what it does about the time when the Lord Jesus Christ returns from heaven to take possession of the earth: *"Thou shalt break them with a rod of iron; thou shalt dash them in pieces like a potter's vessel"* (Psalm 2:9). Sounds a lot like the iron and clay of the feet of that great image in Nebuchadnezzar's dream.

So then, the remnant will be going through that period of time whereby the Lord purges the nation and are to be very cognizant of the various events that transpire around them during that time. They will need to take specific action, depending on where they are and when they see some particular events take place. If they are not watchful, faithful and obedient to what the Lord has commanded for that time, they will be swept away by the destruction that shall come upon the apostate nation and the world of the ungodly—though they themselves are believers and justified unto eternal life. They know that He will not return until those particular things take place.

They also know Daniel's time schedule and the scope of the great tribulation. They are told that only when those various things have transpired are they to lift up their heads, knowing that the time of His return is nearing. Yet, though they know His return to earth is fast approaching, they will be unable to know the day and hour. Why? That is the subject we will now explore and I believe there is much to be gleaned from an examination of this matter and a greater understanding of the timing of the feasts as well.

The Lord Himself has already pointed us back to Daniel in dealing with this subject and I believe that one of the keys to understanding this issue is provided in that book. Throughout Daniel we are constantly confronted with a particular period of time in association with the final world empire that will rule on this earth under the headship of the Antichrist. This period is commonly referred to as Daniel's seventieth week—a seven-year period which is delineated and divided by a number of phrases: a week, in the midst of the week, times, time and half a time, 42 months, 1260 days.

God could not make it any more literal if He tried. The last 3-1/2 years of this time are often called the "great tribulation." It is marked by the abomination of desolation in the temple and the implementing of an extermination policy against Israel by the Antichrist. But the point is that all through Daniel we are presented with this period of time and all fits well and neatly into the time frame set forth. Antichrist is allowed to continue and prosper for the determined period of 42 months and then meets his demise with the return of Jesus Christ to establish the kingdom.

But then, at the very end of Daniel, almost as a footnote, we are confronted with a new schedule—namely, extra days. Up until now it has consistently been 1260 days. But starting in verse 8 of chapter 12 it says, "*And I heard, but I understood not: then said I, O my Lord, what shall be the end of these things? And he said, Go thy way, Daniel: for the words are closed up and sealed till the time of the end. Many shall be purified, and made white, and tried; but the wicked shall do wickedly: and none of the wicked shall understand; but the wise shall understand. And from the time that the daily sacrifice shall be taken away, and the abomination that maketh desolate set up, there shall be **a thousand two hundred and ninety days**. Blessed is he that waiteth, and cometh to the **thousand three hundred and five and thirty days**. But go thou thy way till the end be: for thou shalt rest, and stand in thy lot at the end of the days*" (Daniel 12:8-13).

First of all, Daniel was extremely curious to know more about that final beast and the details of that time but is expressly told that the knowledge is not going to be given to him. It concerns the remnant who will be going through that time and more information would be given about it at a later date.

The running to and fro and increased knowledge of verse 4 of chapter 12 is not a reference to the exponential increase in knowledge and technology that has occurred in our day, although that is quite significant. Daniel was seeking specific knowledge about that period of time and it was not going to be given to him. The issue of the Lord going silent to the nation after the 49 years of rebuilding until Messiah is then declared. They would run to and fro seeking a word from the Lord but would find none (Hosea 5:6,15; Micah 3:4; 5:3; Amos 8:11-13; Psalm 74:9).

This is what, among other things, makes John the Baptist's ministry so significant as the Lord once again began to speak to the nation and what that meant as far as where they were on the time schedule. The knowledge is increased in some measure by Zechariah, as well as the Lord and ministry of the circumcision apostles, but mainly occurs with the arrival of the book of the Revelation when John is given to see that final beast as he is transported by the Spirit into the Lord's Day—the Day of the Lord.

There are three periods outlined in Daniel chapter 12: 1260 days, 1290 days and 1335 days. The last period is often referred to as the extra 75 days because of the extra 30 days of 1290 and 45 days of 1335. But it is my belief, when the starting points are understood, that it should really only be understood as the "extra" 45 days as this period of time is concerned with some particular events. Concerning the 1290 days we are told that it begins from the taking away of the daily sacrifice. If you begin it at the exact 3-1/2 year mark you will indeed go over the 1260 days. But I believe the Lord is here defining the phrase "in the midst of the week" that He had used already in Daniel 9:27.

When you understand just what the Antichrist and his cronies do with respect to Jerusalem and the temple, you understand that it will take more than one day. During that one month midpoint, he will take away the daily sacrifice, set up the abomination of desolation and give them thirty days to either worship and bow down as was demanded by Nebuchadnezzar or suffer from the extermination policy that he will put into effect when he divides the land for gain (Daniel 11:39). Once those thirty days are over, then will begin the great tribulation and determined desolation that is strictly limited to 42 months, during which time the Antichrist is allowed to prevail and prosper in his revealed form.

Then there is the 1335 day period which is marked at its end by the prophesied resurrection which hope Job shared in as well

(Job 14:14). Daniel is told he would be resurrected and granted entrance into the kingdom at the end of those days (Ezekiel 37:11,12; Hebrews 11; Revelation 11:18). What occurs during that period of time between the end of the determined 42 months and the resurrection on day 1335 is obviously of great interest. It is my belief that it is during that time that the fall feasts will be literally fulfilled to the day.

It is generally recognized that Succot represents the kingdom. But it will actually be fulfilled to the day and indeed is what officially marks the beginning of the kingdom. It is essential that Daniel and the other prophetic saints be resurrected before the celebration of the Feast of Tabernacles so that they may join in that great supper of the Lamb that the Lord spoke often of during His earthly ministry. More will be said about this later.

It is important to understand in connection with this that the entire month of Elul which precedes the month of Tishrei is joined with Rosh HaShanah and its ten Days of Awe, and that entire period leading up to Yom Kippur on the tenth of Tishrei is known as the Season of Teshuvah or season of repentance. From the first day of Rosh HaShanah or Tishrei first to the first day of Succot or Tishrei fifteenth is not surprisingly fifteen days. Add that to the month of Elul that precedes it and what do you have? That's right, 45 days.

Simply stated, it is my understanding that once the 42 month or 1260 day period ends, something particular will begin to happen lasting for thirty days in preparation for the Lord's return on Rosh HaShanah, the first of Tishrei. There will then ensue a mighty military campaign, concluding with the utter destruction of the beast and the kings of the earth in what is popularly known as Armageddon. The Lord will then prepare the nation to receive all that had been spoken and promised about the kingdom, including that unique blessing specially connected with Yom Kippur which deals with atonement for the nation, unlike Passover which deals with personal atonement. Finally, the great resurrection takes place and that reborn nation enters the kingdom, celebrates the marriage supper of the Lamb, and the righteous rule of the King of kings and Lord of lords begins. Now, let us return to the first thirty-day period for a closer look.

It is commonly believed that the Lord will return at the very end of Daniel's seventieth week, presumably on the very 1260th day. Some have Him returning a short while before that. This may turn out to be the case but I think not and will endeavor to demonstrate why. It seems clear to me that there is an allotted time whereby complete power is given over to the beast. That last 42 months of Daniel's seventieth week has been set as a determined time whereby he is able to prosper and prevail with no one seemingly being able to stop him. This is the great tribulation and there is no escaping the fact that it *will* consume this earth for the time appointed. It is often thought that because the Antichrist seemingly loses that power after the 1260 days, and we know that he meets his ultimate demise by the coming of the Lord, that the Lord therefore returns at the 1260th day and destroys him. This need not be the case, however, and indeed I don't believe it is.

Let me preface this by saying that I believe the little horn referred to throughout Daniel is the same individual, namely Antichrist. I do not believe that anything refers to Antiochus Epiphanes, Titus the Roman, etc. It seems clear to me that the little horn is the same individual throughout and no more refers to those oppressors than it does Hitler.

"*He shall subdue three kings. And he shall speak great words against the most High, and shall wear out the saints of the most High, and think to change times and laws: and they shall be given into his hand until a time and times and the dividing of time. But the judgment shall sit, and they shall take away his dominion to consume and to destroy it unto the end*" (Daniel 7:25,26).

"*Yea he magnified himself even to the prince of the host, and by him the daily sacrifice was taken away, and the place of his sanctuary was cast down. And an host was given him against the daily sacrifice by reason of transgression, and it cast down the truth to the ground; and it practised, and prospered*" (Daniel 8:11,12).

This issue of the host given to him for that purpose is again emphasized in Daniel 9:26,27 where it declares, "*The* **people** *of the prince that shall come shall destroy the city and the sanctuary; and the end thereof shall be with a flood, and unto the end of the war desolations are determined. And he shall confirm the covenant with many for one week: and in the midst of the week he shall cause the oblation to cease, and for the overspreading of abominations he shall make it desolate, even until the consummation, and that determined shall be poured upon the desolate.*"

"*And arms shall stand on his part, and* **they** *shall pollute the sanctuary of strength, and shall take away the daily sacrifice, and* **they** *shall place the abomination that maketh desolate...Thus shall he do in the most strong holds with a strange god, whom he shall acknowledge and increase with glory: and he shall cause* **them** *to rule over many, and shall divide the land for gain*" (Daniel 11:31,39).

It is crucial to understand the role of the host that is given to him and the determined 42 months that cannot be avoided. When the Lord declares that "*Except those days should be shortened, there would no flesh be saved: but for the elect's sake those days shall be shortened*" (Matthew 24:22), He is amplifying this point. I do not believe He is saying that it will actually be less than 1260 days as it has been specifically determined by the Lord.

The graciousness and mercy is that it will be 1260 days and no more, again because it is a determined period of time. Antichrist will have complete world control and seek to utterly persecute the saints for 42 months but then the timing for something that had been given into his hand will expire. Simply put, at the time of the end, complete rebellion will erupt within his own ten-horn camp and amongst the other kings of the earth at large.

This is seen in Revelation where it states, "*And the ten horns which thou sawest upon the beast, these shall hate the whore, and make her desolate and naked, and shall eat her flesh, and burn her with fire.*" Why? "*For God hath put in their hearts to fulfil his will, and to* **agree,** *and give their kingdom unto the beast,* **until** *the words of God shall be fulfilled. And the woman which thou sawest is that great city, which reigneth over the kings of the earth.*"

Now I differ with many when it comes to the understanding of these passages, both with identity and timing. First, it seems clear to me that this is the literal city of Babylon. She has many daughters and there is great significance to this reaching all the way back to Genesis, but for now I will simply say that you are seeing the fulfillment of the destruction of Babylon that was prophesied long ago but has yet to take place. Contrary to what is often said on the subject, Babylon has never seen the destruction that the Bible says is to come upon her and for that reason alone must show up once again to meet her appointed time.

Furthermore, that mystical aspect of her bloodthirstiness is part of the beast's own system, not something that he is opposed to or seeks freedom from. Most of the objections as to why it cannot possibly be Babylon are simply wrong and are specifically applied to that literal city in the Old Testament itself. It is his capital city and his glory—his queen—as he counterfeits the true Christ who will also be married to His bride, His city, the New Jerusalem. The woman is not a yoke of bondage for the Antichrist but she most certainly is for the ten horns and the rest of the kings of the earth, so much so that they *hate* her. This is part of God's wisdom in once again taking the wise one in his own craftiness. Give him the power he so desperately longs for and it will turn to his utter ruin.

As to the timing, it is generally believed that this destruction of the woman takes place at the midpoint, and that some other major "commercial" city is destroyed at the end. I don't believe that is warranted. First, you are told explicitly just who the woman is. She is that great city. The reason many feel led to differentiate it from the city of chapter 18 is because of a perceived difference in timing. That is, they read chapter 17 as saying that at the midpoint the ten horns destroy the woman and thereby give their power over to the beast. I believe this is inconsistent with all that has gone before in the scriptures leading up to this point.

I believe the explanation is that they agree until a certain time because there is a time determined. The league and covenant is made with the little horn at the beginning of the seventieth week and is in fact what officially starts the clock ticking for that seven-year period (Daniel 11:23). They further agree with him and conspire to exterminate Israel and divide the spoil. This must continue and prosper for the time determined and will last until the appointed time of the end when literally all hell will break loose.

If my understanding is correct, it is this utter rebellion and havoc that will constitute the better part of the thirty days as his total dominion begins to break down after the determined time that had been given to the beast. I also believe this 1 month period has a correlation to the 1 month midpoint of the seventieth week. God throughout the Bible has a tit-for-tat policy, especially as it relates to the nations and their treatment of Israel. The Man of Sin had given Israel 30 days to either change their ways, forsake their religion and worship him, or suffer under his extermination policy.

Likewise, God will give the nations and the armies of the earth thirty days before He puts into effect His extermination policy. That period of time is leading up to one thing—the return of the Lord Jesus Christ to earth in power and great glory. It is during this time of chaos and rebellion that the armies are called to the valley of Megiddo for the great supper of God Almighty. Only at this gathering *they* will be the main course.

It is my understanding that it is at this time that the events recorded in Revelation 16:12-16 will be taking place, "*And the sixth angel poured out his vial upon the great river Euphrates; and the water thereof was dried up, that the way of the kings of the east might be prepared. And I saw three unclean spirits like frogs come out of the mouth of the dragon, and out of the mouth of the beast, and out of the mouth of the false prophet. For they are the spirits of devils, working miracles, which go forth unto the kings of the earth and of the whole world, to gather them to the battle of that great day of God Almighty. Behold, I come as a thief. Blessed is he that watcheth, and keepeth his garments, lest he walk naked, and they see his shame. And he gathered them together into a place called in the Hebrew tongue Armageddon.*"

There is a time when the great gathering begins to take place. I believe it is also significant because of when it takes place. It is part of the sixth vial, which I don't need to tell you comes after the fifth vial. This is significant because the fifth vial brings darkness to the beast's kingdom. In connection with this, note the odd insertion above by the Lord about watching for He comes as a thief. Now granted it would be encouragement, but it still seems to me to be an odd break in the text. I believe we can begin to get a better understanding now by taking all of these myriad events into consideration. We know that the saints are given into his hand for 1260 days. His ability to prevail against them in connection with the great tribulation is a fixed and purposefully determined time.

There will be false prophets claiming that He has returned before the time but it is mere deception *"For as lightning cometh out of the east, and shineth even unto the west; so shall also the coming of the son of man be. For wheresoever the carcasse is, there will the eagles be gathered together. **Immediately after** the tribulation of those days shall the sun be darkened, and the moon shall not give her light, and the stars shall fall from heaven, and the powers of the heavens shall be shaken: And then shall appear the sign of the son of man in heaven"* (Matthew 24:27-30).

The darkness is immediately after the tribulation, but a period of time exists beyond that, although its duration will be unsure for reasons we will discuss. At this time the armies will be gathered to Armageddon and the remnant is exhorted to specially watch, though they will not know the day or hour. There will be many factors working to hinder them from being able to calculate time, not the least of which is their being holed up in their various hiding places where they are miraculously provided for by the Lord in the wilderness as He had done so many times in Israel's history and even in His earthly ministry. But the major reason is because of the darkness that will consume the earth at that particular time and its inextricable connection with His coming.

The fact is that not knowing the day or hour was a prophetic issue. Going back to Zechariah we read, *"And it shall come to pass in that day, that the light shall not be clear, nor dark: But it shall be one day which shall be known to the* LORD, *not day, nor night: but it shall come to pass, that at evening time it shall be light"* (Zechariah 14:6,7).

*"And the Lord shall be seen over them, and his arrow shall go forth as the **lightning**: and the Lord God shall blow the trumpet, and shall go with whirlwinds of the south"* (Zechariah 9:14).

"The earth shall quake before them; the heavens shall tremble: the sun and moon shall be dark, and the stars shall withdraw their shining: And the LORD *shall utter his voice before his army: for his camp is very great: for he is strong that executeth his word: for the day of the* LORD *is **great** and very **terrible**; and who can abide it"* (Joel 2:10,11).

"For I will gather all nations, and bring them down into the valley of Jehoshaphat, and will plead with them there for my people and for my heritage Israel, whom they have scattered among the nations, and parted my land...Proclaim ye this among the Gentiles; Prepare war, wake up the mighty men, let all the men of war draw near; let them come up...Assemble yourselves, and come, all ye heathen, and gather yourselves together round about: thither cause thy mighty ones to come down, O LORD. *Let the heathen be wakened, and come up to the valley of Jehoshaphat: for there will I sit to judge all the heathen round about....Multitudes, multitudes in the valley of decision: for the day of the* LORD *is near in the valley of decision. **The sun and the moon shall be darkened, and the stars shall withdraw their shining**. The* LORD *also shall roar out of Zion, and utter his voice from Jerusalem; and the heavens and the earth shall shake: but the* LORD *will be the hope of his people, and the strength of the children of Israel. So shall ye know that I am the* LORD *your God dwelling in Zion, my holy mountain: then shall Jerusalem be holy, and there shall no strangers pass through her any more"* (Joel 3:2,9,11,12,14-17).

"Therefore I will look unto the LORD; *I will wait for the God of my salvation: my God will hear me. Rejoice not against me, O mine enemy: when I fall, I shall rise; when I sit in **darkness**, the* LORD *shall be **a light** unto me. I will bear the indignation of the* LORD, *because I have sinned against him, until he plead my cause: he will bring me*

*forth to the light, and I shall behold his righteousness. Then **she** that is mine enemy shall see it, and shame shall cover **her** which said unto me, Where is the LORD thy God? Mine eyes shall behold **her**: now shall **she** be trodden down as the mire of the streets"* (Micah 7:7-10). Note that in connection with the darkness is the destruction of that woman. (See also Isaiah 47; Revelation 16:10;17;18).

"*Therefore **wait ye** upon me, saith the LORD, until the day that I rise up to the prey: for my determination is to gather the nations, that I may assemble the kingdoms, to pour upon them mine indignation, even all my fierce anger: for all the earth shall be devoured with the fire of my jealousy*" (Zephaniah 3:8). These are the same events of the gathering of the nations for battle under the sixth vial in Revelation, which is why the angels *pour* out the seven vials wherein is *filled up* the *wrath* of God.

"*But unto you that fear my name shall the **Sun** of righteousness arise with healing in his wings; and ye shall go forth, and grow up as calves of the stall*" (Malachi 4:2). Notice it says *Sun* not *Son*. When you understand the utter darkness that will cover the earth preceding His return, which is marked by Him bursting on the scene as lightning so His coming is unmistakable, the fact of Him arising as the sun bringing deliverance is quite appropriate. This leaves us at the point of waiting for the actual return of the Lord as He breaks through the heavens riding upon that white horse and comes to earth as the mighty man of war to settle His cause with Israel, take possession of the earth and fulfill all of the covenants and promises pertaining to His plans and purposes for the earth.

It is this arrival that I believe is the "hidden day" properly characterized as such for the reasons given thus far. This will mark the arrival and fulfillment of Rosh HaShanah with its blowing of trumpets as the real Joshua, Yeshua, Jesus, goes forth to take the "city." He has already sent His two witnesses into the land and now with His great and mighty host He has come to do battle.

This is the *Great and Terrible* Day of the Lord. "*The LORD shall go forth as a mighty man, he shall stir up jealousy like a man of war: he shall cry, yea roar; he shall prevail against his enemies"* (Isaiah 42:13). As the lion of Judah He will mightily roar as he comes and settles the controversy over Zion. (See also Isaiah. 31:4; Hosea 11:10; Joel 3:16). *"Behold, I will send you Elijah the prophet before the coming of the* **great and dreadful** *day of the LORD"* (Malachi 4:5).

The day of the Lord encompasses the entire fifth and final installment of the fifth course of punishment. It is the Lord's day that John is taken into by the Spirit in the book of Revelation, in much the same way that Ezekiel was transported. The great and terrible Day of the Lord, however, is when the Lord personally returns for battle. The times of the Gentiles have ended and the time is come for the setting up of the righteous government of the King of kings and Lord of lords. It is time for the New Year to begin.

"And in the days of these kings shall the God of heaven set up a kingdom, which shall never be destroyed: and the kingdom shall not be left to other people, but it shall break in pieces and consume all these kingdoms, and it shall stand for ever" (Daniel 2:44).

"There were great voices in heaven, saying, The kingdoms of this world are become the kingdoms of our Lord, and of his Christ; and he shall reign for ever and ever" (Revelation 11:15). But before that rejected stone cut without hands becomes a great mountain it must first smash the image upon its feet. That is what the great and terrible Day of the Lord is all about.

The feet of this image has ten toes. These are the same ten horns of the beast and are the kings that make up the Antichrist's ten nation confederacy. It is interesting to note that the Yamim Nora'im, or Days of Awe from Rosh HaShanah to Yom Kippur, are ten days. If it were representative of Daniel's seventieth week one would think there would be only seven days corresponding to the seven years. But these are truly the Days of Awe when the Messiah comes personally to fulfill these feasts literally and to the day just as He did the spring feasts at His first coming to accomplish the redemptive work.

"*His going forth is prepared as the morning; and he shall come unto us as the rain, as the latter and former rain unto the earth*" (Hosea 6: 3). This is the time of the former rain, the time to water the sun-baked and oppressed land of Yisrael.

During the preceding thirty days of darkness the remnant has been clinging to passages such as Psalm 27, "*The LORD is my light and my salvation; whom shall I fear? The LORD is the strength of my life; of whom shall I be afraid?...And now shall my head be lifted up above mine enemies round about me...I had fainted, unless I had believed to see the goodness of the LORD in the land of the living. Wait on the LORD: be of good courage, and he shall strengthen thine heart: wait, I say, on the LORD.*" But now the waiting is over. "*Arise and shine; for thy light is come, and the glory of the LORD is risen upon thee*" (Isaiah 60:1). (See also Zechariah 9:14-16).

"*Awake, awake, put on strength, O arm of the LORD; awake, as in the ancient days, in the generations of old. Art thou not it that hath cut Rahab, and wounded the dragon?*" (Isaiah 51:9).

These feasts take place in the seventh month and I believe line up with the seventh seal, seventh trumpet and seventh vial of the book of Revelation. This is also the beginning of the civil calendar as Christ takes over the kingdoms of this world, completely destroys the satanic plan of evil and sets up His government to rule and reign over the earth from Jerusalem in the land of Israel. The first item on His agenda will be to deal with the kings of the earth, especially the ten horns. In connection with this it needs to be understood that it is a campaign. The Lord does not immediately set down upon the Mount of Olives. It is indeed the first place that His feet touch down upon when He comes back but He has been rather busy before then.

"*Then shall the LORD go forth, and fight against those nations, as when he fought in the day of battle. And his feet shall stand in that day upon the mount of Olives, which is before Jerusalem on the east*" (Zechariah 14:3,4).

"*And when he had spoken these things, while they beheld, he was taken up; and a cloud received him out of their sight. And while they looked stedfastly toward heaven as he went up, behold, two men stood by them in white apparel; Which also said, Ye men of Galilee, why stand ye gazing up into heaven? This same Jesus, which is taken up from you into heaven, shall so come in like manner as ye have seen him go into heaven. Then returned they unto Jerusalem from the mount called Olivet, which is from Jerusalem a sabbath day's journey"* (Acts 1:9-12).

There are a few things to note. He first goes forth to fight against certain nations outside the land, then His feet stand upon the Mount of Olives and it cleaves in two. He will then make His way to the valley of Jehoshaphat where the nations have been gathered. This route will follow some paths that He had led Israel in before in her history concerning the conquest of the land under Joshua and David, both men of war.

Look at Isaiah 31:4,5: *"So shall the LORD of hosts come down to fight for mount Zion, and for the hill thereof. As birds flying, so will the LORD of hosts defend Jerusalem; defending also he will deliver it; and passing over he will preserve it."* Did you see that? He first does some flying. The other thing to note is that when He does this He fights as He did in the day of battle. When was that? And where was it? *"Wherefore it is said in the book of the wars of the LORD..."* (Numbers 21:14).

This is one of the books that will get opened at that time and as a commanding general He will implement His detailed war plans. The Lord has countless times given Israel a rehearsal and foretaste of things to come, to prepare them for the appointed times and demonstrate His awesome wisdom. He truly is the only one who knows the end from the beginning, the one who dwells in eternity.

This period of time parallels when God first brought the people out of Egypt (Exodus 19:4; Revelation 11:8; 12:14), where they fled from Pharaoh and his armies, were supernaturally provided for in the wilderness and brought into the land that was to be their inheritance where God would make His dwelling place. During their journey they were brought to particular places for no readily apparent reason. Simply stated, there is a particular route which the Lord will take as that man of war. I will leave it to you to search this matter out in Numbers 21:10 ff; Joshua and Habakkuk 3. But furthermore, I believe there is a connection between the ten Days of Awe, the ten horns, the inheritance of Israel and the controversy over Zion. The key to understanding this is identifying just who the ten horns of the beast are.

Chapter Five

Rosh HaShanah

The Great & Terrible
Day of the Lord,
The 10 Horns of the Beast
&
The Significance of the Land of Israel

I t is imperative to keep in mind in this study that the book of Revelation is the full counterpart to Genesis. The Alpha and Omega, the First and the Last, the Beginning and the End. That is who the Lord is and no less is His Word. We will amplify upon this later but it must be noted that God acts with purpose and His actions are reflective and in accordance with His will. He created this earth and all that therein is for a purpose. It was not done in vain.

His plans were interrupted by the activities of a certain serpent in that historical garden whereby man turned over the dominion and possession of earth that had been entrusted to him to that wise and crafty rebellious one who had been known as Lucifer. The Bible records God's concerted and purposeful actions to contend with the dragon, that old serpent, to reconcile this earth back to Himself and repossess it in order to fulfill that which He had purposed for it from the very beginning. Stated another way, from Genesis on through each book of the Scriptures, the Bible is working its way to the book of Revelation.

It is in Revelation where we see the complete and utter demolition of the entire satanic plan of evil actually take place. All throughout the Scriptures we are given glimpses into that time. The prophets function as the word of the Lord comes and speaks to and through them, and we are told many of the things that will be taking place including the activities of God and the activities of the enemy—Satan. We are even given a time schedule for when these things will take place and in what order. But it is in Revelation where we are actually transported with the apostle John into the Lord's Day when these dreadful events will actually take place.

Daniel lived at the beginning of the times of the Gentiles when the final countdown began, anticipating the end of the present rulership of this world when the nations will no longer follow the present course of this world and its god. Daniel was even given to see that final beast with its ten horns. It was this final beast that Daniel was curious about and desired to know more of, but he was expressly told that that particular information and knowledge would not come till later and unto another prophet. Meanwhile, the book was to be sealed and Daniel would go to the grave awaiting the resurrection. It is especially the apostle John to whom that increased knowledge comes and he is taken to the time when those ten horns are crowned.

It is interesting that this parallel knowledge came to the two individuals who in their times were especially singled out for being greatly loved. John is particularly distinguished as "the disciple whom Jesus loved." "*And he said unto me, O Daniel, a man greatly beloved…Now I am come to make thee understand what shall befall thy people in the latter days: for yet the vision is for many days*" (Daniel 10:11,14).

When studying prophecy, especially Revelation, it must be appreciated that the events described and language used have great significance. Information is being given to us and events are occurring for a reason. Revelation is not just a book filled with incoherent, wild apocalyptic and cryptic symbols. Quite the opposite is in fact the case. It is *the* **Revelation**, the unveiling. It is intended to bring about understanding and wisdom. It is very detailed and ordered.

But it must first be appreciated for what and where it is in the Word of God. It must be understood where it and the events described in it fit into the grand plans and purposes of God. Just as you progress in mathematics or language, so too are you to progress through the Bible. To understand the great equations and formulas found in the end, you must first be grounded in the foundations of addition, subtraction, multiplication and so on.

It is no wonder then that when the Lord's means of education through His book is not followed, many are often overwhelmed and find nothing but perplexity and utter confusion. It is quite understandable for this to be the case with the unbeliever who views the Bible as nothing more than the work of men, a collection of interesting writings, rules, uplifting messages and a healthy dose of hallucination. But for those that appreciate the Bible for what it is—truth, the very Word of God—there is much more to be obtained, especially in the realm of understanding. It has been given to us to know His very ways and glory with Him in His matchless wisdom. What a truly awesome thought!

So, as that counterpart to Genesis, all the elements that are found in the book of beginnings are brought together for the end in Revelation. Whether it is the garden, the land of Shinar, the Euphrates river all make their appearance once more as the Lord makes good on His promise to bring an end to the current regime of this world and its bondage of corruption and reconcile all things back unto Himself. *"For the creature was made subject to vanity, not willingly, but by reason of him who hath subjected the same in hope, Because the creature itself also shall be delivered from the bondage of corruption into the glorious liberty of the children of God. For we know that the whole creation groaneth and travaileth in pain together until now"* (Romans 8:20-22).

Every funeral we attend is a vivid reminder of that great rebellious act that took place in the garden so long ago and the curse it brought upon this earth. Thank the Lord that Christ Jesus, the promised seed of the woman, was made that curse for us, took it upon Himself with that horrible crown of the cursed thorns of the ground and nailed it to that dark, bloody cross.

"*Cursed is every one that hangeth on a tree*" (Galatians 3:13, Deuteronomy 21:23).

"*For he hath made him to be sin for us, who knew no sin; that we might be made the righteousness of God in him*" (2 Corinthians 5:21).

But, praise God, when He was taken off that cross and laid in the tomb, He didn't stay there. "*Why seek ye the living among the dead? He is not here, but is risen*" (Luke 24:5,6). Having paid the redemption price He could therefore be the firstfruits of the resurrection glory and all that will entail for this planet. He alone is entitled and able to reconcile this earth, take back what Adam lost and restore this world in accordance with what God had purposed for it.

"*And I saw a strong angel proclaiming with a loud voice, Who is worthy to open the book, and to loose the seals thereof? And no man in heaven, nor in earth, neither under the earth, was able to open the book, neither to look thereon. And I wept much, because no man was found worthy to open and to read the book, neither to look thereon. And one of the elders saith unto me, Weep not: behold, the Lion of the tribe of Juda, the Root of David,* **hath prevailed** *to open the book, and to loose the seven seals thereof. And I beheld, and, lo, in the midst of the elders, stood a Lamb as it had been slain...And he came and took the book out of the right hand of him that sat upon the throne*" (Revelation 5:2-7).

That book includes the title deed to the earth and sets in motion all the things that will take place in accordance with the Lord having *His* day. With that said, let us now return to where it all began, Creation and the Middle East, and perhaps gain some insight into just where those ten horns fit into the plans of both God and the enemy concerning this earth.

It was God's intention from the beginning that earth was to be His residence. It was from earth that He would dwell in the midst of His creation in all the universe. It was given to man to have dominion over all that was concerned with planet Earth. As monarch of the earth Adam was uniquely made in God's image and likeness.

"And God said, Let us make man in our image, after our likeness: and let them have dominion over the fish of the sea, and over the fowl of the air, and over the cattle, and over every creeping thing that creepeth upon the earth" (Genesis 1:26).

"When I consider thy heavens, the work of thy fingers, the moon and the stars, which thou hast ordained; What is man, that thou art mindful of him? And the son of man, that thou visitest him? For thou hast made him a little lower than the angels, and hast crowned him with glory and honour. Thou madest him to have dominion over the works of thy hands; thou hast put all things under his feet: All sheep and oxen, yea, and the beasts of the field; The fowl of the air, and the fish of the sea, and whatsoever passeth through the paths of the seas. O LORD our Lord, how excellent is thy name in all the earth" (Psalm 8:3-9).

The psalms need to be appreciated for their prophetic significance far more than they often are. The above connects the purposes of man and earth with the time when God will be known, recognized and acknowledged in *all* the earth. This is built upon in the Psalms, as well as the prophets which will follow and will have significance for us in the matter at hand in due time.

But more than simply choosing earth in general, God had chosen a particular piece of real estate on this earth that would uniquely serve as His residence. We are introduced to a parcel of land right from the beginning, namely what is designated the land of Eden. Then East in Eden is a garden. What is the significance of this designated boundary of Eden? If you're asking yourself what all this has to do with the ten horns, then please bear with me. We are going somewhere.

Let's go back to what God was doing at the very beginning of creation. *"In the beginning God created the heaven and the earth. And the earth was without form, and void; and darkness was upon the face of the deep. And the Spirit of God moved upon the face of the waters"* (Genesis1:1,2).

What on earth is going on literally? Well, technically, the earth, or dry ground, hasn't appeared yet but never mind. Obviously God is going to form and fill it as He has not created it in vain (Isaiah 45:18). But are we told anything in particular about what is going on here? I believe we are.

"Bless the LORD, O my soul. O LORD my God, thou art very great; thou art clothed with honour and majesty. Who coverest thyself with light as with a garment: who stretchest out the heavens like a curtain: Who layeth the beams of his chambers in the waters" (Psalm 104:1-3).

Now we know why darkness is covering the deep back in Genesis 1:2. Even though God is surrounded by light, He's on the other side of the curtain. I'll leave it to you to study the significance of that as it relates to the tabernacle, temple and so on. But what I am especially concerned with is that He is laying something back there in the waters, namely the beams of *His* chambers. These chambers are uniquely His but He first lays the beams and so far that is all that is in view. There is no record of those chambers being laid upon the beams, not yet anyway.

Having already begun his rebellion and defilement in the heavenly places, the serpent quickly went to work in enticing man to join his rebellion in his attempt to be like the Most High, maker of heaven and earth. He needed to accomplish this before God's plans for this earth were fully realized. That first week would be a trying one, filled with failure and disappointment, and the arrival of those chambers would be delayed. Adam and Eve, among other things, were denied access to the tree of life and driven out of the garden. Also, there were two cherubim angels with flaming swords placed at the east gate of the garden. Again, I leave it to you to study the connection that these elements also have to the "house" of God, the tabernacle and temple.

God made it known at that time that He would contend with Satan over possession of this earth, and that through the seed of the woman He would crush the head of the serpent, even though the serpent would bruise his heel. The serpent grabbed hold and bit the heel of Messiah, the arm of the Lord at the cross and thought he had conquered. Little did he realize that the Lord had him right where he wanted him. The cross was the very means by which the satanic plan of evil was to be thwarted. It is the very heel that the serpent has bitten that will bring him crashing to the ground, crushing his head in utter defeat.

Speaking of when the Lord Jesus Christ will go forth to battle, Habakkuk says, "*Was the LORD displeased against the rivers? Was thine anger against the rivers? Was thy wrath against the sea, that thou didst ride upon thine horses and thy chariots of salvation? The sun and moon stood still in their habitation: at the light of thine arrows they went, and at the shining of thy glittering spear. Thou didst march through the land in indignation, thou didst thresh the heathen in anger. Thou wentest forth for the salvation of thy people, even for salvation with thine anointed; thou woundedst the **head** out of the house of the wicked, by discovering the foundation unto the neck. Selah*" (Habakkuk 3:8,11-14).

"*Awake, awake, put on strength, O arm of the LORD; awake, as in the ancient days, in the generations of old. Art thou not it that hath cut Rahab, and wounded the dragon? Art thou not it which hath dried the sea, the waters of the great deep; that hath made the depths of the sea a way for the ransomed to pass over?*" (Isaiah 51:9,10).

First, it should be noticed that the Lord refers you back to that seed of the woman by calling the arm of the Lord "it." Back to Genesis 3:15, "*I will put enmity between thee and the woman, and between thy seed and her seed; it shall bruise thy head, and thou shalt bruise his heel.*"

He is both *it* and *him* and this is why when He is actually born as that seed of the woman, not the seed of the man, He is referred to rather strangely. "*Then said Mary unto that angel, How shall this be, seeing I know not a man? And the angel answered and said unto her, The Holy Ghost shall come upon thee, and the power of the*

*Highest shall overshadow thee: therefore also **that holy thing** which shall be born of thee shall be called the Son of God"* (Luke 1:34,35).

Also notice that in connection with Christ going out to do battle He seems to have a preoccupation with water. Why is this? Why is He making a point of drying up the waters? We know that four angels came out of the Euphrates in Revelation. Also, the dragon Christ comes to wound is Leviathan, that great beast of the sea. But there is a particular connection with the drying up and the route that He takes through the land as He makes war. This leads us nicely into the next observation.

Let us now skip ahead to the flood. The occurrence of the global cataclysmic flood that took place in the days of Noah is an event I am sure you are well familiar with. It stands as a testimony to the intervention of God in the affairs of men in a big way. God has judged the world before and He will do it again, only this time not with water but fire.

There are now—and will be in the Lord's Day—those in the apostate nation who will be willingly ignorant of the fact that this catastrophic event has taken place. They wish to deny this so as to go along their merry way and further sear their conscience to numb any concern for the coming judgement of this world. These folks are not evolutionists in a strict sense, although they are certainly included in the self-deception. No, the ones specifically referred to by Peter, an apostle of the circumcision, in his letter to the scattered remnant are ones that acknowledge a creation.

"Knowing this first, that there shall come in the last days scoffers, walking after their own lusts, And saying, Where is the promise of his coming? For since the fathers fell asleep, all things continue as they were from the beginning of the creation. For this they willingly are ignorant of, that by the word of God the heavens were of old, and the earth standing out of the water and in the water: Whereby the world that then was, being overflowed with water, perished: But the heavens and the earth, which are now, by the same word are kept in store, reserved unto fire against the day of judgement and perdition of ungodly men" (2 Peter 3:3-7).

These scoffers and mockers will cling to their uniformitarianism in a willful attempt to put the idea of judgement out of their mind. This will bear a particular connection to their denial that Messiah has already come, that he is indeed the Lord Jesus Christ and that He will return to fulfill all that was spoken (see 1 John). They will not respond well to the testimony that declares that by their denial of both Him and the Father, *they* are the true apostates, not the remnant which keeps the testimony of Jesus Christ. By their response they will prove that they are indeed members of that generation of vipers upon whom all the prophesied judgement and destruction will fall as they fill up the measure of their fathers.

Now, in connection with the flood let us turn to the book of Job. Job is set forth as a type of the remnant and, as such, he is told that what he was caused to endure was the result of the Lord's contention with Satan over this earth and God's plans and purposes for it. It is for this reason that the Lord points Job to His acts, particularly as Creator. It is the same thing the remnant will be exhorted to as they go through the time about which the Lord said, "*And because iniquity shall abound, the love of many shall wax cold. But he that shall endure unto the end, the same shall be* **saved**. *And this gospel of the kingdom shall be preached in all the world for a witness unto all nations; and then shall the end come...For then shall be great tribulation, such as was not since the beginning of the world to this time, no, nor ever shall be. And except those days should be shortened, there should no* **flesh** *be* **saved**: *but for the elect's sake those days shall be shortened*" (Matthew 24:12-14,21,22)

"*Behold, we count them happy which endure. Ye have heard of the patience of Job, and have seen the end of the Lord; that the Lord is very pitiful, and of tender mercy*" (James 5:11).

"*For the time is come that judgement must begin at the house of God: and if it first begin at us, what shall the end be of them that obey not the gospel of God? And if the righteous scarcely be saved, where shall the ungodly and the sinner appear? Wherefore let them that suffer according to the will of God commit the keeping of their souls to him in well doing,* **as unto a faithful Creator**" (1 Peter 4:19).

The Lord says something very interesting to Job as He gives him words *with* knowledge. There will be many vying for the ear of the remnant just as Job's "friends," but they have been given particular counsel and they would do well to adhere to it.

Now keeping in mind what we have discussed so far, let's look at Job 38:8,9, where the Lord tells Job in speaking of the flood, "*Or who shut up the sea with doors, when it brake forth, as if it had issued out of the womb? When I made the cloud the garment thereof, and thick darkness a swaddling band for it, And **brake** up for it **my decreed place**, and set bars and doors, And said, Hitherto shalt thou come, but no further: and here shall thy **proud** waves be stayed?*"

I believe there is a reason the Lord calls them proud, and it has to do with Leviathan as that proud one and his cohorts being in them. They are especially interested because they recognize what is set forth in the preceding verses, namely that God had broken up His decreed place. There is a decreed place where the Lord has chosen to put His name, the place of His residence and dwelling.

This issue and geographical area will show up again after the flood. First you have the division of lands according to Noah's sons Japheth, Ham and Shem, and some prophetic utterances involving the course of the people that would come from them. In connection with this we also have recorded an interesting event that occurred involving Ham which resulted in the cursing of his son Canaan. This is highly significant in light of what role the Canaanites will play from this point on in Scripture as it relates to a specific piece of real estate. There is then recorded the incident at the Tower of Babel where man first attempted to set up a world government and religion but was hindered when God divided the languages.

"*And the whole earth was of one language, and of one speech...Go to, let us go down, and there confound their language, that they may not understand one another's speech. So the Lord scattered them abroad from thence upon the face of all the earth: and they left off to build the city*" (Genesis 11:1).

That one language was undoubtedly the original Hebrew, the language of heaven, and there are many fascinating studies that examine the mathematical nature and word roots of Hebrew. But even more fundamental, there are word plays that involve the language and events in the early chapters of Genesis and for those to be true, the language would have to be some form of Hebrew.

This city will show up again in the book of Revelation and it will be located in the same place as the one recorded in Genesis: "*And it came to pass, as they journeyed from the east, that they found a plain in the land of Shinar; and they dwelt there*" (Genesis 11:2).

In connection with this, one should examine closely the prophecies of Zechariah which act as a bridge between the elements found in Daniel and Revelation. Speaking of that coming time Zeachariah says, "*Then the angel that talked with me went forth, and said unto me, Lift up now thine eyes, and seeth what is this that goeth forth. And I said, What is it? And he said, This is an ephah that goeth forth. He said moreover, This is their resemblance through all the earth. And, behold, there was lifted up a talent of lead: and this is a woman that sitteth in the midst of the ephah. And he said, This is wickedness. And he cast it into the midst of the ephah; and he cast the weight of lead upon the mouth thereof. Then lifted I up mine eyes, and looked, and, behold, there came out two women, and the wind was in their wings; for they had wings like the wings of a stork: and they lifted up the ephah between the earth and the heaven. Then said I to the angel that talked with me, Whither do these bear the ephah? And he said unto me, To build it an house in the land of Shinar: and it shall be established, and set there upon her own base*" (Zechariah 5:5-11).

The nations did not like to retain God in their knowledge so God gave them up (see Romans 1:18-32). He did not abandon His plans to contend with the enemy and repossess the earth but the means by which He would accomplish this would be far more focused. The hope of that promised seed of the woman is still alive. The record of His truth and communications to man needed to be preserved. There are things about the nature and power of God which are readily apparent from the awesome creation around us. The mere fact that the naturalist/evolutionist has to attempt to explain why there is an *appearance* of design even though there *really* is no designer speaks volumes.

However, there are things that God wants us to know, things that would be well nigh impossible to know if He didn't tell us. The nations as a whole had become utterly corrupted and that corruption extended to the knowledge of the truth, the godhead, redemption, and the received story in general that had been passed on from Noah and his sons.

All through the biblical account up to this point God has been narrowing the line through which that promised seed would come. When he did come it would be unmistakable who he was and through an extensive amount of prophecies God would prove Himself to be exactly who He claims to be, the Eternal One, the only one who knows the end from the beginning. He has given the precise address of the Messiah and to the honest skeptic there should be no question that, though penned by dozens and dozens of authors, the ultimate author is indeed the God of the Bible and that promised curse-removing redeemer is none other than the God-man, the Lord Jesus Christ.

In connection with this ongoing contention with the serpent and his stronghold over the nations, the Lord called out of that corruption an individual who would later become known as Abraham. God made it clear to Abraham that he would be instrumental in His plans and purposes for this earth. He separated Abraham out and was going to make of him a *great* nation—one that would be uniquely His nation, called by Him, and would be great for that reason. Among other things it would be through this nation that He would preserve the knowledge of the truth and of His ways. It would be through this Shemitic/Hebrew seed that the promised Messiah would come—specifically through Abraham, Isaac and Jacob (Luke 3:23-38). Though there were other children in the line, the blessing and divine purposes would only come through them. God chose Isaac not Ishmael, Jacob not Esau.

This will be relevant for the discussion at hand especially when we deal with the contention over Zion. But this was all very strategic on God's part. The first thing He says to Abraham (Abram at this point) concerning the promise is, "*Now the LORD had said unto Abram, Get thee out of thy country, and from thy kindred, and from thy father's house, unto a **land** that I will shew thee: And I will make of thee a great nation, and I will bless thee, and make thy name great; and thou shalt be a blessing: And I will bless them that bless thee, and curse him that curseth thee: and in thee shall all the families of the earth be blessed*" (Genesis 12:1-3).

Even though the Lord has given up the nations, He has not given up on them. In fact, it is His separating out a nation for Himself that will be the means of reconciling the earth and bringing the nations as such into a relationship with Him. So, far from abandoning His plan, He is actually just beginning to get it underway in earnest. But the issue of a particular land in connection with this calling of Abraham ought to be conspicuous to the reader. Again, there is a particular piece of real estate God is concerned about and He will make it clear that He has some intentions for it. Now let's move ahead to an incident that occurred with Lot.

"*And there was a strife between the herdmen of Abram's cattle and the herdmen of Lot's cattle: and the Canaanite and the Perizzite dwelled then in the land. And Abram said unto Lot, Let there be no strife, I pray thee, between me and thee, and between my herdmen and thy herdmen; for we be brethren. Is not the whole land before thee? separate thyself, I pray thee, from me: if thou wilt take the left hand, then I will go to the right; or if thou depart to the right hand, then I will go to the left. And Lot lifted up his eyes, and beheld all the plain of Jordan, that it was well watered everywhere, before the LORD destroyed Sodom and Gomorrah, **even as the garden of the LORD**, like the land of Egypt, as thou comest unto Zoar. Then Lot chose him all the plain of Jordan; and Lot journeyed **east**: and they separated themselves the one from the other*" (Genesis 13:7-11).

The record of who is in the land will again be significant for our discussion of the contention over Zion. But look again at what is said about the land. It is compared to the garden of the Lord and Lot travels east in it. The connection can be made that this land is indeed part of the Lord's decreed place, broken up at the flood. After this event with Lot takes place the Lord once again reiterates His promise to give the land to Abraham and his seed and tells Abraham to do something very interesting: "*Arise, walk through the land in the length of it and in the breadth of it; for I will give it unto thee*" (Genesis 13:17).

Simply put, this was a "gesture of possession" and was understood as such by the serpent (see Job 1:7; 2:2). The Lord made it clear that He was engaging in the conflict, and in a flagrant manner begins to move in on the enemy's territory and claim a piece of property for Himself.

This land had become a base of operation of sorts for the serpent. He had some individuals in the land and had made it a center of all kinds of abominations and ungodliness. God saw what had become of the land and was sorely grieved but He would not allow that situation to prevail. Ezekiel 16 speaks some interesting things about this issue, especially in relation to Jerusalem as God begins the work He has planned for the city and the land.

"*Now when I passed by thee, and looked upon thee, behold, thy time was the time of love; and I spread my skirt over thee, and covered thy nakedness: yea, I sware unto thee, and entered into a covenant with thee, saith the Lord GOD, and thou becamest mine*" (Ezekiel 16:8).

When God brings Abraham into the land, the Lord had already placed an individual there as His representative. "*And Melchizedek king of **Salem** brought forth bread and wine: and he was the priest of the most high God. And he blessed him, and said, Blessed be Abram of the most high God, **possessor** of heaven and earth: And blessed be the most high God, possessor of heaven and earth: And blessed be the most high God, which hath delivered thine enemies into thy hand. And he gave him tithes of all*" (Genesis 14:18-20).

Again, when Jacob is reminded by the Lord about what He is doing with Abraham's seed, Jacob finally understands just what is at stake with that land. *"And Jacob awaked out of his sleep, and he said, Surely the LORD is in **this place**; and I knew it not. And he was afraid, and said, How dreadful is **this place**! This is none other but **the house of God**, and this is **the gate of heaven**…And this stone, which I have set for a pillar, shall be **God's house**: and of all that thou shalt give me I will surely give the tenth unto thee"* (Genesis 28:16,17,22).

Later after the sojourn in Egypt at the time of the exodus, the Lord makes it clear to Moses that He is going to bring the children of Israel into the promised land He intended to make His dwelling place. What He reveals to Moses in connection with this can be found in what is known as the Law or Torah. *"Thou shalt bring them in, and plant them in **the mountain of thine inheritance**, in the place, O LORD, which thou hast made for thee **to dwell in**, in the Sanctuary, O Lord, **which thy hands have established**. The LORD shall reign for ever and ever"* (Exodus 15:17,18). Moses understood what God's plans were and the role of Israel in connection with that land.

A brief word about the Law needs to be said in connection with what we are speaking about. Along with giving in advance Israel's entire history of failure as found in Leviticus 26, God at that time entered into a covenant with Israel. This covenant acted as an obstacle between the nation and the promises that had been made to Abraham concerning the fulfillment of God's purposes for the earth. It by no means did away with the promises which would be impossible as God had sworn to do them unconditionally. What God enters into with the nation at Sinai is wholly conditional. *If* you obey, then you will be that great nation, kingdom of priests, etc. Basically, God seemingly puts a barrier or obstacle in the way of what He intends to do with this earth.

What He puts on display, however, is that if the nation is going to receive the promises it will only be by His grace and mercy. He also made it clear that He did not choose them because they somehow deserved it. There is no way that they could rely upon their own righteousness and ability to obtain it. They were still children of Adam and God was going to have to accomplish for them what they could not accomplish on their own. When they say, "All that the Lord has said we will do," it stood as a testimony against them. They couldn't do what was commanded as was amply demonstrated in their testings in the wilderness. They had shown their utter failure and inability before the Law had ever been given.

They break the very first two commandments before Moses has even come down from the mount with the tablets of stone! Now, if they want to get those promised blessings as a nation they will need a new covenant that will give them the righteousness God requires. They will need to say what they should have said back at Sinai, and what they will yet say in the future, "*O Israel, return unto LORD thy God; for thou hast fallen by thine iniquity. Take with you words, and turn to the LORD: say unto him, Take away all iniquity, and receive us **graciously**: so will we render the calves of our lips*" (Hosea 14:1,2).

As you know, the tabernacle and temple play a large role in Israel's affairs and for the time the Lord reigns on the earth. They were given rather detailed plans when it came to the production and significance of these houses of worship. One prophet, who was given rather extraordinary information regarding the role that Israel's divine structures will play in that coming time, was Ezekiel. He gives a detailed blueprint with respect to the millenial temple, its attendant features and the division of the land in chapters 40-48.

Let's look particularly at Ezekiel 40:2: "*In the visions of God brought he me into the land of Israel, and set me upon a very high mountain, by which was as **the frame of a city** on the south.*" He then goes on to describe a number of chambers and the functions associated with these chambers as well as the Lord's house. Simply stated, Ezekiel is given to see the beams of the Lord's chambers, the same beams He was laying back in Genesis 1:2, part of the same decreed place broken up during the flood.

Interestingly enough, Ezekiel is only given to see the **frame** of the city, or the beams. It is given to the apostle John to actually see that promised city descend from heaven and rest upon those beams. This is what was delayed by those rebellious events in the garden. But eventually, as He has promised, He will repossess this earth and His dwelling place will at last be with man.

"*And I saw a new heaven and a new earth: for the first heaven and the first earth were passed away; and there was no more sea. And I John saw the holy city, new Jerusalem, coming down from God out of heaven, as a bride adorned for her husband. And I heard a great voice out of heaven saying, Behold, the tabernacle of God is with men, and he will dwell with them, and they shall be his people, and God himself shall be with them, and be their God.* "*...Come hither, I will shew thee the bride, the Lamb's wife. And he carried me away in the spirit to a great and high mountain, and shewed me that great city, the holy Jerusalem, descending out of heaven from God, Having the glory of God...And the wall of the city had twelve* **foundations,** *and in them the names of the twelve apostles of the Lamb.*" (Revelation 21:1-3,9-11).

This "great and high mountain" is the mountain Ezekiel was carried to in the Spirit; and the "great city" is the city Abraham looked for, the city—and also part of the kingdom—which also comes from heaven. It is literally the time of heaven on earth. "*By faith Abraham, when he was called to go out into a place which he should after receive for* **an inheritance,** *obeyed; and he went out, not knowing whither he went. By faith he sojourned in the* **land of promise,** *as in a strange country, dwelling in tabernacles with Isaac and Jacob, the* **heirs** *with him of the same promise: For he looked for a* **city** *which hath* **foundations,** *whose builder and maker is God....But now they desire a better country, that is, an heavenly: wherefore God is not ashamed to be called their God: for he hath prepared for them a city*" (Hebrews 11:8-10,16).

Abraham understood the role that he and the land played in God's plans. This is not about going to heaven, this is about what in heaven is coming to earth as the Lord repossesses it. Even though Abraham was in that land of promise, he was still a stranger in it. The time had not yet come, though he expected it, knowing the plans and purposes of God. What tremendous strength comes to our faith when we are knowledgeable about what God is doing and how we fit into that plan.

By the way, this is what the Lord is referring to when He says, *"Let not your heart be troubled: ye believe in God, believe also in me. In my Father's house are many mansions: if it were not so, I would have told you. I go to **prepare** a **place** for you. And if I go and prepare a place for you, I will come again, and receive you unto myself; that where I am, there ye may be also"* (John 14:1-3).

First of all, if this were heaven the Lord would not need to return to bring His own there so they could enjoy the place He has prepared. That will happen when they die. Failure to understand where you are in the prophetic program in the Gospels has caused much misunderstanding concerning these verses. This is not our catching away, which is part of the mystery of the Body of Christ that will occur for some particular reasons in keeping with who we are and our destiny and bringing an end to the delay in the coming of the Lord's Day of Wrath. The Father's house is a huge subject all throughout the Scriptures.

When the Lord not too long before this said, *"It is written, My house shall be called the house of prayer; but ye have made it a den of thieves"* (Matthew 21:13), was He talking about heaven? No, of course not. In the next few chapters He will say, *"O Jerusalem, Jerusalem, thou that killest the prophets, and stonest them which are sent unto thee, how often would I have gathered thy children together as a hen gathereth her chickens under her wings, and ye would not! Behold, **your** house is left unto you desolate. For I say unto you, Ye shall not see me again henceforth, till ye shall say, Blessed is he that cometh in the name of the Lord"* (Matthew 23:37-39).

He also does not say He will take them back to heaven from whence He came. He says that He is coming back and they will at that time enjoy the place He has provided for them in His Father's house.

"And behold, I come quickly; and my reward is with me, to give every man according as his work shall be. I am Alpha and Omega, the

beginning and the end, the first and the last. Blessed are they that do his commandments, that they may have the right to the tree of life, and may enter in through the gates into the city" (Revelation 22:12-14).

"For the Son of man shall come in the glory of his Father with his angels; and **then** *he shall* **reward** *every man according to his works"* (Matthew 16:27).

"Behold, the LORD hath proclaimed unto the end of the world, Say ye to the daughter of Zion, Behold, thy salvation cometh; behold, his reward is with him, and his work before him. And they shall call them, The holy people, The redeemed of the LORD: and thou shalt be called, Sought out, A city not forsaken" (Isaiah 62:11,12).

Put on display here is the ministry that the remnant will have in fulfillment of God's program for earth with Israel as that kingdom of priests and holy nation in connection with the nations. That city, along with the temple, is heavenly. That is where it is and where it comes from. The Lord is going back to heaven where the millennial temple is located and He is going to prepare a place for them in it. He is then going to return *with* it and the nation will function in accordance with the promises. This is the same house spoken of repeatedly all throughout the Old Testament, and extensively in Ezekiel chapters 40-48 where the functions of those various places are described. Those functions will need to be filled by people and it is the remnant as those priests that will do it.

There are many chambers in connection with Ezekiel's words in these chapters. These are the same chambers of Psalm 104 where the Holy Spirit's actions in Genesis 1:2 are described. But look further down at verse 13 of Psalm 104 where we are told, *"He watereth the hills from his chambers: the earth is satisfied with the fruit of thy works."* This is prophetic. This is what Ezekiel saw in chapter 47.

"Afterward he brought me again unto the door of the house; and behold, waters issued out from under the threshold of the house eastward...Now when I had returned behold, at the bank of the river were very many trees on the one side and on the other. Then

said he unto me, These waters issue out toward the east country, and go down into the desert, and go into the sea: which being brought forth into the sea, the waters shall be **healed**. *And it shall come to pass, that everything that* **liveth**, *which moveth, whithersoever the rivers shall come, shall* **live**: *and there shall be a very great multitude of fish, because these waters shall come thither: for they shall be* **healed**; *and everything shall* **live** *whither the river cometh"* (Ezekiel 47:1,7-9).

Why is it such a great thing for the waters to be healed and to abound with fish? Why is there so much death in association with the waters whereby they need to live? When you understand what will be taking place during the Lord's Day, you appreciate why that river is called the river of life.

"And the second angel poured out his vial upon the sea; and it became as the blood of a dead man: and every living soul died in the sea" (Revelation 16:3; see also Revelation 8:7-11). The remnant will be thankful that they can drink any deadly thing and not have it hurt them (Mark 16:18).

But again, all this will be made new. In connection with that city having descended, *"He shewed me a pure river of water of* **life**, *clear as crystal, proceeding out of the throne of God and of the Lamb. In the midst of the street of it, and on either side of the river, was there the tree of life, which bare twelve manner of fruits, and yielded her fruit every month: and the leaves of the tree were for the* **healing** *of the nations. And there shall be no more curse: but the throne of God and of the Lamb shall be in it; and his servants shall serve him"* (Revelation 22:1-3).

This is the land, this is the city, this is the house and these are the chambers. The fullness of the plans of God are finally realized. I hope you now appreciate the enormous role that the land plays in God's contention for the earth, the role of Israel in that contention and the plans and activities of Satan as he persists in his attempt to be like the most high God, possessor of heaven and earth. We are now ready to examine just who the ten horns of the beast are and why.

Let us return to Genesis. Up until Genesis 15, God repeatedly tells Abraham that He will give him this land. When God actually cuts the unconditional covenant with Abraham in this chapter He tells Abraham, "*In the same day the LORD made a covenant with Abram, saying, Unto thy seed **have I given** this land, from the river of Egypt **unto** the great river, the river Euphrates*" (Genesis 15:18).

This is a done deal, the covenant has been made. As far as God is concerned, it is as good as done. He does not need to come along again and covenant for Israel to have the land. When you understand the way God views these types of issues, you understand what an affront that kind of idea is to the character and fidelity of God.

I believe there is much misunderstanding of the New Covenant when it comes to this point which may reflect a misunderstanding concerning the Mosaic covenant. The *New* Covenant stands in opposition to the *Old* Covenant. God makes it very clear in places like Jeremiah 31 and Ezekiel 36 that the Old Covenant made at Sinai was going to be replaced. It had to be if Israel was ever to get the promises, receive the blessing and be what God had intended for them to be from the beginning, that kingdom of priests and holy nation that will be the blessing for the world.

The two covenants deal with righteousness. The Old covenants for Israel to get the promises based on their performance. He tells them in advance, however, that they will fail and experience all five courses of punishment as seen in Leviticus 26. The New does *not* covenant for the land, throne, kingdom and blessings. Rather, it covenants to give Israel the righteousness they need to obtain all those things that have already been covenanted for in the Abrahamic Covenant, Davidic Covenant and so on.

Now, looking at the previous passage in Genesis 15:18 where God gives Abraham the land, there is something rather odd recorded in the verses immediately following it. It states bluntly, "*...The **Kenites**, and the **Kenizites**, and the **Kadmonites**, And the **Hittites**, and the **Perizzites**, and the **Rephaims**, And the **Amorites**,* and the **Canaanites**, and the **Girgashites**, and the **Jebusites** (Genesis 15:19-21). I suggest you look at the way these verses appear in the text structurally. It is rather conspicuous in its oddity and is meant to get your attention and alert you to something significant.

Again, they are in the land so the subject is certainly relevant enough. But the way in which the Lord tells you this is rather strange. If you count the above names you will find that there are ten. It is my belief that these are none other than the ten horns of the beast. Their names will change throughout history and the Scriptures, but these ten nations are constantly in view when it comes to the land, the satanic plan of evil and the contention over Zion.

I realize this is not in line with the position that the ten horns will be ten European nations as is commonly taught and believed by many Bible prophecy teachers. This obviously relates nicely to the popular idea of the European Union as a revived Roman Empire. But I believe that the Scriptures are very clear on this matter and if you have been following the argument thus far, the true identity of those horns is quite natural. I am sure that the European Union will probably play a significant role in the geopolitics of the coming time. I am not even discounting that they may play an extremely important role during the days of the beast. Time will tell.

It would appear that the West for the most part will be more involved with trade and commerce and seek to prosper from whatever relationship they have with the beast. It is Magog who acts as the forceful one on behalf of the other Japhetic nations, the isles of the Gentiles, and leads the coalition also made up of the other sons of Ham and Shem that have apparently not appreciated the oppressive activities of the beast and want a piece of the action themselves.

"*Wherefore it shall come to pass, that when the Lord hath performed **his whole work** upon mount Zion and on Jerusalem, I will punish the fruit of the **stout heart** of the **king of Assyria**, and the glory of **his high looks**...be not afraid of **the Assyrian**...And the*

LORD of hosts shall stir up a scourge for him according to the slaughter of Midian at the rock of Oreb" (Isaiah 10:24,26).

You can also read about the division of nations and the mingled people of the ten toes of Nebuchadnezzar's image in Jeremiah 25:12-38, as well as the drinking that will be going on with the woman of Revelation. Notice again that God prefaces it by saying, *"And I will bring upon that land all my words which I have pronounced against it, even all that is written in this book, which Jeremiah hath prophesied against all the nations"* (Jeremiah 25:13).

The mingled people and other kings of the earth can also be seen in Jeremiah 50:37, 41-46. Finally, this issue is once again seen in Ezekiel 30:5, *"Ethiopia, and Lybia, and Lydia, and all the mingled people, and Chub, and the men of the land that is in league, shall fall with them by the sword."*

There is going to be an interesting array of a confederation of forces at the time of the end. Magog will figure very prominently as it leads a coalition of forces with the kings of the East into the land to contend with the beast, the Assyrian who will rule from Babylon. What seems clear from Scripture, however is that the ten horns are not European nations and, further, we are not left in the dark as to who they are. We need to briefly examine Daniel as this is the source of most of the ideas concerning the European Union.

— Chapter Six —

The Contention Over Zion

The Times of the Gentiles,
The Ten Horns of the Beast
&

The Book of Daniel

Five revelations are given in Daniel and they are given in a particular order. With the coming of the Babylonian captivity, the kingdom is officially stripped from the nation and the Times of the Gentiles begins as the fifth course of punishment arrives for the southern kingdom of Judah. There is general agreement as to who the first three kingdoms are that rule successively because we are told explicitly who they are. The first is Babylon, the second is Media/Persia, the third is Grecia.

To be brief I will not address here all that is commonly said concerning the visions of Daniel. I do not believe, however, that what is commonly attributed to Antiochus Epiphanes, Ptolemy, and others is what is being talked about at all, although I do believe it begins to get close to appreciating what is presented. I believe it is the same little horn that is being referred to in the different visions. Unless there is strong indication to the contrary from the text, I see no warrant for interpreting otherwise. Also, the various information that is given when connected seems to cement the issue, for me anyway.

A failure to appreciate the way God presents information has also contributed to misperception when it comes to Daniel, the prophets and especially Revelation. God will first give you the basic scope of a period of time. Then He will go back and give you further details about that time and build upon the previous revelations. This should be no surprise as you are introduced to this method in the very beginning with the basic scope of the creation week given in Genesis 1:1-2:3. Further details are then given in the following verses as to what took place on day six.

We are told in Daniel what the prophesied fifth and final course of punishment for Israel will be like. We are told it will consist of five installments lasting seventy weeks, what God will and will not be doing during that time, and who the nations are—besides Babylon—that will yet serve themselves of Israel once the seventy years of captivity are up (Jeremiah 25:11-14). I will simply say that the fourth installment was when Christ was born and ministered to the nation. This was after the 400 years of silence from God that had preceded Christ's and John the Baptist's arrival. When we understand Daniel's time schedule, we understand why they proclaimed that the time had come and the kingdom of heaven was at hand. After the seventy weeks are up, that's it.

The fifth installment, or the Lord's Day, would come upon the nation after the Messiah had been cut off out of the land of the living (crucified) and returned to His Father in heaven. Their response to the Son would determine what would happen to them out there in the Day of the Lord. This was a huge subject of prophecy and is expressed in passages such as Psalm 2:12, "*Kiss the Son, lest he be angry, and ye **perish** from the way, when his wrath is kindled but a little. Blessed are all they that put their trust in him*" and John 3:16, "*For God so loved the world, that he gave his only begotten Son, that whosoever believeth in him should not **perish**, but have everlasting life.*"

It is Daniel 8:21-25 and Daniel chapter 11 that I believe helps us better appreciate how God tells us to look at the successive kingdoms. "*And the rough goat is the king of Grecia: and the great horn that is between his eyes is the first king. Now that being broken, whereas four stood up for it, four kingdoms shall stand up out of it, but not in his power. And in the latter time of their kingdom, when the transgressors are come to the full, a king of fierce countenance, and understanding dark sentences shall stand up. And his power shall be mighty, but not by his own power: and he shall destroy wonderfully, and shall prosper, and practise, and shall destroy the mighty and the holy people. And through his policy also he shall cause craft to prosper in his hand; and he shall magnify himself in his heart, and by peace shall destroy many: he shall also stand up against the Prince of princes; but he shall be broken without hand*" (8:21-25).

This information is building upon the revelation given in chapter 7 and will be built upon itself in the fifth and final revelation given in chapters 11 and 12. But it should be noticed that what God is concerned with is the fourfold breakdown of the Grecian Empire. He is doing this because He wants you to be able to identify geographically where the Antichrist is coming from. When the Romans came, they left in place the basic structure that existed in the Middle East under Greece. It truly was a Greco-Roman world with a Greek East and dominating Hellenistic culture. Regardless of how you describe it historically, however, the Scripture is concerned with the divided Grecian kingdom. When the apostle Paul divides the world, He says there is no difference between the Jew and Greek.

When you read in Luke 2:1, "*And it came to pass, that there went out a decree from Caesar Augustus, that all the world should be taxed,*" you know that you are at least in the time of the third Grecian kingdom of brass for you were told in Daniel 2:39, "*And after thee shall arise another kingdom inferior to thee, and another third kingdom of brass, which shall bear rule over all the earth.*"

Furthermore, we are put on notice that we are in the next phase of that Grecian kingdom when, immediately after we are told about all the world being taxed, we read, "*And this taxing was first made when Cyrenius was governor of Syria*" (Luke 2:2). This is one of the quarters of Alexander's divided kingdom. We are alerted to the fact that we are in the time of the fourfold break-down when we are repeatedly confronted in the Gospels with those that Rome permitted to exercise a certain amount of sover-eignty within the province of Syria. These rulers are called tetrar-chs, which means a ruler of one-fourth of a given territory and/or ruler of part of a divided kingdom. Geographically, it is out of this fourfold division of the Grecian kingdom that the beast, the man of sin, the Antichrist will come. He will make an agreement, a league, and put together a ten nation confederacy. We are told in Daniel that He will come from one of those four sections which raises our curiosity as to which one. In keeping with the progres-sive revelations, we will be given the details in Daniel's fifth reve-lation in chapter 11 as to which of those four sections he arises from. Actually, the information given about his geographical ori-gin in Daniel should be no surprise as he has already been identi-fied as the Assyrian throughout the prophets.

We haven't the space here to address the various geographical areas of modern day Syria, the kingdom and province of Syria, "greater" Syria, Assyria, etc. It should simply be noted that they are not all the same. At times we are speaking of countries, at other times we are speaking of far larger regions. As individual "countries" Syria and Assyria are different, both historically and as identified in Scripture, although Assyria did bear rule over Syria for a time. Syria is quite identifiable enough even today as found on modern maps. Assyria, however, is found basically in what is today northern Iraq.

Now let's look at chapter 11 when the seventy-year captivity is over. "*Also I in the first year of Darius the Mede, even I, stood to con-firm and to strengthen him. And now will I shew thee the truth. Behold, there shall stand up yet three kings in Persia; and the fourth shall be far richer than they all: and by his strength through his riches he shall stir up all against the realm of Grecia*" (Daniel 11:1,2).

Again, the first installment of the seventy years is over. What has just been described in verses 1 and 2 is the second empire that will serve itself of Israel, during which the nation will be rebuilding the city and temple in troublous times as laid out in chapter 9. During this empire the second installment will end with the close of the ministries of Zechariah, Haggai and Malachi. With the closing of the book of Malachi the third installment begins to come upon the nation and they experience the famine of hearing a word from the Lord as He goes silent to the nation until the time for the bringing forth of the Messiah has come. This is why we have nothing in our Bible between Malachi and Matthew. If we do, as interesting and informative as it may be, it isn't from God.

"And a mighty king shall stand up, that shall rule with great dominion, and do according to his will" (Daniel 11:3). This is Alexander the Great, the king of Grecia, the great horn of Daniel 8:21. He comes to power during the third installment, the time that God has gone silent to the nation, and he is instrumental in preparing the region by his spread of Greek culture and the Greek language. He had a great vision for that region which vision the Romans patterned and followed. *"And when he shall stand up, his kingdom shall be divided toward the four winds of heaven; and not to his posterity, **nor according to his dominion** which he ruled: for his kingdom shall be plucked up even for others beside those"* (Daniel 11:4).

This is the next stage in the succession of empires that will have a bearing on Israel, the land, and the city of Jerusalem—the next phase of that great image that was seen by Nebuchadnezzar and also seen in the vision of the beasts. This is the fourfold division phase of the Grecian Kingdom. It is during this stage that the fourth installment will commence with the arrival of the Messiah, the preaching of the kingdom of heaven as at hand, and the cutting off and withdrawal of the Messiah. Now we already know from the previous visions that the little horn, the Antichrist, is going to arise from one of these four Grecian heads.

"Therefore the he goat waxed very great: and when he was strong, the great horn was broken; and for it came up four notable ones toward the four winds of heaven. And out of one of them came

forth a little horn, which waxed exceeding great, toward the south, and toward the east, and toward the pleasant land. And it waxed great, even to the host of heaven; and it cast down some of the host and of the stars to the ground, and stamped upon them. Yea, he magnified himself even to the prince of the host, and by him the daily sacrifice was taken away, and the place of his sanctuary was cast down. And an host was given him against the daily sacrifice by reason of transgression, and it cast down the truth to the ground; and it practiced, and prospered" (Daniel 8:8-12).

Many interesting things can be noticed here, not the least of which is that he is *given* what he has, and this is in connection with the ruling princes in heavenly places that correspond to nations, the same princes that hindered Gabriel when he was on his way to see Daniel in chapter 9. This is why the beast in Revelation has all the features of the dragon, except with the beast the ten horns are crowned.

Remember how Satan tempted the Lord: *"And the devil, taking him up into an high mountain, shewed unto him all the kingdoms of the world in a moment of time. And the devil said unto him, All this power will I give thee, and the glory of them: for that is delivered unto me; and to whomsoever I will I give it. If thou therefore wilt worship me, all shall be thine"* (Luke 4:5-7).

There is one coming who will accept that offer and he will worship the dragon who has given him all that he has. *"But in his estate shall he honour the God of forces: and a god whom his fathers knew not shall he honour with gold, and silver, and with precious stones, and pleasant things. Thus shall he do in the most strong holds with a strange god, whom he shall acknowledge and increase with glory: and he shall cause **them** to rule over many and shall divide the land for gain"* (Daniel 11:38,39).

But as I said, he will come out of one of the four Grecian heads and it is going to be in the latter time. This is the information we are given beginning in verse 5 and running all the way through to the end of chapter 11. We are told just where he arises from and I will simply say that he is the king of the North (not Russia, by the way, nor the various forces associated with Gog and Magog). That is a different coalition of forces that will come against him at the time of the end, when all hell literally breaks loose and his power breaks down. He is the Assyrian and with verse 5 of chapter 11 we are brought to the commencement of the fifth and final installment, or the Lord's Day.

Now I want you to follow me here because this is important. I believe what is recorded in Daniel 11:5-20 is the beginning of sorrows talked about by the Lord in Matthew 24:4-8 which also match up with the first four seals in Revelation chapter 6. These are not just any old wars and famines but some particular chaos and circumstances out of which the Antichrist will arise. We are given a hint about this as the Lord makes it clear that He is giving an exposition of Daniel 11 and 12. He uses the phrase "nation against nation and kingdom against kingdom" (compare with Isaiah 19). There will be a great deal of turmoil within the nations themselves as well as amongst each other.

But if I am correct, then look closely at what will occur in this fifth installment that is yet to come. All of the verses from 5 to 20, except one, are concerned with the king of the North at that time and his various activities as they relate to the king of the South and the glorious land. In verse 19 it is said of him, "*Then he shall turn his face toward the fort of his own land: but he shall stumble and fall, and not be found.*"

That's king of the North #1. Keep track. Then in one verse, and one verse only, we are told concerning king of the North #2. "*Then shall stand up in his estate a raiser of taxes in the glory of the kingdom: but **within few days** he shall be destroyed, neither in anger, nor in battle.*"

It's interesting that the Lord makes sure to point some things out to us here about both individuals, especially as to how they die or don't die. Again, to me it seems rather strange and conspicuous and I, for one, think that the Lord wants to alert us to something. Notice that neither one is killed by the sword. I leave it to you to search out the significance of that.

Now arises that infamous deceitful little horn with the big mouth that comes to power on a platform of peace and unity in light of the tremendous turmoil that has rocked that region. *"And in his estate shall stand up a vile person, to whom they shall not give the honour of the kingdom: but he shall come in peaceably, and obtain the kingdom by flatteries"* (Daniel 11:21).

Unlike his fathers, he will treat Israel favorably and share the wealth with them. If the remnant is abiding in the wisdom, so that they may be counted among the wise ones in Israel, they will be prepared for him.

"He that goeth about as a talebearer revealeth secrets: therefore meddle not with him that flattereth with the lips" (Proverbs 20:19).

"He that hateth dissembleth with his lips, and layeth up deceit within him; When he speaketh fair, believe him not: for there are seven abominations in his heart. Whose hatred is covered by deceit, his wickedness shall be shewed before the whole congregation...A lying tongue hateth those that are afflicted by it; and a flattering mouth worketh ruin" (Proverbs 26:22-26,28).

"A man that flattereth his neighbor spreadeth a net for his feet" (Proverbs 29:5; see also 28:11-28).

"Here is wisdom. Let him that hath understanding count the number of the beast: for it is the number of a man; and his number is Six hundred threescore and six" (Revelation 13:18).

That is king of the North #3. *He* is the Antichrist and continues until the end, when Christ returns and shows him just what kind of power lies in the tongue (James 3:5-12; Revelation 19:15).

With that little lesson in addition, let us now turn to Revelation chapter 17. Remember, John has been taken by the Spirit into the fifth installment, the Lord's Day. What he sees, therefore, is what is taking place *at that time.* Now we are given a review of the history of the satanic plan of evil, but when it says in verse 18 of this chapter, *"And the woman which thou sawest is that great city, which reigneth over the kings of the earth,"* it is speaking of the literal city of Babylon, in the land of Shinar which will be reigning at that time.

Looking at Revelation 17:8-11 we read, *"The beast which thou sawest was, and is not; and shall ascend out of the bottomless pit, and go into perdition: and they that dwell on the earth shall wonder, whose names were not written in the book of life from the foundation of the world, when they behold the beast that was, and is not, and yet is. And here is the mind which hath wisdom. The seven heads are seven mountains, on which the woman sitteth. And there are seven kings."*

Now before we go any further, let me ask you a question. If we are in the fifth installment, how many kings of the North should we expect to see in the fifth installment according to Daniel 11? That's right, three.

*"And there are seven kings: five are fallen, and **one is**, and the **other** is not yet come; and when he cometh, he must continue **a short space**. And the **beast** that was, and is not, even **he is the eighth**, and is of the seven, and goeth into perdition"* (verse Revelation 17:10,11).

Doesn't this look an awful lot like what is stated in Daniel 11, even down to the second king of the North continuing a short space or few days. Then, just as recorded in Daniel 11:21-45, the little horn makes the league and puts together his confederacy of ten nations.

*"And the ten horns which thou sawest are ten kings, which have received no kingdom as yet; but receive power as kings one hour with the beast. These have one mind, and shall give their power and strength unto the beast. These shall make war with the Lamb, and the Lamb shall overcome them: for he is Lord of lords, and King of kings: and they that are with him are called, and chosen, and faithful...For God hath put in their heart to fulfil his will, and to **agree**, and give their kingdom unto the beast, until the words of God shall be fulfilled"* (Revelation 17:12-14,17).

Again, Antichrist is the Assyrian, the king of the North, and he initially brings peace, prosperity and security to the region that has so long desired it. But deceit is in his heart. He makes an agreement and forms a confederacy among those ten nations that have always been involved in the contention over Zion in their contest for the land. We have already seen them in Genesis 15:19.

Before we go any further, let's review the totality of what we have seen. With all this detail of the later revelations given to Daniel, we can now look back to Nebuchadnezzar's image with a full understanding and appreciation of the outline it gives. Simply stated, Nebuchadnezzar was *given* a particular kingdom by the Lord. The statue is concerned with a particular area of real estate and the control and domination of it and the form it takes. So the image basically represents the Middle East more or less especially in the relationship it has to Palestine and Jerusalem.

First, Babylon, the lion beast or golden head is given the kingdom. After that, the two arms and breast of the silver Medo-Persian bear beast takes over. We here have development as it is told to "arise and devour much flesh." After that we finally see the Grecian kingdom arise and are told that it bears rule over "all the earth." There isn't much further to go once you have that. What takes place afterward happens from the viewpoint of being within that kingdom of the Greeks. This is the leopard beast with four wings and the brass belly and thighs.

Initially, with that first king, it is viewed as *one* corresponding to the belly. However, that kingdom will be divided. Remember, while the leopard beast itself is divided into four sections, we are only looking at the statue, not Europe. That region is divided into two of the four sections of the divided Grecian Kingdom. The two thighs of brass are the north country and the south country (Daniel 11:4; Zechariah 6:1).

Following these two sections we then move into the legs of iron. This marks the coming of the fourth beast and sees the arrival of the Assyrian dragon and his horns. It is at this point that the dragon takes control of that which God had given to Nebuchadnezzar and the hands it subsequently passed through.

"*Behold, I will send and take all the families of the north, saith the LORD, and Nebuchadrezzar the king of Babylon, my servant, and will bring them against **this land**, and the inhabitants thereof, **and against all these nations round about**…And this whole land shall be a desolation, and an astonishment; and **these nations** shall serve the king of*

*Babylon seventy years. And it shall come to pass, when seventy years are accomplished, that I will punish the king of Babylon, and that nation, saith the LORD, for their iniquity, and the land of the Chaldeans…and I will bring upon that land **all my words** which I have pronounced against it, **even all** that is written in this book, which Jeremiah hath prophesied against all nations. For many nations and great kings **shall serve themselves of them also**: and I will recompense them according to their deeds, and according to the works of their own hands"* (Jeremiah 25:9,11,12-14. See also Ezekiel 31, 32).

The emergence of this exceeding dreadful and terrible diverse beast will be marked by the "beginning of sorrows." Assyria comes out of the north country and begins to cause trouble and clash with the king of the South, Egypt, as he stirs up those ancient horns and builds up his influence and power. This period of time sees two of these kings of the North. Then the little horn arises and puts together his confederacy of ten horns. This is the feet and ten toes of iron mixed with clay. These ten toes are in the land of the statue and five are from the north country and five are from the south country. They are the nations "round about" Israel. They agree to give their kingdom to the beast and they are crowned as they receive power as kings one "hour" with the beast. Here in Daniel we see the earthly view where they make their league for one "week" or seven years. In Revelation, however, we are given to see the events taking place in heaven, and in heavenly time it is but one "hour." These ten toes are the final stage of that kingdom, that statue, that land.

Let us turn to Psalm 83 which prophetically describes the league and agreement which we have just read about.

*"Keep not thou silence, O God: hold not thy peace, and be not still, O God. For, lo, thine enemies make a tumult: and they that hate **thee** have lifted up the head. They have taken **crafty counsel** against thy people, and **consulted** against thy **hidden ones**. They have said, Come, and let us cut them off from being a nation; that the name of Israel may be no more in remembrance. For they have **consulted** together with **one consent**: they are **confederate** against thee: The tabernacles*

of Edom, and the Ishmaelites; of Moab, and the Hagarenes; Gebal, and Ammon, and Amalek; the Philistines with the inhabitants of Tyre; Assur also is joined with them: they have helpen the children of Lot. Selah. Do unto them as unto the Midianites; as to Sisera, as to Jabin, at the brook of Kison" (verse Psalm 83:1-8).

If we count the nations above, we will find not surprisingly that there are ten. The names may change but geographically they are the same ten. These are not just any ten nations and they are certainly not European nations. They are the nations that are "round about" Israel, that are part of the dragon's contention over the land and over Zion. They are the nations that the dragon has used in his constant affliction of Israel throughout Scripture. The children of Lot, the Ammonites and the Moabites are the ones who instigate this thing. Assur, or Assyria, conspicuously mentioned last, plays a unique role in bringing them together.

The special contention that the dragon has with the woman is especially related to conflict that has existed between her "seed" and his "seed." She of course has an ultimate seed that is brought forth who is none other than the Messiah, Jesus of Nazareth, the Lord Jesus Christ. The dragon too has an ultimate seed who is none other than the *Anti*christ. But just as God has been working through a particular general seed and people, so too has the dragon his people in connection with the land that the woman's children are to occupy and have dominion over.

That woman is crucial in God's plans for this earth and Satan has known that from the time she came on the scene. The dragon's footprints can be seen all throughout the Bible as he rises up time and again through his horns in his policy of evil against the woman. Some of the most notable of his seed are Balak-king of the Moabites, Goliath the Philistine, Haman the Amalekite, and Herod the Edomite to name a few. Here is a sampling of one of the dragon's horns, and please notice the context, especially as it relates to the use of God's compound name.

"And Joshua discomfited Amalek and his people with the edge of the sword. And the LORD said unto Moses, Write this for a memorial

*in a book, and **rehearse** it in the ears of Joshua: for I will utterly put out the remembrance of Amalek from under heaven. And Moses built an altar, and called the name of it **Jehovah-nissi:** For he said, Because the LORD hath sworn that the LORD will have **war** with Amalek **from generation to generation***" (Exodus 17:13-16).

"*Therefore it shall be, when the LORD thy God hath given thee rest from all thine enemies **round about, in the land** which the LORD thy God giveth thee for an inheritance **to possess it,** that thou shalt blot out the remembrance of Amalek from under heaven; thou shalt not forget it*" (Deuteronomy 25:19).

That dragon knows what that woman means to God in His plans for earth and Satan has tried to enact his extermination policy on more than one occasion. When God resumes His prophetic program with Israel, the time will be winding down to when He is finally going to fulfil the rest of His compound names. It is at the midpoint of Daniel's seventieth week that Satan will go all out in his attempt to prevail in his contention over earth.

"*And the great dragon was cast out, that old serpent, called the Devil, and Satan, which deceiveth the whole world: he was cast out into the earth, and his angels were cast out with him…Therefore rejoice, ye heavens, and ye that dwell in them. Woe to the inhabiters of the earth and of the sea! For the devil is come down unto you, having **great** wrath, because he knoweth that he hath but a short time…And the dragon was wroth with the woman, and went to make war with the remnant of her seed, which keep the commandments of God, and have the testimony of Jesus Christ*" (Revelation 12:9,12,17).

The land that has been promised to Abraham extends from the river of Egypt unto the river Euphrates. That obviously presents quite a problem for these nations as they occupy the territory that God has claimed for Himself through Israel and the territory that He says they will occupy during the kingdom.

It should be pointed out in dealing with this issue, there is one which bears a special relationship to the dragon and that is Assyria which is distinct from the others the dragon has used in their relationship to the land. The dragon has most certainly instituted a certain policy in connection with the arrival of the woman in world affairs and her relationship to the land. But he was around before she ever became an issue. Remember, he is that *old* serpent.

Knowing that this land was to be the place of God's residence containing the beams of His chambers, Satan all throughout Scripture pursues a deliberate policy of defiling the land. He is a consummate counterfeit above all else. His ultimate objective is to be like "*the most high God, the possessor of heaven and earth*" (Genesis 14:22) and to rule over this earth just as the Lord intends to. He too has a particular land that is the home of "his ways," and as the land of the Lord has a woman associated with it, so too does this land have a woman associated with it. And as the Lord is to rule and reign over this earth from a particular city, so too does that serpent have a city in that land from which he will rule over the nations and his "law" will go forth. Rather than Jerusalem, the serpent has his own city that he wants to establish as the "gate of heaven" (Genesis 28:17).

This is not the place to delve into these issues in depth but let me point out that Satan has already tried to establish this once in the days of Nimrod and the tower of Babel. He was hindered from accomplishing that when the Lord confused the languages, and since that time Satan has been unable to establish his global kingdom over this earth and obtain through his "god"-man the open worship that he craves and desires to flaunt in the face of almighty God.

"...*even of that horn that had eyes, and a mouth that spake very great things, whose look was more stout than his fellows*" (Daniel 7:20).

"*And his power shall be mighty, but not by his own power: and he shall destroy wonderfully, and shall prosper, and shall destroy the mighty and holy people. And through his policy also he shall cause craft to prosper in his hand; and he shall magnify himself in his heart, and by peace shall destroy many; he shall also stand up against the Prince of princes; but he shall be broken without hand*" (Daniel 8:24,25).

"*And after the league made with him he shall work deceitfully: for he shall come up, and shall become strong with a small people...And the king shall do according to his will; and he shall exalt himself, and magnify himself above every god, and shall speak marvelous things against the God of gods, and shall prosper till the indignation be accomplished: for that that is determined shall be done*" (Daniel 11:23,36).

"*Let no man deceive you by any means: for that day shall not come, except there come a falling away first, and that man of sin be revealed, the son of perdition; Who opposeth and exalteth himself above all that is worshipped; so that he as God sitteth in the temple of God, shewing himself that he is God*" (2 Thessalonians 2:3,4).

"*And they worshipped the dragon which gave power unto the beast: and they worshipped the beast, saying, Who is like unto the beast? Who is able to make war with him? And there was given unto him a mouth speaking great things and blasphemies; and power was given unto him to continue forty and two months. And he opened his mouth in blasphemy against God, to blaspheme his name, and them that dwell in heaven. And it was given unto him to make war with the saints, and to overcome them: and power was given him over all kindreds, and tongues, and nations. And all that dwell upon the earth shall worship him, whose names are not written in the book of life of the Lamb slain from the foundation of the world*" (Revelation 13:4-8).

I strongly recommend that you read through the book of Proverbs to glean a full description of this character where all his various characteristics are pulled together. That book will give full notice to the remnant at that time and they will be able to identify him for who he is as that "man of sin," "son of perdition," "wicked one," etc. "*Here is **wisdom**. Let him that hath **understanding** count the number of the beast: for it is the number of a **man**; and his number is Six hundred threescore and six*" (Revelation 13:18).

"*And the LORD said, Behold, the people is one, and they have all one language; and this they begin to do: and now nothing will be restrained from them, which they have imagined to do*" (Genesis 11:6).

Those barriers are being broken down and we are fast becoming that one world and great global community. The dragon awaits the time when all things are ready for him to finally grasp that which he has desired for so long. Man needs a leader and instinctively has a desire for a center of worship and activity that represents all that he is and all that he can achieve. The global community will require nothing less and the dragon will be happy and eager to provide it for them. He is a sentimental serpent and cares just as much about real estate as God does. When the time comes, he will offer this world an ancient love whose roots reach deep into the sand.

"*And I said, What is it? And he said, This is an ephah that goeth forth. He said moreover, This is their resemblance through **all the earth**. And behold, there was lifted up a talent of lead: and this is **a woman** that sitteth in the midst of the ephah. And he said, This is **wickedness**. And he cast it into the midst of the ephah; and he cast the weight of lead upon the mouth thereof. Then lifted I up mine eyes, and looked, and, behold, there came out two women, and the wind was in their wings; for they had wings like the wings of a stork: and they lifted up the ephah between the earth and the heaven. Then said I to the angel that talked with me, Whither do these bear the ephah? And he said unto me, To build it an house in **the land of Shinar**: and it shall be established, and set there upon **her own base**"* (Zechariah 5:5-11).

Oh memories, sweet memories. Things just haven't been the same since she was disrupted and dislodged from her home so long ago. "*Stand now with thine enchantments, and with the multitude of thy sorceries, wherein thou hast laboured **from thy youth**; if so be thou shalt be able to profit, if so be thou mayest prevail…Thus shall they be unto thee with whom **thou hast labored**, even thy merchants, **from thy youth**"* (Isaiah 48:12,15). No matter, she will yet get her chance to rule and reign as that lady of kingdoms back where she belongs. It feels so good to be back home.

She is an old whore. She has been working for a long time in spreading her abominations. Through her harlotry she has brought many daughters into this world but she is the proud mother of them all. She, with that old serpent, has flaunted her seeming success in corrupting this earth with her fornications. Nevertheless, as Jezebel of old, she will meet her humiliating end and be fed to the dogs.

"*And he said, Throw her down. So they threw her down: and some of her blood was sprinkled on the wall, and on the horses: and he trode her underfoot...In the portion of Jezreel shall dogs eat the flesh of Jezebel: And the carcase of Jezebel shall be as dung upon the face of the field in the portion of Jezreel; so that they shall not say, This is Jezebel*" (2 Kings 9:33,36,37).

"*Call together the archers against Babylon: all ye that bend the bow, camp against her: for she hath been proud against the LORD, against the Holy One of Israel*" (Jeremiah 50:29).

"*Behold, I am against thee, O destroying mountain, saith the LORD, which destroyest all the earth: and I will stretch out mine hand upon thee, and roll thee down from the rocks, and will make thee a burnt mountain*" (Jeremiah 25:25).

"*Rejoice not against me, O mine enemy: when I shall fall, I shall arise; when I sit in darkness, the LORD shall be a light unto me...Then she that is mine enemy shall see it, and shame shall cover her which said unto me, Where is the LORD thy God? Mine eyes shall behold her: now shall she be trodden down as the mire of the streets*" (Micah 7:8,10).

"*And the fifth angel poured out his vial upon the seat of the beast; and his kingdom was full of darkness; and they gnawed their tongues for pain...And the ten horns which thou sawest upon the beast, these shall hate the whore, and shall make her desolate and naked, and shall eat her flesh, and burn her with fire. For God hath put in their hearts to fulfil his will, and to agree, and give their kingdom unto the beast, until the words of God shall be fulfilled. And the woman which thou sawest is that great city which reigneth over the kings of the earth*" (Revelation 16:10; 17:16-18) Those words are the words in the Euphrates river that speak of *all* the evil that is to come upon Babylon.

"For her sins have reached unto heaven, and God hath remembered her iniquities. Reward her even as she rewarded you, double according to her works; in the cup which she hath filled fill to her double. How much she hath glorified herself, and lived deliciously, so much torment and sorrow give her: for she saith in her heart, I sit a queen, and am no widow, and shall see no sorrow...And a mighty angel took up a stone like a great millstone, and cast it into the sea, saying, Thus with violence shall that great city Babylon be thrown down, and shall be found no more at all" (Revelation 18:5-7,21).

As I said, we cannot here explore this in detail. However, I will say that this woman and her land have a very special and mystical relationship with the Assyrian and is conspicuously pointed out all through the Scriptures.

*"And Cush begat **Nimrod**: he began to be a mighty hunter before the LORD: wherefore it is said, Even as Nimrod the mighty hunter before the LORD. And **the beginning of his kingdom** was Babel, and Erech, and Accad, and Calneh, in the land of Shinar. Out of that land went forth **Asshur**, and builded Ninevah, and the city Rehoboth, and Calah"* (Genesis 10:9-11).

*"Behold **the land of the Chaldeans**; this people was not, till the **Assyrian** founded it for them that dwell in the wilderness"* (Isaiah 23:13).

*"And this man shall be the peace, when the **Assyrian** shall come into our land: and when he shall tread in our palaces, then shall we raise against him seven shepherds, and eight principal men. And they shall waste the **land of Assyria** with the sword, and the **land of Nimrod** in the entrances thereof: thus shall he deliver us from the Assyrian, when he cometh into our land, and when he treadeth within our borders"* (Micah 5:5,6).

It is to the Assyrian that the dragon wishes to give his power and receive the honor and worship that he believes is due him. But, as always, it is the true God and He alone that is "the only wise God" (1 Timothy 1:17). Just as He has done in the past, the Lord will once again take this "wise" and haughty one in his own craftiness. The great oppressor will be given all that he ever wanted and will find that it brings his doom. Just when he thinks he has captured his long sought-after prize, he will find himself in a trap as his kingdom crumbles around him.

It will be very difficult for the faithful at that time. But if they seek after true wisdom and place their trust in the Lord they will be able to endure, knowing the wisdom and instruction of the Lord. It will appear as though the Lord has sold all that he has over to the enemy. The title "the prince of the kings of the earth" (Revelation 1:5) that rightfully belongs to Christ in light of the redemptive work will be held by the Antichrist. Christ, as that sinless man, after His resurrection declared, "*All power is given unto me in heaven and in earth*" (Matthew 28:18). Yet, when the man of sin arrives on the scene, "*Even him, whose coming is after the working of Satan with all power and signs and lying wonders*" (2 Thessalonians 2:9).

Nevertheless, the Lord truly is the only wise God. He knows exactly what He is doing. By selling all that He has, He is going to end up getting both His hidden treasure and the whole field (Matthew 13:44). His "hidden ones" will make up His jewels at that time and Israel will be the peculiar treasure God intends for her to be. It is through this process that God intends to get the whole earth back as His possession. (Proverbs 21:19,20; Psalm 2:8;13; 17:7-14; 27:5; 57-63; 83:3; 135:4; Isaiah 26:20; Ezekiel 30:12; Malachi 3:17; Hebrews 1:2; 2:8; Revelation 1:5; 5; 13:7).

"*The fear of the LORD is the beginning of knowledge: but fools despise wisdom and instruction*" (Proverbs 1:7).

"*Be not wise in thine own eyes: fear the LORD, and depart from evil...Envy thou not the oppressor, and choose none of his ways. For the froward is abomination to the LORD: but his secret is with the righteous. The curse of the LORD is in the house of the wicked: but he blesseth the habitation of the just...The wise shall inherit glory: but shame shall be the promotion of fools*" (Proverbs 3:7,31,32,33,35).

"*Frowardness is in his heart, he deviseth mischief continually; he soweth discord. Therefore shall his calamity come suddenly; suddenly shall he be broken without remedy*" (Proverbs 6:14,15).

"The fear of the LORD is to hate evil: **pride***, and* **arrogancy***, and the evil way, and the* **froward mouth***, do I hate. Counsel is mine, and sound wisdom: I am understanding; I have strength. By me kings reign, and princes decree justice. By me princes rule, and nobles, even all the judges of the earth…I lead in the way of righteousness, in the midst of the paths of judgement; That I may cause those that love me to inherit substance; and I will fill their treasures"* (Proverbs 8:13-21).

"As a dog returneth to his vomit, so a fool returneth to his folly. Seest thou a man **wise in his own conceit***? There is more hope of a fool than of him"* (Proverbs 26:11,12).

When that time comes it is the fear of the Lord they are to have, not the fear of that wicked one. He is going to meet his humiliating and horrific end and the one who couldn't keep his mouth shut will be brought low to the sides of the pit, unable to speak his seductive words for quite some time.

"And fear not them which kill the body, but are not able to kill the soul: but rather fear him which is able to destroy both soul and body in hell" (Matthew 10:28).

"Hell and destruction are before the LORD: how much more then the hearts of the children of men?" (Proverbs 15:11).

"Wherefore it shall come to pass, that when the Lord hath performed his **whole work** *upon mount Zion and on Jerusalem, I will punish the fruit of the* **stout** *heart of the* **king of Assyria***, and the glory of his* **high looks***. For he saith, By the strength of my hand I have done it, and by my wisdom; for I am prudent: and I have removed the bounds of the people, and have robbed their treasures, and I have put down the inhabitants like a valiant man: And my hand hath found as a nest the riches of the people: and as one gathereth eggs that are left, have I gathered all the earth; and there was none that moved the wing, or opened the mouth, or peeped. Shall the axe boast itself against him that shaketh it? As if the rod should shake itself against them that lift it up, or as if the staff should lift up itself, as if it were no wood. Therefore shall the Lord, the Lord of hosts, send among his fat ones leanness; and under his glory he shall kindle a*

*burning like the burning of fire. And the light of Israel shall be for a fire, and his Holy One for a flame: and it shall burn and devour his thorns and his briers in one day; And shall consume the glory of his forest, and of his fruitful field, **both soul and body**: and they shall be as when a standard-bearer fainteth...For though thy people Israel be as the sand of the sea, yet **a remnant** of them shall return: the consumption decreed shall overflow with righteousness. For the* **Lord** **GOD** *of hosts shall make a consumption, even* **determined** *in the midst of all the land.* **Therefore** *thus saith the* **Lord GOD** *of hosts, O my people that dwellest in Zion,* **be not afraid** *of the* **Assyrian**: *he shall smite thee with a rod, and shall lift up his staff against thee, after the manner of Egypt. For yet a very little while, and the indignation shall cease, and mine anger in their destruction. And the LORD of hosts shall stir up a scourge for him according to the slaughter of Midian at the rock of Oreb"* (Isaiah 10:12-27).

"That thou shalt take up this proverb against the king of Babylon, and say, How hath the oppressor ceased! The golden city ceased! The LORD hath broken **the staff** *of the wicked, and* **the scepter** *of the rulers. He who smote the people in wrath with a continual stroke, he that ruled the nations in anger, is persecuted, and none hindereth...Thy* **pomp** *is brought down to the grave...How art thou fallen from heaven , O Lucifer, son of the morning! How art thou cut down to the ground,* **which didst weaken the nations!**...*thou shalt be brought down to hell, to the sides of the pit. They that see thee shall narrowly look upon thee, and consider thee, saying, Is this the man that made the earth to tremble, that did shake kingdoms...But thou art cast out of thy grave like an abominable branch...Thou shalt not be joined with them in burial"* (Isaiah 14:4-6,11,12,14-16,19,20).

"Fear, and the pit, and the snare, are upon thee, O inhabitant of the earth. And it shall come to pass, that he who fleeth from the noise of the fear shall fall into the pit; and **he that cometh up out of the pit** *shall be taken in the snare: for the windows from on high are open, and the foundations of the earth do shake..And it shall come to pass in that day, that the LORD shall punish the host of the high*

ones that are on high, and the kings of the earth upon the earth" (Isaiah 24:17,18,21).

*"Awake, awake, put on strength, O **arm of the LORD**; awake, as in the ancient days, in the generations of old. Art thou not it that hath cut Rahab, and wounded the dragon?…I, even I, am he that comforteth you: who art thou, that thou shouldest be afraid of a man that shall die, and of the son of man which shall be made as grass…Therefore hear now this, thou afflicted, and drunken, but not with wine: Thus saith **thy Lord the LORD**, and thy God that pleadeth the cause of his people, Behold, I have taken out of thine hand the cup of trembling, even the dregs of the cup of my fury; **thou shalt no more drink it again: But I will put it into the hand of them that afflict thee**; which have said to thy soul, Bow down, that we may go over: and thou hast laid thy body as the ground, and as the street, to them that went over"* (Isaiah 51:9,12,21-23).

*"Flee out of the midst of Babylon, and deliver every man his soul: be not cut off in her iniquity; for **this is the time of the LORD's vengeance**; he will render unto her a recompence. Babylon hath been a golden cup in the LORD's hand, that made all the earth drunken: the nations have drunken of her wine; therefore the nations are mad. Babylon is suddenly fallen and destroyed: howl for her…And I will punish Bel in Babylon, and **I will bring forth out of his mouth** that which he hath swallowed up: and the nations shall not flow together any more unto him: yea, the wall of Babylon shall fall"* (Jeremiah 51:6,7,8,44. Read Isaiah 47 and Jeremiah 25:12-38; 50; 51 for further details of this event involving Gog's coalition of forces and the kings of the east).

Now before we go into the Lord's Day with the apostle John, let's just take note of a very particular action that Jeremiah took and perhaps gain some insight into the events we have been looking at.

*"So Jeremiah wrote in a book **all** the evil that should come upon Babylon, even **all** these words that are written against Babylon. And Jeremiah said to Seraiah, When thou comest to Babylon, and shalt see, and shalt read **all** these words; Then shalt thou say, O LORD,*

thou hast spoken against this place, to cut it off, that none shall remain in it, neither man nor beast, but that it shall be desolate for ever. And it shall be, when thou hast made an end of reading this book, that thou shalt bind a stone to it, and **cast it into the Euphrates:** *And thou shalt say, Thus shall Babylon sink, and shall not rise from the evil that I will bring upon her: and they shall be weary. Thus far are the words of Jeremiah"* (Jeremiah 51:60-64).

Do you recall something else in the Bible that has an uncanny resemblance to this? It's when Babylon finally gets the destruction that she is promised in connection with the EUPHRATES river drying up.

"And the sixth angel poured out his vial upon the great river **Euphrates;** *and the water thereof was dried up, that the way of the kings of the east might be prepared. And I saw three unclean spirits like frogs come* **out of the mouth of the dragon,** *and* **out of the mouth** *of the beast, and* **out of the mouth** *false prophet. For they are the spirits of devils, working miracles, which go forth unto* **the kings of the earth and of the whole world,** *to gather them to the battle of that great day of God Almighty. Behold, I come as a thief. Blessed is he that watcheth, and keepeth his garments, lest he walk naked, and they see his shame. And he gathered them together into a place called in the Hebrew tongue Armageddon"* (Revelation 16:12-16).

Pay close attention to whose mouth those spirits come out of. Sounds an awful lot like what we saw above in Jeremiah 51:44 in connection with this event, doesn't it? The passage then goes on to describe Babylon's destruction in chapters 17 and 18 of Revelation. No wonder such a big issue is made of *remembrance* when we are told, *"...and great Babylon* **came in remembrance** *before the God, to give unto her the cup of the wine of the fierceness of his wrath"* (Revelation 16:19).

Friends, the fact of the matter is that the Lord has not performed His *whole* work upon Mount Zion and Jerusalem. Nor has *all* the evil come upon Babylon that has been decreed. Jeremiah's scroll was in the literal land of Shinar. It was in the literal city of Babylon. It was a literal scroll and it was literally thrown into the

Euphrates river. And yes, you guessed it, that was not a symbolic Euphrates river but the literal one. That curse is still in the Euphrates river, and you can be sure that when it gets dried up in the Lord's Day, according to all that has been written, Babylon will come in remembrance before the Lord and she will get her promised destruction. There is so much more that could be said about this issue but I hope this will suffice.

And speaking of remembering, I have not forgotten about the fear of the Lord and the promised punishment for the dragon and his cronies. Remember, the Lord is using this breakdown in the Antichrist's kingdom to gather *all* the armies of the kings of the earth into one place. In addition to the passages I gave you before concerning the details of this event, you may also want to review Ezekiel 38 and 39 as well as Daniel 11:40-45.

God is not only concerned about dealing with the beast or his horns. He is truly multi-cultural and as we circle back to Genesis, He wants to deal with all the sons of Japheth, Ham and Shem. The events which transpire during Rosh HaShanah and the Days of Awe are going to have a global impact. Nevertheless, the Lord still has something special for the beast and his prophet. While Gog will have a cemetery named after him to stand as a testimony during the millennium, he is still going to have to settle for a regular burial just like all the rest assembled there. Our two stars, however, are going to be reminded of just who they should have been fearing during their short reign on earth (Matthew 10:28)

"*And I saw the beast, and the kings of the earth, and their armies, gathered together to make war against him that sat on the horse, and against his army. And the beast was taken, and with him the false prophet that wrought miracles before him, with which he deceived them that had received the mark of the beast, and them that worshipped his image. These both were cast **alive into a lake of fire** burning with brimstone. And the remnant were slain with the sword of him that sat upon the horse, which sword proceeded out of his mouth: and all the fowls were filled with their flesh*" (Revelation 19:19-21).

It is very interesting that when Christ taught the remnant about fearing the one who is able to destroy both soul and body in hell, He immediately follows it with, *"Are not two sparrows sold for a farthing? And one of them shall not fall on the ground without your Father. But the very hairs of your head are all numbered. Fear not therefore, ye are of more value than many sparrow."* (Matthew 10:29-31).

"Behold the fowls of the air: for they sow not, neither do they reap, nor gather into barns; yet your heavenly Father feedeth them. Are ye not much better than they?" (Matthew 6:26). They will certainly have plenty of provision at that time.

To sum up, during the Great and Terrible Day of the Lord, the ten Days of Awe when the Lord returns for battle, He will *visit* the horn nations and *personally* deal with them and remove their kingdoms as Israel finally receives the promises and blessings and the *full* inheritance of the possession that is rightfully theirs according to the word and purpose of God. It is at this time that God finally puts an end to the ancient controversy over Zion.

However, He is not just to be Lord of Israel in the promised land. It is from that land that Christ is to be Lord of *all* the earth. The time for repossession has arrived when His name is finally "hallowed" in all the earth. The assembled armies of the nations as a whole get dealt with at Armageddon. Just before and during this time there will be utter confusion and it will truly be as in the day of Midian when every man's sword was against his fellowman as the beast's power over the nations begins to fall apart. Interestingly, in the days of Midian there was also the immediate bursting forth of light in the darkness and the blowing of trumpets.

In connection with this whole issue of Christ visiting the horns of the beast and removing them from the land, I strongly suggest you examine the following passages: Isaiah chapters 13-19; Jeremiah chapters 46-50; Ezekiel chapters 25-31. We will briefly look at a few choice excerpts to amplify upon this basic concept.

"Behold, the day of the LORD cometh, cruel both with wrath and fierce anger, to lay the land desolate: and he shall destroy the sinners thereof out of it" (Isaiah 13:9).

"*Concerning Edom, thus saith the LORD of hosts; Is wisdom no more in Teman? Is counsel perished from the prudent? Is their wisdom vanished? Flee ye, turn back, dwell deep, O inhabitants of Dedan; for I will bring the calamity of Esau upon him, the time that I will visit him...Therefore hear the counsel of the LORD, that he hath taken against Edom; and his purposes, that he hath purposed against the inhabitants of Teman: Surely the least of the flock shall draw them out: surely he shall make their habitations desolate with them. The earth is moved at the noise of their fall, at the cry the noise was heard in the Red Sea. Behold, he shall come up and fly as the eagle, and spread his wings over Bozrah: and at that day shall the heart of the mighty men of Edom be as the heart of a woman in her pangs*" (Jeremiah 49:7,8,20-22).

"*Thus saith the Lord GOD; Because the Philistines have dealt by revenge, and have taken vengeance with a despiteful heart, to destroy it for **the old hatred**. Therefore thus saith the Lord GOD; Behold, I will stretch out mine hand upon the Philistines, and I will cut off the Cherethims, and destroy the remnant of the sea coast. And I will execute great **vengeance** upon them with furious rebukes; and **they shall know that I am the LORD**, when I shall lay my **vengeance** upon them*" (Ezekiel 25:15-17).

"*For my sword shall be bathed in heaven: behold, it shall come down upon Idumea, and upon the people of my curse, to judgement. The sword of the Lord is filled with blood, it is made fat with fatness, and with the blood of lambs and goats, with the fat of the kidneys of rams: for the Lord hath a sacrifice in Bozrah, and a great slaughter in the land of Idumea...For it is the day of the LORD's **vengeance**, and the year of recompences for **the controversy of Zion**" (Isaiah 34:5,6,8).

"*Who is this that cometh up from Edom, with dyed garments from Bozrah? This that is glorious in his apparel, travelling in the greatness of his strength? I that speak in righteousness, mighty to save. Wherfore art thou red in thine apparel, and thy garments like that treadeth in the winefat? I have trodden the winepress alone; and of the people there was none with me: for I will tread them in mine anger, and trample them in my fury; and their blood shall be sprinkled upon my garments, and I will stain my raiment. For the day of* **vengeance** *is in mine heart, and the year of my redeemed is come. And I looked, and there was none to help; and I wondered that there was none to uphold: therefore mine own arm brought salvation unto me; and my fury, it upheld me. And I will tread down the people in mine anger, and make them drunk in my fury, and I will bring down their strength to the earth.* (Isaiah 63:1-6).

"*O LORD, why hast thou made us to err from thy ways, and hardened our heart from thy fear?* **Return** *for thy servants' sake, the tribes of thine* **inheritance***. The people of thy holiness have* **possessed** *it but a little while: our adversaries have trodden thy sanctuary. We are thine: thou never barest rule over them; they were not called by thy name. Oh that thou wouldest rend the heavens, that thou wouldest come down, that the mountains might flow down at thy* **presence***, As when the melting fire burneth, the fire causeth the waters to boil,* **to make thy name known to thine adversaries***, that the nations may tremble at thy* **presence**" (Isaiah 63:17–64:2).

"*Hear the word of the Lord, ye that tremble at his word; Your brethren that hated you, that cast you out* **for my name's sake***, said, Let the LORD be glorified: but he shall* **appear** *to your joy, and they shall be ashamed*" (Isaiah 66:5).

"*Let God arise, let his enemies be scattered: let them also that hate* **him** *flee from before him. As smoke is driven away, so drive them away: as wax melteth before the fire, so let the wicked perish at the* **presence** *of God. But let the righteous be glad; let them rejoice before God: yea, let them exceedingly rejoice. Sing unto God, sing praises to his name: extol him that* **rideth upon the heavens** *by his name JAH, and rejoice before him…To him that* **rideth** *upon the heavens of heavens, which were of old; lo, he doth send out his voice, and that a mighty voice. Ascribe ye strength unto God: his excellency is over Israel, and his strength is in the clouds. O God, thou art terrible out of thy holy places: the God of Israel is he that giveth strength and power unto his people. Blessed be God*" (Psalm 68:1-4,33-35).

*"And I fell at his feet to worship him. And he said unto me, See thou do it not: I am thy fellowservant, and of thy brethren that have the testimony of Jesus: worship God: for the testimony of Jesus is the spirit of prophecy. And I saw **heaven opened**, and behold a white **horse**; and he that sat upon him was called Faithful and True, and in righteousness he doth judge and make war. His eyes were as a flame of fire, and on his head were many crowns; and he had a name written, that no man knew, but he himself. And he was clothed with a vesture dipped in blood: and his name is called The Word of God. And the armies of heaven followed him upon white horses, clothed in fine linen, white and clean. And out of his mouth goeth a sharp sword, that with it he should smite the nations: and he shall rule them with a rod of iron: and he treadeth the winepress of the fierceness and wrath of Almighty God. And he hath on his vesture and on his thigh a name written, KING OF KINGS, AND LORD OF LORDS"* (Revelation 19:10-16).

It is the events of the Great and Terrible Day of the Lord, involving what is commonly known as Armageddon, that will bring about the finalization of the Lord's repossession of this earth. He has already gathered *all* the armies of the nations into one place in the valley of Megiddon for the purpose of His arrival to do battle. In connection with this we are introduced once again to the sons of Shem, Ham and Japheth.

The end result of these awesome days is that the nations will then without a doubt know that He is the Lord. This is repeatedly spoken of throughout the prophets in anticipation of that promised day of blessing for the world. During this conflict the horns of the beast are completely destroyed and God finally fulfills His purposes for the land.

If my understanding is correct, while both the ten horns and the Magog coalition of forces will be involved in this final battle, only the rest of the other nations besides the beast's horns are left after this momentous event. The land of the horns is swallowed up as the borders of the land are extended according to the promise. This is why the incident involving the nations which takes place one thousand years later is referred to as Gog and Magog.

*"And it shall come to pass in that day, that the LORD shall pun-
ish the host of the high ones that are on high, and **the kings of the
earth** upon the earth.* And they shall be gathered together, as prison-
ers are gathered in the pit, and shall be shut up in the prison, and
after many days shall they be visited"* (Isaiah 24:21,22).

*"And I saw the beast, **and the kings of the earth**, and their
armies, gathered together to make war against him that sat on the
horse, and against his army...And I saw an angel come down from
heaven, having the key of the bottomless pit and a great chain in his
hand. And he laid hold on the dragon, that old serpent, which is the
Devil, and Satan, and bound him a thousand years, And cast him
into the bottomless pit, and shut him up, and set a seal upon him,
that he should deceive **the nations** no more, till the thousand years
should be fulfilled: and after that he must be loosed a little season...And when the thousand years are expired, Satan shall be
loosed out of his prison, And shall go out to deceive **the nations**
which are in the four quarters of the earth, Gog and Magog, to gather
them together to battle: the number of whom is as the sand of the
sea"* (Revelation 19:19; 20:1-3,7,8).

The end result of the Great and Terrible Day of the Lord will
be the supper of the great God and the "hallowing" of God's name
as all the world finally knows that He is the Lord. This is not the
supper for his redeemed, however. Here the armies of the nations
are the main entrée.

*"Thus will I **magnify** myself, and **sanctify** myself; and I will be
known in the eyes of many nations, and they shall know that I am
the LORD...Thou shalt fall upon the mountains of Israel, thou, and
all thy bands, and the people that is with thee: I will give thee unto
the ravenous birds of every sort, and to the beasts of the field to be
devoured... And I will send a fire on Magog, and among them that
dwell carelessly in the isles: and they shall know that I am the
LORD. So will I make my holy name known in the midst of my people Israel; and I will not let them pollute my holy name any more:
and the heathen shall know that I am the LORD, the Holy One in
Israel. And, thou son of man, thus saith the Lord GOD; Speak unto*

every feathered fowl, and to every beast of the field, Assemble your-
selves, and come; gather yourselves on every side to my sacrifice that
I do sacrifice upon the mountains of Israel, that ye may eat flesh,
and drink blood...And I will set my glory among the heathen, and
all the heathen shall see my judgement that I have executed, and my
hand that I have laid upon them" (Ezekiel 38:23; 39:4,6,7,17, 21).

   "And I saw an angel standing in the sun; and he cried with a loud
voice, saying to all the fowls that fly in the midst heaven, Come and
gather yourselves together unto the supper of the great God; That ye
may eat the flesh of kings, and the flesh of mighty men, and the flesh
of horses, and of them that sit on them, and the flesh of all men, both
free and bond, both small and great" (Revelation 19:17,18).

   First the Lord assembles the armies of the earth for the slaugh-
ter, then He assembles the fowls and beasts for the clean-up feast.
The net result of the Days of Awe, the Great and Terrible Day of
the Lord, will be the universal recognition of the King of kings.
The impact that these events will have on the nations is enormous
and is the subject of much prophecy in the Scriptures. At that time
His name will be magnified and they will know that He is the
Lord.

   *"Our Father which art in heaven, **Hallowed** be thy name. Thy*
*kingdom **come**. Thy will be done in earth, as it is in heaven"*
(Matthew 6:9). This was to be the desire and cry of the hearts of
the remnant in Israel as they stood, and will yet stand, on the
doorstep of the fulfillment of the covenants and promises. God's
name will be sanctified and He will be King of all the earth as
Israel finally fulfills her "great commissions" and ministry to the
nations.

   As the Days of Awe come to an end on the tenth of Tishrei,
Yom Kippur acts as a bridge capping off and bringing to an end
the entire forty day season of Teshuvah "repentance," and preparing in light of it for the next feast five days later, the Festival of
Succot. The next event in the prophetic scenario to take place is
the gathering of the remnant from the nations to bring them into
the land, and the sitting of the judgement to decide what the

rewards will be for various individuals as they inherit the kingdom, especially in connection with the city. This issue of rewards is one of the major issues in the Gospels, in perfect keeping with what had already been laid out in the prophetic scriptures. I will say more on this in the next chapter.

Let us now leave this chapter with Psalm 18 before us and in so doing review the entire period of time leading up to the Lord's appearance on Rosh HaShanah, the ensuing battle of His Great and Terrible Day, the deliverance and gathering into the land, and the blessedness of the kingdom and the rewards associated with it. It is a bit long, but it is worth it.

*"I will love thee, O LORD, my strength. The LORD is my rock, and my fortress, and my deliverer; my God, my strength, in whom I will trust; my buckler, and the horn of my salvation, and my high tower. I will call upon the LORD, who is worthy to be praised: so shall I be saved from mine enemies. The sorrows of death compassed me, and the floods of ungodly men made me afraid. The sorrows of hell compassed me about: the snares of death prevented me. In my distress I called upon the LORD, and cried unto my God: he heard me out of his temple, and my cry came before him, even into his ears. Then the earth shook and trembled; the foundations also of the hills moved because he was wroth. There went up a smoke out of his nostrils, and fire out of his mouth devoured: coals were kindled by it. He bowed the heavens also, and **came down:** and **darkness** was under his feet. And he **rode** upon a cherub, and did **fly:** yea, he did **fly** upon the wings of the wind. He made **darkness** his **secret** place; his pavilion round about him were **dark** waters and thick clouds of the skies. At the **brightness** that was before him his thick clouds passed, hail stones and coals of fire. The Lord also thundered in the heavens, and the Highest gave his voice; hail stones and coals of fire. Yea, he sent out his arrows and scattered them; and he shot out lightnings, and discomfited them. Then the channels of **waters** were seen, and the **foundations** of the world were discovered at thy rebuke, O LORD, at the blast of the breath of thy nostrils. He sent from above, he took me, he drew me out of many waters. He delivered me from the strong*

*enemy, and from them which hated me: for they were too strong for me. They prevented me in the day of my calamity: but the LORD was my stay. He brought me forth also into a large place; he delivered me, because he delighted in me. The LORD **rewarded** me **according** to my righteousness; **according** to the cleanness of my hands hath he **recompensed** me. For I **have kept** the ways of the LORD, and have not wickedly departed from my God. For all his judgements were before me, and I did not put away his statutes from me. I was also upright before him, and I kept myself from mine iniquity. Therefore hath the LORD **recompensed** me **according** to my righteousness, **according** to the cleanness of my hands in his eyesight. With the merciful thou wilt shew thyself merciful; with an upright man thou wilt shew thyself upright; With the pure thou wilt shew thyself pure; and with the froward thou wilt shew thyself froward. For thou wilt save the afflicted people; but wilt bring down high looks. For thou wilt light my candle: the LORD my God will enlighten my darkness...Thou hast enlarged my steps under me, that my feet did not slip. I have pursued mine enemies, and overtaken them: neither did I turn again till they were consumed. I have wounded them that were not able to rise: they are fallen under my feet. For thou hast girded me with strength unto the battle: thou hast subdued under me those that rose up against me. Thou hast also given me the necks of mine enemies; that I might destroy them that hate me. They cried, but there was none to save them: even unto the LORD, but he answered them not. Then did I beat them small as the dust before the wind: I did **cast them out** as the dirt in the streets. Thou hast delivered me from the strivings of the people; and thou hast made me the head of the heathen: a people whom I have not known shall serve me. As soon as they hear of me, they shall obey me: the strangers shall submit themselves unto me. The strangers shall fade away, and be afraid out of their close places. The LORD liveth; and blessed be my rock; and let the God of my salvation be exalted. It is God that avengeth me, and subdueth the people under me. He delivereth me from mine enemies: yea, thou liftest me up above those that rise up against me: thou hast delivered me from **the violent man**. Therefore will I give* *thanks unto thee, O LORD, among the heathen, and sing praises unto thy name. Great deliverance giveth he to his king; and sheweth mercy to his anointed, to David, and to his seed for evermore"* (Psalm 18:1-28, 36-50). I hope this strikes you as being related to the Sermon on the Mount because that is indeed what the Lord is talking about here.

TIMES OF THE GENTILES
The 5th Course of Punishment
(Leviticus 26:27-46)

Gold Head (Dan 2:38)
BABYLON—The Kingdom is stripped from Israel

70 YEAR CAPTIVITY (Dan 9:2; II Chron 36:20,21)

THE **LION** OF DAN 7:4—(Jer 52:31-34)
1st Installment Lev 26:34,35
City and Temple sacked and burned

The Two Arms of the Silver Breast (Dan 2:32,39)
MEDIA-PERSIA—Daniel's Seventy Weeks Begin

49 YEARS OF REBUILDING (Dan 9:25; II Chron 36:22,23)

THE **BEAR** Of DAN 7:5—(Is 45:14; Esther 1:1)

THE RAM OF DAN 8:
DAN 11:2
2nd Installment
City and Temple rebuilt

BEARS RULE OVER ALL THE EARTH

The Brass Belly (Daniel 2:39)
GRECIA—Rules with Great Dominion

SILENCE (Ps 74:9; Amos 8:11-13; Micah 3:4; 5:3; Hosea 5:6,15)

THE **LEOPARD** OF DAN 7:6

THE GOAT OF DAN 8
DAN 11:3
3rd Installment
Famine of hearing the word of the Lord

THE DIVIDED GRECIAN KINGDOM
Days of the Messiah
(Lev 26:40,41; Is 40:3; Dan 9:26; The Dominion passes to the Two Thighs of Brass
Hos 2:14; Mal3:1; Mt 3:1; Lk 2:1,2; Mt 2:13-23)

THE **4 WINGS & HEADS OF THE LEOPARD**
DAN 7:6

THE **4 KINGDOMS THAT STAND UP OUT OF THE
NATION. ANTICHRIST COMES OUT OF ONE OF
THEM WHICH IS WHY HE IS LATER IDENTIFIED
AS THE KING OF THE NORTH.**
DAN 8:8
DAN 11:4
During this time God breaks the silence of the **3rd
Installment**. The nation is confronted by John the
Baptist. Messiah comes in His earthly ministry and
fulfills the spring feasts. The city and temple are left
for the coming desolation (Mt. 23:38). All that then
remains is for Christ to have His Day of Wrath which
He has prepared His little flock to go through.

The South Country   **The North Country**

The rejected stone returns
(Dan 2:34,44; Ps 2:9)

DAN 11:5 The latter time of their kingdom (Dan 8:23)

(IRON) Daniel's 4th Beast Emerges (Zech 6:1)
10 KINGS ARISE OUT OF THIS KINGDOM

The Ancient and Perpetual Hatred (Gen 15; Ps 83; Ez 25:15; 35:5)

EDOM
ISHMAELITES
MOAB
HAGARENES
GEBAL
AMMON
AMALEK
PHILISTINES
TYRE
ASSYRIA

THE LORD'S DAY—(Mt 24:1-31)
Beginning of Sorrows-Daniel's 4th Beast Arrives
(Dan 2:40; 7:7; 11:5) **"Strong Exceedingly" Diverse**
KING OF THE
NORTH #6 DIES
(Dan 11:5-19; Rev 17:10)

RAISER OF TAXES
AFTER FEW DAYS KING OF THE
NORTH #7 DIES
(Dan 11:20; Rev 17:10)

KING OF THE NORTH #8—THE BEAST (Iron/Clay)
(Dan 11:21; Rev 17:11)—(Gen 10:10; 11:1-4; Zech 5:5-11;
Rev 17:3,9,10)
The little horn, the vile person rises up with a small
people. He is diverse from the first. He is given his
power from the dragon. He makes his league and the
10 horns are crowned as they receive power as kings
one hour with the beast. Dan 7:8,20,24; 8:9,23; 9:26,27;
11:21-45; Rev 13; 17:12
"And in the days of these kings shall the God of heaven
set up a kingdom." Dan 2:44
Christ returns, smashes the image and sets up a kingdom that shall never be destroyed.

The Land of Canaan and the contention over Zion
The Kings of the Earth and Armageddon
(The Sons of Japheth, Ham, Shem and that Great City)
Gen 10; 11; Ezra 9:1-4; Ps 106:35-48; Is 19; 24:21; Jer 25:20-38; 50:37-46;
Ez 38; 39; Dan 11:40-45; Rev 16:12-17:1,2; 19:19-21

Chapter Seven

Yom Kippur

The Day of Atonement
&
The Rebirth of the Nation

*S*o the house of Israel shall know that I am the LORD their God *from that day forward. And the heathen shall know that the house of Israel went into captivity for their **iniquity**: because they trespassed against me, therefore hid I my face from them, and gave them into the hand of their enemies: so fell they by the sword. According to their uncleanness and according to their transgressions have I done unto them, and hid my face from them. Therefore thus saith the Lord GOD; Now will I bring again the captivity of Jacob, and have mercy upon the whole house of Israel, and will be jealous for my holy name; After that they have borne their shame, and all their trespasses whereby they have trespassed against me, when they dwelt safely in their land, and none made them afraid. When I have brought them again from the people, and gathered them out of their enemies' lands, and am sanctified in them in the sight of many nations; Then shall they know that I am the LORD their God, which caused them to be led into captivity among the heathen: but I have gathered them unto their own land, and have left none of them any more there. Neither will I hide my face any more from them: for I* have poured out my spirit upon the house of Israel, saith the Lord GOD" (Ezekiel 39:22-29).

This is the next event on the prophetic calendar to take place after the Days of Awe. But just what does the Lord mean when He tells Israel that at that time and forever more they will know that *He* is the Lord. Don't they know that is who He is? Isn't that a fundamental pillar of biblical Judaism? They do indeed know that is who He is, but do they know *who* He is? Alas, only a small remnant will—the little flock—who will carry the testimony of Jesus Christ against the spirit of Antichrist and the false doctrine associated with it that denies that Jesus is the Christ and, therefore, Messiah has *already come* in the flesh. These are the scoffers, mockers and scorners in the nation. They will be urging the reception of another who comes in his own name, an idol shepherd.

As Christ approached the hour when He would be pierced on that tree and cut off out of the land of the living, He declared, "*O Jerusalem, Jerusalem, thou that killest the prophets, and stonest them which are sent unto thee, how often would I have **gathered** thy children together, even as a hen gathereth her chickens under her wings, and ye would not! Behold, your house is left unto you desolate. For I say unto you, Ye shall not see me henceforth, till ye shall say, Blessed is he that cometh in the name of the Lord*" (Matthew 23:37-39).

"*And the LORD shall be seen over them, and his arrow shall go forth as the lightning: and the Lord GOD shall blow the trumpet, and shall go with whirlwinds of the south...And it shall come to pass in that day, that I will seek to destroy all the nations that come against Jerusalem. And I will pour upon the inhabitants of Jerusalem, the spirit of grace and of supplications: and they shall look upon **me** whom they have pierced, and they shall mourn for **him**, as one mourneth for **his only son**, and shall be in bitterness for him, as one that is in bitterness for his firstborn*" (Zechariah 9:14; 12:9,10)

I encourage you to read Psalm 22, which vividly puts on display the experience of the Lord when, as that Passover Lamb, He was pierced for the transgression of His people. It is a marvelous example of the detail of biblical prophecy and the efforts of the Lord to leave no doubt as to just *who* He is.

*"And then shall appear the sign of the Son of man in heaven: and then shall all the tribes of the earth mourn, and they shall see the Son of man coming in the clouds of heaven with power and great glory. And he shall send his angels with a **great** sound of a trumpet, and they shall gather together his elect from the four winds, from one end of heaven to the other."* (Matthew 24:30,31).

*"And it shall come to pass in that day, that the LORD shall beat off from the channel of the river unto the stream of Egypt, and ye shall be gathered one by one, O ye children of Israel. And it shall come to pass in that day, that the **great** trumpet shall be blown, and they shall come which were ready to perish in the land of Assyria, and the outcasts in the land of Egypt, and shall worship the LORD in the holy mount in Jerusalem"* (Isaiah 27:12,13).

This is the blowing of the *great* trumpet on Yom Kippur, which marks the end of the Days of Awe and the beginning of something new. It is also the trumpet of the Jubilee, the fiftieth year. The end of Daniel's seventy weeks, 490 years or 49 x 10, has come. This final gathering into the land for the purpose of receiving the inheritance and the fulfillment of the long-awaited promises and blessing is inextricably tied up with the New Covenant.

Yom Kippur is a *national* issue. It is about *national* atonement. This is in contrast to the Passover where each man had to take the lamb for his household. If a Jew did not apply the blood of the lamb to the doorpost of his house, he would not be spared the judgement that would come upon Egypt with the Angel of Death. Likewise, if an Egyptian came under the blood by coming under the roof of an Israelite, he would be spared.

Yom Kippur is for a *nation* that is in covenant relationship with the Lord. It is inextricably part of the Law and testifies to Israel's failure under the conditional covenant they had entered into. They can be spared because of the sacrifice but they obviously do not deserve it, they are not *naturally* righteous or worthy to obtain the unconditional promises made unto the fathers based on that conditional covenant. If they are to obtain the promised blessings, it will be only through the Lord's graciousness and mercy. He is the one who will have to accomplish the work for them and He is able to do it because He paid the redemption price. He bore the full penalty on the cross for their sinfulness so they could be made fit in God's sight to be utilized by Him in His plans and purposes for earth as laid out in the Abrahamic Covenant. Yom Kippur is for a people who have already been redeemed by the blood of the Passover Lamb.

The old conditional covenant ensured Israel a long history of curses, five courses of punishment in all. Having locked themselves into that system by entering into that contract, they are forced to experience the long history laid out in Leviticus 26 and, thereby, learn the hard way that they are not naturally fit to be utilized by God in His plan and purpose for earth. Everything that would happen was spelled out to the letter. As the various courses came upon them, God made it clear that He was simply keeping His end of the bargain according to the terms of the contract. He told them in advance that they were going to be in material breach of that contract. Therefore, under that contract they would not get the promises.

Yet, He made it equally clear that they *were* going to get the promises. In keeping with this, He made it clear that the day was going to come when He would make a *New* Covenant with the house of Israel and the house of Judah: "**Not** *according to the covenant that I made with their fathers in the day that I took them by the hand to bring them out of the land of Egypt; which my covenant they brake, although I was an husband unto them, saith the* LORD" (Jeremiah 31:32). And indeed this must be the case if they are ever to get the promises.

The five courses must come upon Israel. But now, the entire five Courses have run their course. The fifth installment to the fifth Course has come to an end. There are no more to come. The time to be blessed and enter into that promised joy has arrived.

The nation will no longer be under the old contract but will finally obtain the sonship position and finally fulfill what they were called for in the first place. The time for the "rebirth" of the nation has come. This is what the Lord was referring to when He told Nicodemus, "**Ye** must be born again" (John 3:7).

When Nicodemus seemed perplexed, the Lord squarely reproved him and said, "*Art thou a master of Israel, and knowest not these things?*" (John 3:10). The Lord was speaking nothing new here. There was no reason for ignorance on this subject unless Nicodemus bought into the leaven of the apostate rulers who in their pride and self-righteousness thought they were naturally holy and righteous as pure children of Abraham. They did not see a need for a rebirth.

But Nicodemus was a master of Israel. He was supposed to be one who had mastered the subject and doctrine of Israel and all that pertained to it. He was supposed to know all the ins and outs of what God had revealed concerning His program with Israel, and yet he was ignorant of this most fundamental truth concerning the nation and its need for a rebirth as a nation. The Lord says *ye* must be born again, plural. This is addressed to a nation that is in covenant relationship with the Lord.

It is true that we—as ones who have trusted in the Lord Jesus Christ and His sacrifice alone for our salvation—are *begotten* of God, as the apostle Paul tells us. But there is particular terminology used here as the Lord functions as that "*minister of the circumcision for the truth of God, to confirm the promises made unto the fathers*" (Romans 15:8).

The Gentiles as such are not in view here. The Lord is speaking of those things that prophetically concern the nation, but this leads up to the real issue: The righteous nation that will inherit those promises is made up of begotten individuals "*which were born, not of blood, nor of the will of man, but of God*" (John 1:13).

This is in keeping with James' words to the scattered remnant, "*Of his own will begat he us with the word of truth, that we should be **a kind of firstfruits** of his creatures*" (James 1:18).

They anticipate that time when *all* Israel will be holy. That is what the Lord is referring to, the prophesied and necessary rebirth of the nation. The Lord makes it clear with all the terminology that He uses—water, wind, Spirit—that He is referring back to some particular things that have been prophetically declared concerning the New Covenant and the time when the nation, as a nation, enters into the promises. A host of scriptures should have been running through Nicodemus' mind as the Lord was speaking—Isaiah chapters 40 and 66 and Ezekiel chapters 36 and 37, to name just a few.

In connection with this I suggest you read through the book of Hosea. It needs to be understood that at the beginning of the Fifth Course of Punishment God pronounced an official declaration over the nation of "not my people." This is not something that was pronounced upon them because of the crucifixion. This is the position of the nation from the beginning of the Fifth Course until the end of Daniel's seventy weeks when the nation, through the New Covenant, is once again declared by God to be "my people."

The Lord is going to purge the nation in the furnace of affliction that will come upon the earth and all that will be left of Israel is a righteous remnant. This is what He was preparing the people for in the Gospels. He was calling the seed out of Jacob who would be the firstfruits of the righteous nation to come. Their response to the Son was going to determine how they would fare in the coming Day of the Lord.

This is what the Lord refers Nicodemus to in the oft-quoted scripture, "*For God so loved the world, that he gave his only begotten Son, that whosoever believeth in him should not perish, but have everlasting life*" (John 3:16).

"*Kiss the **Son**, lest he be angry, and ye **perish** from the way, when his wrath is kindled but a little. Blessed are all they that put their trust in him*" (Psalm 2:12).

"*Plead with your mother, plead: for she is not my wife, neither am I her husband: let her therefore put away her whoredoms out of* *her sight, and her adulteries from between her breasts; **Lest** I strip her naked, and set her as in the day that she was born, and make her as a wilderness, and set her like a dry land, and slay her with thirst...Therefore, behold, I will allure her, and bring her into the wilderness, and speak comfortably unto her. And I will give her vineyards from thence, and the valley of Achor for a door of hope: and she shall sing there, as in the days of her youth, and as in the day when she came up out of Egypt. And it shall be at that day, saith the LORD, that thou shalt call me Ishi; and shalt call me no more Baali. For I will take away the names of Baalim out of her mouth, and they shall no more be remembered by their name. And in that day will I make a covenant for them with the beasts of the field and with the fowls of heaven, and with the creeping things of the ground: and I will break the bow and the sword and the battle out of the earth, and will make them to lie down safely. And I will betroth thee unto me for ever; yea, I will betroth thee unto me in righteousness, and in judgement, and in lovingkindness, and in mercies. I will even betroth thee unto me in faithfulness: and thou shalt know the Lord...And I will sow her unto me in the earth; and I will have mercy upon her that had not obtained mercy; and I will say to them which were not my people, Thou art my people; and they shall say, Thou art my God"* (Hosea 2:2,3,14-20,23).

That is more or less the gospel of the kingdom that was being preached by the Lord and the twelve as being at hand. First, there will be the purging of the final installment and then the restoration. The Lord begins to woo Israel with the arrival of the fourth installment and the preaching of John the Baptist, the prophesied messenger who was to prepare the way of the Lord. The Lord had declared He would bring Israel into the wilderness when He did this and this is why John is the voice crying in the wilderness where he does his preaching and water baptizing.

This is also why John said, *"He that hath the bride is the bridegroom: but the friend of the bridegroom, which standeth and heareth him, rejoiceth greatly because of the bridegroom's voice: this my joy therfore is fulfilled"* (John 3:29). The Body of Christ is nowhere in view here. The apostle Paul has not been raised up as a brand new apostle yet, the dispensation of the grace of God to the Gentiles has not been ushered in yet, and the revelation of the mystery has not been made known yet. Just as John had already declared, "*And I knew him not: but that he should be made manifest to Israel, therefore am I come baptizing with water*" (John 1:31).

There should not be any misunderstanding if you have been following the scriptures up to this point. The Lord will talk about the great marriage supper that will take place after He returns and sets up the kingdom. You will see the prophesied restoration marriage in connection with the complete fulfillment of the prophetic program at the end of the book of Revelation. This is a national issue and is one of restoration in fulfillment of the entire prophetic purposes for Israel and earth and is made possible because of the righteousness that is given the nation through the New Covenant. Moses could not lead them into the land. He could only stand as a witness against them for their utter failure in the light of the holiness of God. Only Joshua—Yeshua—Jesus, could actually bring them into the promised inheritance.

The time has come for the Lord to turn the captivity of Israel, gather them into the land, and bring them as a *nation* under the New Covenant. This is when *all* Israel is saved and there is much made of this issue all throughout the Old Testament. I believe there are two aspects to this particular subject. First, there is going to be a resurrection of all of the *justified* individuals of the Old Testament.

Technically, the Old Testament doesn't start until Exodus 20 and is still in effect into the New Testament but I will use it as it is generally understood, that is Genesis through Malachi. So then, the resurrection referred to above is the first resurrection. Now, not all Old Testament saints are members of the nation of Israel; i.e., Abel, Noah, etc. And not all members of the nation were justified. But all those who were *justified* members of the nation will be resurrected and enjoy the blessings of the kingdom. More will be said about this later.

There have been some who have taught that verses such as the ones dealing with Ezekiel's dry bones mean that every single member of the nation of Israel will be resurrected and have the benefit of forgiveness of sins, even though they were unjustified when they died. This seems clearly erroneous to me and the Scriptures are pretty clear on this matter. The rulers in Israel whom the Lord condemned were not justified and, unless they responded to Him and decided to believe God like their father Abraham, their only hope was to be raised up at the second resurrection, the resurrection of the unjust, where they would be cast into the lake of fire. This is the teaching throughout Scripture but this belief about Israel is often held by those who believe the Scripture teaches the idea of "universal reconciliation." I will say more about this later but for now I will simply say that I believe they are wrong.

Some also believe the resurrection of the dead is not at all in view in places like Ezekiel's vision but rather that it refers only to Israel becoming a nation again. It is often believed that the vision refers to what took place in 1948 with the recognition of Israel. I believe they are both wrong. The resurrection and rebirth of the nation is the same one foretold by all the prophets. It takes place at the end, after the events of Daniel's seventy weeks, the great tribulation, and the Great and Terrible Day of the Lord, when the Lord returns and gathers them into the land under the New Covenant. This national resurrection is also tied to the resurrection of individuals, but only *justified* Israelites and other justified Old Testament saints will be raised up. The vision of the dry bones leads us to the second part of this issue.

One of the things that the Lord's Day of Wrath accomplishes is the purging and purifying of the nation. Only a very small remnant will be left of the nation when the Lord returns to perform the sure mercies of David and restore the kingdom to Israel. Everything will have been utterly devastated just as it was with Job. But, just as Job is set forth as a type of the remnant, so will their end be as Job's. There is much to be studied and appreciated concerning this but we don't have the space here.

It is important to understand two things in connection with the subject at hand. First, after the Lord forced Job to go through this experience as part of His contention with Satan over earth, He says two things. "*And the LORD **turned the captivity** of Job, when he prayed for his friends: also the LORD gave Job **twice as much** as he had before. Then came there unto him **all** his brethren, and **all** his sisters, and **all** they that had been of his acquaintance before, and did eat bread with him **in his house**: and they bemoaned him, and comforted him over all the evil that the LORD had brought upon him...So the LORD blessed the latter end of Job more than his beginning*" (Job 42:10-12).

It is interesting to note that in the next few verses there is a resurrection of His children in view. But first notice that the Lord strangely characterizes the experience Job was in as "captivity" which the Lord "turns": "*And it shall come to pass, when **all** these things are come upon thee, and thou shalt call them to mind among all the nations, whither the LORD thy God hath driven thee...That then the LORD thy God will **turn thy captivity**, and have compassion upon thee, and will return and gather thee from all the nations, whither the LORD thy God hath scattered thee. If any of thine be driven out unto the outmost parts of heaven, from thence will the LORD thy God gather thee, and from thence will he fetch thee: And the LORD thy God will bring thee into the land which thy fathers possessed, and thou shalt possess it; and he will do thee good, and multiply thee above thy fathers. And the LORD thy God will circumcise thine heart, and the heart of thy seed, to love the LORD thy God with all thine heart, and with all thy soul, that thou mayest live*" (Deuteronomy 30:1,3-6).

I hope it is obvious by this point what this is referring to. Notice also how many times it says that *God will* be the one to do all of it. Furthermore, it is all made possible because of the circumcision of the heart which takes place and the giving of the spirit made possible by the New Covenant.

Then there is the blessing of the kingdom and the double portion: "*And strangers shall stand and feed your flocks, and the sons of* *the alien shall be your plowmen and your vinedressers. But ye shall be named the Priests of the LORD: men shall call you the Ministers of our God: ye shall eat the riches of the Gentiles, and in their glory shall ye boast yourselves. For your shame ye shall have **double**; and for confusion they shall rejoice in their portion: therefore in their land they shall possess the **double**: everlasting joy shall be unto them. For I the LORD love judgement, I hate robbery for burnt offering; and I will direct their work in truth, and I will make an everlasting covenant with them. And their seed shall be known among the Gentiles, and their offspring among the people: all that see them shall acknowledge them, that they are the seed which the LORD hath blessed"* (Isaiah 61:5-9).

Let us now briefly look at some scriptures which amplify this issue of the remnant. *"And it shall come to pass in that day, that the **remnant** of Israel, and such as are **escaped** of the house of Jacob, shall no more again stay upon him that smote them; but shall stay upon the Holy One of Israel, in truth. The **remnant** shall return, even the **remnant** of Jacob, unto the mighty God. For though thy people Israel be as the sand of the sea, yet a **remnant** of them shall return: the consumption decreed shall overflow with righteousness. For the Lord GOD of hosts shall make a consumption, even determined, in the midst of all the land"* (Isaiah 10:20-23).

This is what the Lord was preparing His little flock for while He was here on the earth, *"For as a snare shall it come on **all** them that dwell on the face of the **whole** earth. Watch ye therefore, and pray always, that ye may be accounted worthy to **escape** all these things that shall come to pass, and to **stand** before the Son of man"* (Luke 21:35,36).

These are the ones that endure till the end and are also the same hidden ones that we will encounter later in Isaiah. *"And it shall come to pass in that day, that the Lord shall set his hand again the **second** time to recover the **remnant** of his people, which shall be left"* (Isaiah 11:11).

"For the Lord will have mercy on Jacob, and will yet choose Israel, and set them in their own land: and the stranger shall be

joined with them, and they shall cleave to the house of Jacob. And the people shall take them, and bring them to their place: and the house of Israel shall possess them in the land of the LORD for servants and handmaids: and they shall take them captives, whose captives they were; and they shall rule over their oppressors. And it shall come to pass in the day that the LORD shall give thee rest" (Isaiah 14:1-3).

"*Open ye the gates, that **the righteous nation** which keepeth the truth may enter in...Thy dead men shall live, together with my dead body shall they arise. Awake and sing, ye that dwell in the dust: for thy dew is as the dew of herbs, and the earth shall cast out the dead. Come, my people, enter thou into thy chambers, and shut thy doors about thee: **hide** thyself as it were for a little moment, until the indignation be overpast. For, behold, the LORD cometh out of his place to punish the inhabitants of the earth for their iniquity: the earth also shall disclose her blood, and shall no more cover her slain"* (Isaiah 26:2, 19-21).

Remember Psalm 83 and the ten horns of the beast: "*They have taken crafty counsel against thy people, and consulted against **thy hidden ones**. They have said, Come, and let us cut them off from being a nation; that the name of Israel may be no more in remembrance"* (Psalm 83:3,4).

Not to worry, those dry bones can and will live just as surely as those horns will suffer annihilation when they come in remembrance before the Lord. He will keep His word. Beware the wrath of the Lamb!

"*Strengthen ye the weak hands, and confirm the feeble knees. Say to them that are of a fearful heart, Be strong, fear not: behold, your God will come with vengeance, even God with a recompence; he will come and save you...And the **ransomed** of the LORD shall return, and come to Zion with songs and everlasting joy upon their heads: they shall obtain joy and gladness, and sorrow and sighing shall flee away"* (Isaiah 35:3,4,10).

This is when the Lord turns their sorrow into dancing as they move from Yom Kippur on to the blessings of Succot.

"*For the LORD shall comfort Zion: he will comfort all her waste places; and he will make her wilderness **like Eden**, and her desert **like*** *the garden of the LORD; joy and gladness shall be found therein, thanksgiving, and the voice of melody...And I have put my words in thy mouth, and I have covered thee in the shadow of mine hand, that I may plant the heavens, and lay the foundations of earth, and say unto Zion, Thou art my people"* (Isaiah 51:3,16).

There is a reason why this comparison is made. As we have already seen, this land is His decreed place, the same decreed place that had been broken up at the time of the flood. The time for the fulfillment of His purposes for earth is come.

"Therefore my people shall know my name: therefore they shall know in that day that I am he that doth speak: behold, it is I. Break forth into joy, sing together, ye waste places of Jerusalem: for the LORD hath comforted his people, he hath redeemed Jerusalem" (Isaiah 52: 6,9). You are told in Isaiah 53 just how He is able to accomplish the redemption.

"For thy Maker is thine husband; the LORD of hosts is his name; and thy Redeemer the Holy One of Israel; The God of the whole earth shall he be called. For the LORD hath called thee as a woman forsaken and grieved in spirit, and a wife of youth, when thou wast refused, saith thy God. For a small moment have I forsaken thee; but with great mercies will I gather thee. In a little wrath I hid my face from thee for a moment; but with everlasting kindness will I have mercy on thee, saith the LORD thy Redeemer" (Isaiah 54:5-8).

It is because of the accomplished redemption as ministered through the New Covenant that He is able to perform this mercy. But once again, it is only by His mercy and grace. Under that old contract God had every right to wipe out the nation as He had told Moses. They simply would never be able to be what He called them to be on their own. Israel would need His grace, they would need Him to perform the work that they were unable to do. This would be accomplished through the obedient servant that they are constantly told to behold all throughout Isaiah and the prophets. He stands in contrast to the nation, the disobedient servant. That servant, the Redeemer, the *Lord GOD*, is none other than the Lord Jesus Christ, the anointed one, the arm of the Lord.

"*And he saw that there was no man, and wondered that there was no intercessor: therefore his arm brought salvation unto him; and his righteousness, it sustained him. For he put on righteousness as a breastplate, and an helmet of salvation upon his head; and he put on the garments of vengeance for clothing, and was clad with zeal as a cloak. According to their deeds, accordingly he will repay, fury to his adversaries, recompense to his enemies; to the islands he will repay recompence. So shall they fear the name of the LORD from the west, and his glory from the rising of the sun. When the enemy shall come in like a flood, the Spirit of the LORD shall lift up a standard against him. And the* **Redeemer** *shall come to Zion, and unto them that turn from transgression in Jacob, saith the LORD. As for me, this is my covenant with them, saith the LORD; My spirit that is upon thee, and my words which I have put in thy mouth, shall not depart out of thy mouth, nor out of the mouth of thy seed, nor out of the mouth of thy seed's seed, saith the LORD, from henceforth and for ever*" (Isaiah 59:16-21).

"*Thy people also shall be* **all** *righteous: they shall inherit the land for ever, the branch of my planting, the work of my hands, that I may be glorified. A little one shall become a thousand, and a small one a strong nation: I the LORD will hasten it in his time*" (Isaiah 60:21,22).

"*Thou shalt no more be termed Forsaken; neither shall thy land any more be termed Desolate: but thou shalt be called Hephzibah, and thy land Beulah: for the LORD delighteth in thee, and thy land shall be* **married.** *For as a young man marrieth a virgin, so shall thy sons marry thee: and as the bridegroom rejoiceth over the bride, so shall thy God rejoice over thee...And they shall call them the holy people, The* **redeemed** *of the LORD: and thou shalt be called, Sought out, A* **city** *not forsaken*" (Isaiah 62:4,5,12).

We will see this restoration and marriage at the end of Revelation as we approach Succot where the subject will be that great marriage supper of the Lamb. "*But be ye glad and rejoice for ever in that which I create: for, behold, I create Jerusalem a rejoicing, and her people a joy. And I will rejoice in Jerusalem, and joy in my people: and the voice of weeping shall be no more heard in her, nor the voice of crying"* (Isaiah 65:18,19). This is why it says in Revelation that God wipes all the tears from their eyes, the time of the promised joy has come.

*"Who hath heard such a thing? Who hath seen such things? Shall the earth be made to bring forth in one day? Or shall a nation be born at once? For as soon as Zion travailed, she brought forth her children. Shall I bring to the birth, and not cause to bring forth? saith the LORD: shall I cause to bring forth, and shut the womb? Saith God. Rejoice ye with Jerusalem, and be glad with her, all ye that love her: rejoice for joy with her, all ye that mourn for her...And when you see this, your heart shall rejoice, and your bones shall flourish like an herb: and the hand of the LORD shall be known toward his servants, and his indignation toward his enemies....And I will set a sign among them, and I will send those that **escape** of them unto the nations"* (Isaiah 66:8-10,14,19).

*"Alas! For that day is great, so that none is like it: it is even the time of Jacob's trouble; but he shall be **saved out of it**...For I will restore **health** unto thee, and I will **heal** thee of thy wounds, saith the LORD; because they called thee an Outcast, saying, This is Zion, whom no man seeketh after. Thus saith the LORD; Behold, I will bring again the captivity of Jacob's tents, and have mercy on his dwellingplaces...And ye shall be my people, and I will be your God"* (Jeremiah 30:7,17,18,22).

*"For thus saith the LORD; Sing with gladness for Jacob, and shout among the chief of the nations: publish ye, praise ye, and say, O LORD, save thy people, the **remnant** of Israel. Behold, I will bring them from the north country, and gather them from the coasts of the earth...They shall come with **weeping**, and with supplications, will I lead them: I will cause them to walk by the rivers of waters in a straight way, wherein they shall not stumble...He that scattered Israel will gather him, and keep him, as a shepherd doth his flock. For the LORD hath **redeemed** Jacob, and **ransomed** him from the hand of him that was stronger than he"* (Jeremiah 31: 7-11).

*"Behold, the days come, saith the LORD, that I will make a new covenant with the house of Israel, and with the house of Judah: **Not***

according to the covenant that I made with their fathers in the day that I took them by the hand to bring them out of the land of Egypt; which my covenant they brake, although I was an **husband** *unto them, saith the LORD: But this shall be the covenant that I will make with the house of Israel; After those days, saith the LORD, I will put my law in their inward parts, and write it in their hearts; and will be their God, and they shall be my people...for I will forgive their iniquity, and I will remember their sin no more"* (Jeremiah 31:31-34).

"Behold, **I will** *gather them out of all countries, whither I have driven them in mine anger, and in my fury, and in great wrath; and* **I will** *bring them again unto this place, and* **I will** *cause them to dwell safely: And they shall be my people, and I will be their God: And* **I will** *give them one heart, and one way, that they may fear me for ever, for the good of them, and of their children after them: And I will make an everlasting covenant with them, that I will not turn away from them, to do them good; but* **I will** *put my fear in their hearts, that they shall not depart from me"* (Jeremiah 32:37-40).

"Behold, I will bring it health and cure, and I will cure them, and will reveal unto them the abundance of peace and truth. And I will cause the captivity of Judah and the captivity of Israel to return, and will build them, as at the first. And I will cleanse them from all their iniquity, whereby they have sinned against me; and I will pardon all their iniquities, whereby they have sinned, and whereby they have transgressed against me. And it shall be to me a name for joy, a praise and an honor before all the nations of the earth, which shall hear all the good that I do unto them: and they shall fear and tremble for all the goodness and for all the prosperity that I procure unto it...Behold, the days come, saith the LORD, that I will perform that good thing which I have promised unto the house of Israel and to the house of Judah...In those days shall Judah be saved, and Jerusalem shall dwell safely: and this is the name wherewith she shall be called, **The LORD our righteousness"** (Jeremiah 33:6-9,14,16).

"And I will bring Israel again to his habitation...In those days, and in that time, saith the LORD, the iniquity of Israel shall be

sought for, and there shall be none; and the sins of Judah, and they shall not be found: for I will pardon them whom I reserve" (Jeremiah 50:19,20).

*"For thus saith the Lord GOD; I will even deal with thee as thou hast done, which hast despised the oath in breaking **the covenant**. Nevertheless I will remember **my covenant** with thee in the days of thy youth, and I will establish unto thee **an everlasting covenant**. Then thou shalt remember thy ways, and be ashamed, when thou shalt receive thy sister, thine elder and thy younger: and I will give them unto thee for daughters, but **not according to thy covenant**. And I will establish **my covenant** with thee; and thou shalt know that I am the LORD: That thou mayest remember, and be confounded, and never open thy mouth any more because of thy shame, **when I am pacified** toward thee for all that thou hast done, saith the Lord GOD"* (Ezekiel 16:59-63).

Now this passage may be a little difficult to parse out but initially recognizing that there are several covenants being spoken about is a good start. You need to understand Israel's history and what took place back in Deuteronomy chapters 29 and 30, what is often called the Palestinian Covenant or the second giving of the Law. It is a little misnamed and often gives the wrong impression as to what it actually covenants for. This is the covenant the Lord made with Israel, *"**beside** the covenant which he made with them in Horeb"* (Deuteronomy 29:1).

It must be understood that this comes on the heels of the making of the old contract where they demonstrated their utter failure to be able to live up to it. This consequently becomes a "dead issue" with God and He has it placed in a coffin or ark where it will remain. This covenant that is made *beside* that one is the provision for their failure to keep the Law Covenant. In other words, it anticipates the New Covenant. The Lord promises here that He will put His name Jehovah and His grace into effect on their behalf in light of their failure. Then He adds the provision to make the New Covenant with them at a later time after this Old Covenant has run its course. It is the New Covenant that is foretold in chapter 30 of Deuteronomy, and it is *God* who will accomplish all of these things for Israel. This becomes the *living* issue between Him and Israel from this point on.

"*And I will bring you out from the people, and will gather you out of the countries wherein ye are scattered, with a mighty hand, and with a stretched out arm, and with fury poured out. Like as I pleaded with your fathers in the wilderness of the land of Egypt, so will I plead with you, saith the Lord GOD. And I will cause you to pass under the rod, and I will bring you into the bond of the covenant: And I will purge out from among you the rebels, and them that transgress against me: I will bring them forth out of the country where they sojourn, and they shall not enter into the land of Israel...For in mine holy mountain, in the mountain of the height of Israel, saith the Lord GOD, there shall **all** the house of Israel, **all** of them in the land, serve me: there will I **accept** them...I will accept you with your sweet savour, when I bring you out from the people, and gather you out of the countries wherein ye have been scattered; and I will be **sanctified** in you before the heathen. And ye shall know that I am the LORD, when I shall bring you into the land of Israel, into the country for the which I lifted up mine hand to give it to your fathers...And ye shall know that I am the LORD, when I have wrought with you for my holy name's sake, not according to your wicked ways, nor according to your corrupt doings, O ye house of Israel, saith the Lord GOD*" (Ezekiel 20:34,36-38,40-42,44).

"*And I will multiply men upon you, **all** the house of Israel, even **all** of it: and the cities shall be inhabited, and the waste places shall be builded...A new heart also will I give you, and a new spirit will I put within you: and I will take away the stony heart out of your flesh, and I will give you an heart of flesh. And I will put my spirit within you, and cause you to walk in my statutes, and ye shall keep my judgements, and do them. And ye shall dwell in the land that I gave to your fathers; and ye shall be my people, and I will be your God...Thus saith the Lord GOD; in the day that I shall have cleansed you from all your iniquities I will also cause you to dwell in the cities, and the wastes shall be builded...And they shall say, This* land that was desolate is become **like the garden of Eden**...*Thus saith the Lord GOD; I will yet for this be enquired of by the house of Israel, to do it for them; I will increase them with men like a flock. As* **the holy flock,** *as the flock of Jerusalem in her solemn feasts; so shall the waste cities be filled with flocks of men: and they shall know that I am the LORD"* (Ezekiel 36:10,26-28,35,37,38).

"*Then he said unto me, Son of man, these bones are the* **whole** *house of Israel: behold, they say, Our bones are dried, and our hope is lost: we are cut off for our parts. Therfore prophesy and say unto them, Thus saith the Lord GOD; Behold, O my people, I will open your graves, and bring you into the land of Israel. And ye shall know that I am the LORD, when I have opened your graves, O my people, and brought you up out of your graves, And shall put my spirit in you, and ye shall live, and I shall place you in your own land: then shall ye know that I the LORD have spoken it, and performed it, saith the LORD"* (Ezekiel 37:11-14).

At this time the Lord will take both houses of Judah and Israel and they will no longer be divided. "*And I will make them one nation in the land upon the mountains of Israel; and one king shall be king to them all: and they shall be no more two nations, neither shall they be divided into two kingdoms any more at all...Moreover I will make a covenant of peace with them; it shall be an everlasting covenant with them: and I will place them, and multiply them, and will set my sanctuary in the midst of them for evermore. My tabernacle also shall be with them: yea, I will be their God, and they shall be my people. And the heathen shall know that I the LORD do sanctify Israel, when my sanctuary shall be in the midst of them for evermore"* (Ezekiel 37: 22,26-28).

"*I am the good shepherd, and know my sheep, and am known of mine. As the Father knoweth me, even so know I the Father: and I lay down my life for the sheep. And other sheep I have, which are not of this fold: them also I must bring, and they shall hear my voice; and there shall be one fold, and one shepherd. Therefore doth my Father love me, because I lay down my life, that I might take it up again. No man taketh it from me, but I lay it down of myself. I have power to lay it down, and I have power to take it again. This commandment have I received of my Father"* (John 10:14-17).

As a minister of the circumcision, it is this issue of uniting both houses of Israel that the Lord was talking about when He spoke of the fold. There will most certainly be a place for Gentiles in the coming kingdom and we will have reason to discuss it as we approach Succot. The issue of Gentile salvation was a huge issue of prophecy in accordance with God's program concerning the nation of Israel, the nations and the earth. We, however, as members of the Body of Christ, are partakers of something about which God had said nothing. The first time we are introduced to this separate program of which we are a part is with the raising up of the apostle Paul and his epistles. It is with Paul that God makes known this great mystery. More will be said about this later but it should be understood that only when He is finished with this mystery program will He resume His program with Israel as laid out in the Scriptures.

*"For I would not, brethren, that ye should be wise in your own conceits, that blindness **in part** is happened to Israel, **until** the fulness of the Gentiles be come in. And so **all** Israel shall be saved: as it is written, There shall come out of Sion the Deliverer, and shall turn away ungodliness from Jacob: For this is my covenant unto them, when I shall take away their sins. As concerning the gospel, they are enemies for your sakes: but as touching the election, they are beloved for the fathers' sakes. For the gifts and calling of God are without repentance"* (Romans 11:25-29).

*"For I could wish that myself were accursed from Christ for my brethren, my kinsmen according to the flesh: Who are Israelites; to whom **pertaineth** the adoption, and the glory, and the covenants, and the giving of the law, and the service of God, and the promises; Whose are the fathers, and of whom as concerning the flesh Christ came, who is over all, God blessed for ever. Amen"* (Romans 9:3-5).

Well, this is it—that great Day of Atonement for the nation. Yom Kippur is the most solemn day of the Jewish calendar, to the Jewish people what Easter is to the Christian world. Even if they are not found in synagogue any other day of the year, Jews will be in attendance on Yom Kippur. Actually, that connection is quite proper. When I say Easter, I do so because that is how it is basically referred to in our society. The actual holiday of Easter has always been a pagan festival and its celebration has a long history.

We need not here go into the history of the corruption of Christendom and its baptizing of paganism. It simply needs to be understood that the events which Christians remember and celebrate are the sacrifice of the crucifixion during Passover and the glorious resurrection on the feast of firstfruits. It is on the basis of what takes place during the spring feasts that the fall feasts are able to follow, especially the Day of Atonement.

The Lord is able to perform all that will take place on Yom Kippur because of what He accomplished at Passover. Christ can bring this great national atonement because of the completed redemptive work of the cross of Calvary. He had stretched forth his hands on the doorposts and bloodied the lintel with that ugly crown of the curse on His head as darkness crept in and covered the land.

"Who hath believed our report? And to whom is the arm of the LORD revealed? For he shall grow up before him as a tender plant, and as a root out of a dry ground: he hath no form nor comeliness; and when we see him, there is no beauty that we should desire him. He is despised and rejected of men; a man of sorrows, and acquainted with grief: and we hid as it were our faces from him; he was despised, and we esteemed him not. Surely he hath borne our griefs, and carried our sorrows: yet we did esteem him stricken, smitten of God, and afflicted. But he was wounded for our transgressions, he was bruised for our iniquities: the chastisement of our peace was upon him; and with his stripes we are healed. All we like sheep have gone astray; we have turned every one to his own way; and the LORD hath laid on him the iniquity of us all. He was oppressed, and he was afflicted, yet he opened not his mouth: he is brought as a lamb to the slaughter, and as a sheep before her shearers is dumb, so he opened not his mouth. He was taken from prison and from judgement: and who shall declare

his generation? For he was cut off out of the land of the living: for the transgression of my people was he stricken. And he made his grave with the wicked, and with the rich in his death; because he had done no violence, neither was their any deceit in his mouth. Yet it pleased the LORD to bruise him; he hath put him to grief: when thou shalt make his soul an offering for sin, he shall see his seed, he shall prolong his days, and the pleasure of the LORD shall prosper in his hand. He shall see of the travail of his soul, and shall be satisfied: by his knowledge shall my righteous servant justify many; for he shall bear their iniquities. Therefore will I divide him a portion with the great, and he shall divide the spoil with the strong; because he hath poured out his soul unto death: and he was numbered with the transgressors; and he bare the sin of many, and made intercession for the transgressors" (Isaiah 53:1-12).

The detail of this prophecy is absolutely marvelous, even down to Christ being numbered as a common criminal as He hung between those two thieves, and yet He would somehow be in the grave of the wealthy. Compare this with the Gospel accounts. He was keeping that Passover seder for the last time before He offered Himself up as the sacrifice.

*"And as they were eating, Jesus took bread, and blessed it, and brake it, and gave it to the disciples, and said, Take, eat; this is my body. And he took the cup, and gave thanks, and gave it to them, saying, Drink ye all of it; For this is my blood of the **new** testament, which is shed for many for the remission of sins. But I say unto you, I will not drink henceforth of this fruit of the vine, until I drink it new with you in my Father's kingdom"* (Matthew 26:26-29).

As Isaac, the faithful son of the father, Christ carries on His back the wood of the altar He is to be sacrificed upon. Up that dreadful mount He goes, the horrible place of the skull, where it would seem that the only chance for hope, the Son of Promise, is going to be lost. There will be no voice from heaven this time to stop the impending scene.

"And Abraham stretched forth his hand, and took the knife to slay his son. And the angel of the LORD called unto him out of

heaven, and said, **Abraham, Abraham:** and he said, Here am I. And he said, Lay not thine hand upon the lad, neither do thou any thing unto him: for now I know that thou fearest God, seeing thou hast not withheld thy son, thine **only** son from me" (Genesis 22:11,12).

No, the only cry that would be heard that day is, "**My God, my God,** why hast thou forsaken me? Why art thou so far from helping me, and from the words of my roaring?" (Psalm 22:1). As the Son, He was forsaken by both His Father and the Holy Spirit, disrupting the blessed union of the godhead that had existed since eternity.

"*For he hath made him* **to be sin** *for us, who knew no sin; that we might be made the righteousness of God*" (2 Corinthians 5:21).

"*Thou art of purer eyes than to behold evil, and canst not look on iniquity*" (Habakkuk 1:13).

We cannot even begin to imagine what it meant for a holy and righteous God to be made sin for us and to have all the filth and vileness of our wickedness laid upon Him. But, thank God, Christ did not shrink from the work that He had come to do. "*Now is my soul troubled; and what shall I say? Father, save me from this hour: but* **for this cause** *came I unto this hour*" (John 12:27).

There, on that cross, as the serpent lifted up in the wilderness, the curse of sin was judged and when the Lord saw it He was satisfied. "*When Jesus therefore had received the vinegar, he said, It is finished: and he bowed his head, and gave up the ghost*" (John 19:30). Oh, there is bitterness associated with the Passover, but what greater glories there are to follow because of it.

There would be no sparing of the son this time around, as with Isaac, because at last, in the mount of the Lord, He provides *Himself* a lamb. He is Jehovah-Jireh, the Lord is my provider. He is the great Redeemer. Oh, praise God, for the faithfulness of Abraham. Even though it seemed contrary to all he knew of God that such a request should be made of him, he was obedient nevertheless.

Because of his obedience, we have set forth in advance one of the greatest and most detailed pictures of what the Lord was going to accomplish for His people: He would give His only Son, the only way to remedy the plague that had come upon the human race. He, as wholly man and wholly God, was the only one who could make propitiation for the people. He had no sins of His own to pay for and, as such, could be that great substitute taking upon Himself the judgement that you and I so rightly deserve.

Of course the picture does not end there. Abraham truly *believed* God. He knew that Isaac was the son of promise. He believed that God *was* going to perform exactly what He said He would through his seed. The LORD had gone through the trouble of making Isaac's birth a miraculous one just so Abraham would realize that this was not going to be accomplished by "*the will of the flesh, nor of the will of man, but of God*" (John 1:13).

The only alternative to God's gracious performance of His promise is a system of bondage based on a performance of the flesh. They had tried that with Hagar but, alas, the product of that union is not according to the promise. So, if God was requiring him to give up this only son of promise, then fine. But then God would *have* to raise him up again because He *must* keep His word and He promised to do this mighty work through Isaac.

"*By faith Abraham, when he was tried, offered up Isaac: and he that had received the promises offered up his only begotten son, Of whom it was said, That in Isaac shall thy seed be called: Accounting that God was able to raise him up, even from the dead; from whence also he received him in a figure*" (Hebrews 11:17-19).

That is faith. That is what you call *believing* God's word. He *knew* God. He was able to place his trust in what God had said because He had proven Himself to be trustworthy. You and I can place our souls in His hands and stake our claims on what He has said because He has always performed His word. He has gone out of His way to give us this supernatural living Book so that if we are honest, we can clearly see that He is who says He is. And because He has been 100 percent on target so far, we can logically and reasonably expect that all He has proclaimed about our situation and what is to come will indeed come to pass.

It is not a blind faith, or at least it should not be. He expects us to believe what He has said as the God of the Bible because He is convinced that He has thoroughly made His case. Through His word, and the performance of it, He has amply demonstrated that He is who He says He is and can be trusted. Blind faith is dangerous as there will be many who claim to speak on His behalf; the major game of Satan is spiritual deception. Yet He makes it clear that these are not to be followed after. Why? Because He has made His case, a case that no one else can make.

"To whom will ye liken me, and make me equal, and compare me, that we may be like? They lavish gold out of the bag, and weigh silver in the balance, and hire a goldsmith; and he maketh it a god: they fall down, yea, they worship. They bear him upon the shoulder, they carry him, and set him in his place, and he standeth; from his place shall he not remove: yea, one shall cry unto him, yet can he not answer, nor save him out of his trouble. Remember this, and shew yourselves men: bring it again to mind, O ye transgressors. Remember the former things of old: for I am God, and there is none else; I am God; and there is none like me. Declaring the end from the beginning, and from ancient times the things that are not yet done, saying, My counsel shall stand, and I will do all my pleasure: Calling a ravenous bird from the east, the man that executeth my counsel from a far country: yea, I have spoken it, I will also bring it to pass; I have purposed it, I will also do it. Hearken unto me, ye stouthearted, that are far from righteousness: I bring near my righteousness; it shall not be far off, and my salvation shall not tarry: and I will place salvation in Zion for Israel my glory" (Isaiah 46:5-13).

But now the time has come for Him to perform the oath He had sworn unto their fathers. *"...the year of my redeemed is come"* (Isaiah 63:4). The tenth of Tishrei, the awesome Day of Atonement for the nation has arrived. All Israel will be saved and the righteous reborn nation will enter into that great promised inheritance of the kingdom. It is the final removal of sin for the nation so that they might finally inherit and receive the promises.

*"For on that day shall the priest make an atonement for you, to cleanse you, that ye may be clean from **all** your sins before the LORD...And he shall make an atonement for the holy sanctuary,*

and he shall make an atonement for the tabernacle of the congrega-tion, and for the altar, and he shall make an atonement for the priests, and for **all** *the people of the congregation*" (Leviticus 16:30,33).

Let us now turn to the second aspect of Yom Kippur. We have already examined it in connection with what it brings to an end and I spoke earlier of how it acts as a bridge. The Fifth Course of Punishment is over, the Season of Teshuvah including the Days of Awe are completed, that great gathering in the land has taken place and the national atonement has been applied under the New Covenant. We will now look to the other side of the bridge of this awesome day—the next feast, Succot, with all the attending joy of the kingdom. But first, some preparations need to be made before the nation actually enters into the blessedness of that time. It is to those preparations that we now turn.

— Chapter Eight —

The Five Intervening Days

*The Fulfillment
of the
Abrahamic Covenant
&*

Rewards in the Kingdom

W e are now fast approaching that joyous time of the Feast of Tabernacles. From Yom Kippur, the tenth of Tishrei, until Succot, the fifteenth of Tishrei, is a five-day period. I am convinced that there is significance to this number of days. The Lord has carefully chosen in advance these feasts to manifestly display in detail a particular truth concerning the appointed times when He comes to the nation and fulfills the various aspects of His name.

Again, He specifically designed for there to be a five-day period between Yom Kippur and Succot. Why? If you have even a cursory knowledge of the Scriptures, you realize that numbers are very significant to God. I am not talking about the speculation concerning various codes embedded in the text and other ideas often thought of in connection with numerology. I am speaking of what is plainly on the surface involving a clear correlation between various numbers and their consistent identification and association with various themes and concepts.

One example would be the number 6, especially the number 666 associated with the beast in Revelation and the "unholy trinity" counterfeit. It is said there that it is the number of a man. Man was created on day 6 of the creation week. Of the ten commandments, the first four have to do with our relationship to God, the last *six* concern our relationship to man. The number 6 is one short of 7 and the number 7 is identified with the idea of completeness in the Bible. It is, therefore, most often connected with the Lord Himself and the idea that man is incomplete without His Maker. The same could be said of the number 12, 3 and so on.

The list that could be compiled of the significance of various numbers is virtually endless and many works are devoted to this topic alone. But again, it should be fairly obvious to those who know God's ways that He did not just pick five days out of the blue. The key to understanding this issue, then, is to see where, if at all, the Lord points us to the number 5 and what it is most often associated with. Now, even without knowing the significance of the issue of *five* days, if you are familiar with the prophetic scenario, you know the basic order that events will follow. After the Lord returns, He will judge the nations in connection with entrance into the kingdom and judge His remnant in connection with the level of position, privilege and reward they will have in the kingdom—degrees of blessedness in that kingdom if I can put it that way (Psalm 120–134). I think it is quite interesting to see just how the Lord treats this issue of 5 in the Scriptures.

I encourage you to study the full contexts of the following verses as there is much to be learned. This first example involving Joseph's brethren being brought into his presence after his long absence from them following their rejection of him is especially interesting to me. They had convinced their father Jacob that Joseph was dead, but the next time they would see him he would be on the throne.

"*And they sat before him, the firstborn according to his birthright, and the youngest according to his youth: and the men marvelled one at another. And he took and sent messes unto them from before him: but Benjamin's mess was five times so much as any of theirs. And they drank, and were merry with him*" (Genesis 43:33,34).

"To all of them he gave each man changes of raiment; but to Benjamin he gave three hundred pieces of silver, and five changes of raiment" (45:22).

"And he took some of his brethren, even five men, and presented them unto pharaoh...The land of Egypt is before thee; in the best of the land make thy father and brethren to dwell; in the land of Goshen let them dwell: and if thou knowest any men of activity among them, then make them rulers over my cattle...And Jacob blessed Pharaoh, and went out from before Pharaoh. And Joseph placed his father and his brethren, and gave them a possession in the land of Egypt, in the best of the land...And Joseph nourished his father, and his brethren, and all his father's household, with bread, according to their families" (Genesis 47:2,6,10,11,12).

Go through the book of Joshua and I think you will find that the number 5 is conspicuous in dealing with blessing and inheritance of the land and judgement on kings and nations.

"And five cubits was the one wing of the cherub, and five cubits was the other wing of the cherub: from the uttermost part of the one wing unto the uttermost part of the other was 10 cubits" (1 Kings 6:24).

For now, simply notice that it deals with the temple and the division of ten with five on one side and five on the other. *"And he made two chapiters of molten brass, to set upon the tops of the pillars: the height of the one chapiter was five cubits, and the height of the other chapiter was five cubits...And he made a molten sea, ten cubits from the one brim to the other: it was round all about, and his height was five cubits...And he put five bases on the right side of the house, and five on the left side of the house: and he set the sea on the right side of the house eastward over against the south...And the candlesticks of pure gold, five on the right side, and five on the left, before the oracle"* (1 Kings 7:16,23,39,49).

Again, notice this division and the right and the left issue. See also 2 Chronicles in further amplification of this. *"In that day shall five cities speak the language of Canaan, and swear to the LORD of hosts; one shall be called, The city of destruction. In that day shall there be an altar to the LORD in the midst of the land of Egypt, and* *a pillar at the border thereof to the LORD... In that day shall Israel be the third with Egypt and with Assyria, even a **blessing** in the midst of the land: Whom the LORD of hosts shall **bless**, saying, **Blessed** be Egypt my people, and Assyria the work of my hands, and Israel mine inheritance"* (Isaiah 19:18,19,24,25).

There are more examples but this will suffice for now. We will see all of these elements pulled together in the Gospels, but right now let us take a very brief look at the things associated with the observance of Yom Kippur.

One of the key features of Yom Kippur is the involvement of goats—specifically, involving two goats and the casting of lots. *"And Aaron shall cast lots upon the two goats; one lot for the LORD, and the other lot for the scapegoat"* (Leviticus 16:8). The one that had the Lord's lot fall on him was slain, but the one upon whom fell the lot to be the scapegoat was allowed to live. There is a right-hand versus left-hand issue here and this also will be significant for what we will see shortly.

We are not finished looking at the issues associated with the number 5 by any means. However, I want to now take a brief interlude and discuss some fundamentals of the reward issue with Israel, the Lord's earthly ministry and the kingdom. It is my aim that once these issues are grasped, we will be in a better position to return to the timetable and see the connection with these numbers by examining the relevant passages in the Gospels.

It is important to remember that in the Gospels, we are in the climactic stage of God's program with Israel. The preaching of John the Baptist puts the nation on notice that the fourth installment in the Fifth Course of Punishment has arrived (Leviticus 26:40), beginning the days of Messiah. This means that only the fifth installment is left after this and then the glorious kingdom as foretold by the prophets. This is why both John and the Lord preach that the kingdom of heaven is "at hand."

Daniel's time schedule was winding down and the Messiah was in their midst fulfilling His ministry. The gospel of the kingdom could not have been preached at any time before this because the time had not yet come. The ministry was one of preparation, both for the Lord's Day of Wrath that was going to come to purge the nation and the kingdom to follow. This is why Christ performs certain signs and miracles. First, He proves that He is who He claims to be, the Son of David, the Son of God. But He also performs the signs of the kingdom, those things which will characterize that glorious age.

One of the main issues in this ministry of preparation was for the Lord Himself to magnify the law and make it honorable (Isaiah 42:21). He begins to do this with the Sermon on the Mount and throughout His ministry, as He did not come to abolish the law but fulfill it. Now before we actually talk about that well-known sermon I want you to look closely at a passage from the psalms:

*"But unto the wicked God saith, What hast thou to do to declare my statutes, or that thou shouldest take my covenant in thy mouth? Seeing thou hatest instruction, and castest my words behind thee. When thou sawest a thief, then thou consentedst with him, and hast been partaker with adulterers. Thou givest thy mouth to evil, and thy tongue frameth deceit. Thou sittest and speakest against thy brother; thou slanderest thine own mother's son. These things hast thou done, and I kept silence; thou thoughtest that I was altogether such an one as thyself: but I will reprove thee, and set them in order **before thine eyes**. Now consider this, ye that forget God, lest I tear you in pieces, and there be none to deliver. Whoso offereth praise glorifieth me: and to him that ordereth his conversation aright will I shew the salvation of God"* (Psalm 50:16-23).

This is the Sermon on the Mount, folks and He begins at that time to set things straight *before their eyes*. All throughout the Lord's earthly ministry, those wicked rulers that rule this people demonstrate that they do indeed hate His instruction. Those that responded to the Lord, became part of His little flock and separated themselves from that apostate nation, would have the opportunity to receive the promised deliverance in that time of wrath to come. Those who were still joined to the apostate nation, however, would be destroyed when the overflowing scourge and desolation came.

That is the issue I now want to focus on. According to the prophetic program, the Lord would come as the seed of the woman, the Son of David, call a seed out of Jacob that would be accounted to Him a generation—His brethren, accomplish the redemptive work by being that great sacrifice and rise from the dead. Having successfully accomplished the redemptive work, He would then be entitled to receive the kingdom and implement all the events that would enable the repossession of this earth and the setting up of that kingdom. *"And Jesus came and spake unto them, saying, All power is given unto me in heaven and in earth"* (Matthew 28:18).

He was then to return to heaven and sit down at the Father's right hand (Psalm 110:1) where He would remain seated *until* the time came to make His enemies His footstool. At that time He would arise and have His Day of Wrath. He was, therefore, going to prepare the remnant of Israel for the time that He would no longer be among them. He would return at the very end of His Day of Wrath as laid out in Matthew 24, but they were going to have to go through a time of unparalleled distress that would come upon both the land and all the earth. The issue then was to endure unto the end, he that did so would be *saved* (Matthew 24:13).

This is *not* salvation from the penalty of their sins. If they don't have that, then they would not be a member of the remnant at all and wouldn't even qualify for what the Lord speaks of here. The salvation spoken of is the same deliverance we saw back in Psalm 50:23, namely *physical* salvation. *"For then shall be great tribulation, such as was not since the beginning of the world to this time, no, nor ever shall be. And except those days should be shortened, there should no flesh be saved: but for the elect's sake those days shall be shortened"* (Matthew 24:21,22).

During that time they will need to be abiding in Christ and His words and obeying all that He has instructed them in His ministry and through the epistles written to them (Hebrews to Revelation).

"And the dragon was wroth with the woman, and went to make war with the remnant of her seed, which keep the commandments of God, **and** *have the testimony of Jesus Christ"* (Revelation 12:17). *"Here is the patience of the saints: here are they that keep the commandments of God,* **and** *the faith of Jesus"* (Revelation 14:12). If they do this they will follow such commandments as, *"Ye shall not make any cuttings in your flesh for the dead, nor print any marks upon you: I am the LORD"* (Leviticus 19:28).

The remnant will have no problem when confronted with the issue of receiving the mark of the beast. If they are abiding in the wisdom, they will not be taken in by that coming king's flatteries. The list could go on and on. This issue of wisdom will be a huge factor at that time. *"And they that* **understand** *among the people shall* **instruct** *many...And some of them of* **understanding** *shall fall...And they that be* **wise** *shall shine as the brightness of the firmament; and they that turn many to righteousness as the stars for ever and ever"* (Daniel 11:33,35; 12:3).

They will also need to strictly obey what the Lord has instructed them. When they see that abomination of desolation they are to flee, period. If they don't, they will be taken in the judgement that falls upon the city. *"Let him which is on the housetop not come down to take any thing out of his house: Neither let him which is in the field return back to take his clothes"* (Matthew 24:17,18).

But, they might ask, What will I eat? Surely I will starve out there. What will I wear? Surely I need a coat or I will freeze to death. Ah, but if they abide in the Lord and obey what He has said, He has already prepared them for this. *"Therefore take no thought saying, What shall we eat? or, What shall we drink? or, Wherewithal shall we be clothed? Take therefore no thought for the morrow: for the morrow shall take thought for the things of itself. Sufficient unto the day is* **the evil** *thereof"* (Matthew 6:31,34).

We need to examine this in light of the things they will be praying about as outlined in the Lord's prayer. This is not just any old evil. *"A* **prudent** *man* **foreseeth** *the evil, and* **hideth** *himself: but* the *simple* pass on, and are punished...That I might make thee know the **certainty** of the words of truth; that thou mightest answer the words of truth to them that send unto thee?" (Proverbs 22:3,21). I encourage you to look at the full contexts of these passages and see the awesome detail of the warnings concerning the temptations they will face at that time.

The so-called "Lord's prayer" is a wonderful example of the Lord preparing His remnant for the coming time of trouble, and then the inheriting of the earth. The rest of the apostate nation, because of their refusal to offer the prophesied and required repentance would be doomed and left for the desolater. However, those who were faithful to Christ would be provided for during that time. "*Ask and it shall be given **you**; seek, and ye shall find; knock, and it shall be opened unto **you**"* (Matthew 7:7).

There are many prophetic scriptures on this matter but I will simply offer a few choice examples here:

"**Depart from evil, and do good; seek** *peace, and pursue it. The eyes of the LORD are upon **the righteous**, and his ears are open unto **their** cry. The face of the LORD is against them that do evil, to cut off the remembrance of them from the earth. The **righteous** cry, and the LORD heareth, and delivereth **them** out of all their troubles. The LORD is nigh unto **them** that are of a broken heart; and saveth such as be of a contrite spirit"* (Psalm 34:14-18).

"*And when **ye** spread forth your hands, I will hide mine eyes from **you**: yea, when **ye** make many prayers, I will not hear: your hands are full of blood"* (Isaiah 1:15).

"**Blessed** *are all **they** that **wait** for him. For the people shall dwell in Zion at Jerusalem: thou shalt weep no more: he will be very **gracious** unto **thee** at the voice of **thy** cry; when he shall hear it, he will answer **thee**"* (Isaiah 30:18,19).

"*For I know the thoughts that I think toward **you**, saith the LORD, thoughts of peace, and not **evil**, to give you an expected end. Then shall **ye** call upon me, and ye shall go and pray unto me, and I will hearken unto **you**. And **ye** shall **seek** me, and find me, when ye shall **search** for me with all your heart"* (Jeremiah 29:11-13).

*"Therefore will I also deal in fury: mine eye shall not spare, neither will I have pity: and though **they** cry in mine ears with a loud voice, yet will I not hear **them**"* (Ezekiel 8:18. See also Psalm 18:41; 27; 50; 70 and Isaiah 26).

One of the particular applications of this provision can be seen in Isaiah 65, *"Therefore will I number **you** to the sword, and **ye** shall all bow down to the slaughter: **because** when I called, **ye** did not answer; when I spake, **ye** did not hear; but did evil before mine eyes, and did choose that wherein I delighted not. **Therefore** thus saith the Lord GOD, Behold, **my** servants shall **eat**, but **ye** shall be hungry: behold, **my** servants shall **drink**, but **ye** shall be thirsty: behold, **my** servants shall rejoice, but **ye** shall be ashamed: Behold, **my** servants shall sing for joy of heart, but **ye** shall cry for sorrow of heart, and vexation of spirit."* (Isaiah 65:12-14. See also Isaiah 4:6; 8:20,21; 32:2; 33:16; 48:21; 58:11).

Here is the great doctrine of the stone that the house of Israel is to be built upon. There is a time coming when a king of fierce countenance, the Antichrist, will arise with a small people and will enter into a league with Israel and the ten horns which surround her. Out of the wars and turmoil that will be going on, he will provide the peace and safety that has so long been desired until he is revealed.

*"Wherefore hear the word of the LORD, ye **scornful men**, that rule this people which is in Jerusalem. Because ye have said, We have made a covenant with death, and with hell are we at agreement; when the overflowing scourge shall pass through, it shall not come unto us: for we have made lies our refuge, and under falsehood have we hid ourselves: Therefore thus saith the Lord GOD, Behold, I lay in Zion for a foundation a stone, a tried stone, a precious cornerstone, a sure foundation: he that believeth shall not make haste. Judgement also will I lay to the line, and righteousness to the plummet: and the hail shall sweep away the refuge of lies, and the waters shall overflow the hiding place. And your covenant with death shall be disannulled, and your agreement with hell shall not stand; when the overflowing scourge shall pass through, then ye shall be trodden down by it...Now*

*therefore be ye not **mockers**, lest your bands be made strong: for I have heard from the Lord GOD of hosts a consumption, even determined upon the whole earth. Give ye ear, and hear my voice; hearken, and hear my speech"* (Isaiah 28:14-18,22,23).

You will encounter all these particulars in the book of the Revelation. It is interesting that Peter, when writing to the remnant that will be going through that time to come, mentions both that stone and the mockers. Finally, the Lord Himself declared, *"Therefore whosoever heareth these sayings of mine, and doeth them, I will liken him unto a **wise** man, which built his house upon a rock: And the rain descended, and the floods came, and the winds blew, and beat upon that house; and it fell not: for it was founded upon a rock. And every one that heareth these sayings of mine, and doeth them not, shall be likened unto a **foolish** man, which built his house upon the sand: And the rain descended, and the floods came, and the winds blew, and beat upon that house; and it fell: and **great** was the fall of it"* (Matthew 7:24-27).

Before we move on, I want to reinforce the various things we have been looking at by looking at some verses in Isaiah. This passage reviews the issues that will face the remnant from the time after the crucifixion and the laying of the cornerstone until the end of the fifth installment, especially as it relates to the ministry of the twelve apostles and the coming beast.

*"**Associate** yourselves, O ye people, and ye shall be broken in pieces; and give ear, all ye of far countries: gird yourselves, and ye shall be broken in pieces. **Take counsel** together, and it shall come to nought; speak the word, and it shall not stand: for God is with us. For the LORD spake thus to me with a strong hand, and instructed me that I should not walk in the way of this people, saying, Say ye not, **A confederacy**, to all them to whom this people shall say, **A confederacy**; neither fear ye their fear, nor be afraid. Sanctify the LORD of hosts himself; and let him be your fear, and let him be your dread. And he shall be for a **sanctuary**; but for a stone of stumbling and for a rock of offence to both the houses of Israel, for a gin and for a snare to the inhabitants of Jerusalem. And many among them shall stumble, and*

*fall, and be broken, and be snared, and be taken. Bind up **the testimony**, seal **the law** among my **disciples**. And I will **wait** upon the LORD, that hideth his face from the house of Jacob, and I will look for him. Behold, I and the children whom the LORD hath given me are for **signs** and for **wonders** in Israel from the LORD of hosts, which dwelleth in mount Zion. And when they shall say unto you, Seek unto them that have familiar spirits, and unto wizards that peep, and that mutter: should not a people seek unto their God? For the living to the dead? To **the law** and to **the testimony**: if they speak not according to this word, it is because there is no light in them. And they shall pass through it, hardly bestead and hungry: and it shall come to pass, that when they shall be hungry, they shall fret themselves, and curse their king and their God, and look upward. And they shall look unto earth; and behold trouble and darkness, dimness of anguish; and they shall be driven darkness"* (Isaiah 8:9-22).

I highly recommend that you read 1 John in connection with this. If you really understand this passage, you should have little difficulty in grasping what is occurring in the Gospels, Acts 1-7, and the circumcision epistles (Hebrews to Revelation). I will not here address the mystery epistles of Paul (Romans to Philemon) addressed to you and me as members of the Body of Christ as it is not the place.

You should be able to understand by now this issue of the remnant versus the apostate nation. *"And I will bring forth a seed out of Jacob, and out of Judah an inheritor of my mountains: and mine elect shall inherit it, and my servants shall dwell there"* (Isaiah 65:9). This is who the Lord is preparing in the Gospels, and the twelve continue that ministry after He has departed to sit at the Father's right hand. All of this was well prophesied in the Scriptures. However, there is also the doctrine of the remnant *within* the remnant and it is in the Lord's discussions about this subject that the issue of rewards figures prominently. This is the wise versus foolish issue and the standard is faithfulness.

Now, let me make one thing clear: The subject is *not* salvation from the debt of our sins and being given a justified position before God. We could never earn or merit that by our works. And this is not mystery truth by any stretch of the imagination. Today, there is also the issue of being *"dead with Christ from the rudiments of the world"* (Colossians 2:20), but that is a different matter in accordance with who we are in the current mystery program of God. That is, while justification is by faith in the prophetic program, sacrifices, water baptisms, circumcision, etc., are still part of the program. This justification issue is the whole testimony of the prophetic scriptures as I hope has been clear from our discussion of the New Covenant (Romans 3:20,21; 4:2,6; Galatians 3:21).

This kind of salvation has *always been* by grace through faith. *"Abraham **believed** God, and it was counted unto him for righteousness"* (Romans 4:3; Genesis 15:6). If justification was by the Law, then no one except Christ could ever be justified before God. Nevertheless, God almost killed Moses because he neglected the circumcision of his son! (Exodus 4:24) Today it is faith *alone*.

The Law was never given to justify anyone unto eternal life. It was a schoolmaster showing them the need for a substitute Redeemer and their inadequacy before God. When they believed they needed substitution, God justified them. Then came the "faith *of* Jesus Christ," the faithful performance and obedience of Jesus Christ. *"For the life of the flesh is in the blood: and I have given it to you upon the altar to make an atonement for your souls: for it is the blood that maketh an atonement for the soul"* (Leviticus 17:11). *"Without shedding of blood is no remission."* (Hebrews 9:22) What the blood of other animal substitutes could only *cover*, the blood of the tried and precious Lamb of God removed and took away forever making that justified one perfect (Hebrews 8–10).

The Sermon on the Mount is not about telling how an Israelite can get justified unto eternal life or how to become a member of the remnant. The Sermon on the Mount is addressed to those who are *already* members of the remnant, those who had already believed the gospel of the kingdom. By the very nature of grace and justification, we cannot lose it once we have it. If we cannot earn it then we cannot earn it, period. If for some reason you have trouble with this, then I suggest you go back and get thoroughly grounded in the book of Romans where this issue is made clear. A large price was paid for that grace; be careful not to slander it.

Rewards, however, can be lost or gained and just because you are a justified saint doesn't guarantee that you will be spared the physical destruction that will come upon the earth. Here, obedience is at a premium. Unlike certain of the Pharisees and other leaders in the nation whose father is the devil, these individuals can rightfully claim God as their Father. The issue for them is rewards and good *works*. Go through the Sermon on the Mount and see how many times the word *reward* appears. A reward is something you earn and merit. You *deserve* what you receive and that is why you get it. This is the exact opposite of grace and salvation from the penalty of your sin before God. In fact, this is what the leaders in Israel failed to understand in their thinking that they were naturally worthy and holy before God. (See Luke 18:10-14).

The rewards issue involves those who are already justified. Faithfulness during that coming time of trouble will determine what is received after it is over. This is where the subject of blessedness enters in connection with the coming kingdom and the rejoicing of Succot. In fact, the entire fifth book of the psalms (chapters 107-150) is all about the Everlasting Father and His blessings. There are blessings associated with that kingdom and a member of the remnant's conduct and faithfulness will determine just how blessed they will be in that time. If you don't like that idea, remember that God seems to care an awful lot about it and sets it forth as a *major* issue before the remnant. Their rewards are in heaven, with that great city in which is the Lord's house.

When Christ returns at the end of having His Day, He will then distribute the rewards and various positions in that kingdom. He is going to set up His government, His royal house, His holy hill and a host of other positions concerning rulership, the temple and the ministries to the nations. Just being in that kingdom is a great blessing, obviously, but as I said, there are also degrees of blessedness. Let's look at some passages that touch on this topic.

"*Behold, the Lord GOD will come with strong hand, and **his arm** shall rule for him: behold, his reward is **with** him, and his work before him*" (Isaiah 40:10).

"*Behold, thy salvation cometh; behold, his reward is **with** him, and his work before him. And they shall call them, the holy people, The **redeemed** of the LORD: and thou shalt be called, Sought out, A city not forsaken*" (Isaiah 62:11,12). See also Psalm 15; 24; 19:11; Proverbs 11:18; 24:14,20; 25:22).

"*Rejoice, and be exceeding glad for **great** is your **reward in heaven**"* (Matthew 5:12).

"*Take heed that ye do not **your** alms before men, **to** be seen of them: otherwise ye have no **reward** of your Father which **is in heaven**...and thy Father which seeth in secret himself shall **reward** thee **openly**...shall reward thee **openly**...shall reward thee **openly**"* (Matthew 6:1,4,6,18).

"*He that receiveth you receiveth me, and he that receiveth me receiveth him that sent me. He that receiveth a prophet in the name of a prophet shall receive a prophet's **reward**; and he that receiveth a righteous man in the name of a righteous man shall receive a righteous man's **reward**. And whosoever shall give to drink unto one of these little ones a cup of cold water only in the name of a disciple, verily I say unto you, he shall in no wise **lose his reward**"* (Matthew 10:40-42).

"*Rejoice ye in that day, and leap for joy: for, behold, your **reward** is **great in heaven**...and your **reward** shall be **great**"* (Luke 6:23,35).

"*For ye had compassion of me in my bonds, and took joyfully the spoiling of your goods, **knowing** in yourselves that ye have **in heaven** a better and an enduring substance. Cast not away therefore your confidence, which hath **great recompence of reward**...For yet a little while, and he that shall come will come, and will not tarry*" (Hebrews 10:34,35,37).

"*Look to yourselves, that we **lose not** those things which **we have** wrought, but that we receive a **full reward**"* (2 John 8).

So, once again, when the Lord said, "*In my Father's house are many mansions: if it were not so, I would have told you. I go to prepare a place for you. And if I go and prepare a place for you, I will come again, and receive you unto myself; that where I am, there you may be also.*" (Jn 14:2,3), He was talking about the gathering that will take place at the great trump on Yom Kippur when He gathers them back into the land from where they have been scattered in fulfillment of all the promises of the prophetic scriptures. The issue for the remnant is not their going to heaven, but rather those things in heaven coming back with the Lord to earth.

"*Blessed is the man that doeth this…Even unto them will I give in **mine house** and within my walls **a place** and a name better than of sons and of daughters: I will give them an everlasting name, that shall not be cut off…Even them will I bring to my holy mountain, and make them joyful in **my house** of prayer: their burnt offerings and their sacrifices shall be accepted upon mine altar; for **mine house** shall be called an house of prayer for all people. The Lord GOD, which gathereth the outcasts of Israel saith, Yet will I gather others to him, beside those that are gathered unto him.*" (Isaiah 56:5,7,8. For the details about this house and associated ministries see Ezekiel chapters 40–48).

The Lord is in perfect keeping with the prophetic scenario. "*For the Son of man shall come in the glory of his Father with his angels; and **then** he shall **reward** every man **according to his works**"* (Matthew 16:27).

For some this will not be a pleasant experience. He will be sure to "reward" his enemies, they will get what they deserve.

"*And the nations were angry, and thy wrath is come, and the time of the dead, that they should be judged, and that thou shouldest give **reward** unto thy servants the prophets, and to the saints, and to them that fear thy name, small and great; and shouldest destroy them which destroy the earth*" (Revelation 11:18). "*And, behold, I come quickly; and my reward is **with** me, to give every man **according as his work** shall be*" (Revelation 22:12).

The seven churches of the remnant of Israel in the book of Revelation are quite naturally presented with this issue of rewards.

They are the ones to whom the circumcision epistles minister as they experience the sequence of events in the fifth installment, the Lord's Day. We are there given specifics as to certain rewards. Time does not allow to fully explore this issue, but I will simply point out for now that access to the tree of life will be quite beneficial for those that are left standing before the Lord in their physical bodies (John 11:25,26; Revelation 2:7). Once again the return to Genesis, the garden and the original purposes for earth should be clearly seen, even down to the very rewards that will exist at that coming time.

Touching upon the great escape that is to take place at that time for the faithful, "*Therefore we ought to give the more earnest heed to the things which we have heard, lest at any time we should let them slip. For if the word spoken by angels was stedfast, and every transgression and disobedience received a just recompence of reward; How shall we escape, if we neglect so great salvation; which at the first began to be spoken by the Lord, and was confirmed unto us by them that heard him; God also bearing them witness, both with signs and wonders, and with divers miracles, and gifts of the Holy Ghost, according to his own will?*" (Hebrews 2:1-4. See also Isaiah 8:16-18 on the ministry of the twelve.).

"*And take heed to yourselves, lest at any time your hearts be overcharged with surfeiting, and drunkeness, and cares of this life, and so that day come upon you unawares. For as a snare shall it come on all them that dwell on the face of the whole earth. Watch ye therefore, and pray always, that ye may be accounted worthy to escape all these things that shall come to pass, and to stand before the Son of man.*" (Lk 21:34-36). But again, everything included in the book of Revelation is in complete keeping with the prophetic program.

Let me say, too, that many of those that are to be resurrected on that last day of Daniel 12 also have an expectation of reward in that kingdom and look forward to that city.

"*By faith Abraham, when he was called to go out into a place which he should after receive for an inheritance, obeyed; and he went out, not knowing whither he went. By faith he sojourned in the* *land of promise, as in a strange country, dwelling in tabernacles with Isaac and Jacob, the **heirs** with him of the same promise: For he looked for a city which hath **foundations**, whose builder and maker is God*" (Hebrews 11:8-10).

The Lord Jesus Christ will bring that city from heaven with him when He returns.

"*These all died in faith, not having received the promises, but having seen them afar off, and were persuaded of them, and embraced them, and confessed that they were strangers and pilgrims on the earth. For they that say such things declare plainly that they seek a country. And truly , if they had been mindful of that country from whence they **came out**, they might have had opportunity to have **returned**. But now they desire a better country, that is, an heavenly: wherefore God is not ashamed to be called their God: for he hath **prepared** for them a city*" (Hebrews 11:13-16).

"*The land shall not be sold for ever: for **the land is mine**; for ye are strangers and sojourners **with me***" (Leviticus 25:23). "*And Jacob awaked out of his sleep, and he said, Surely the LORD **is in this place**; and I knew it not. And he was afraid, and said, How dreadful is **this place**! This is none other but **the house of God**, and **this is the gate of heaven**... And this stone, which I have set for a pillar, **shall be God's house***" (Genesis 28:16,17,22).

"*By faith Moses, when he was come to years, refused to be called the son of Pharaoh's daughter; Choosing rather to suffer affliction with the people of God, than to enjoy the pleasures of sin for a season; Esteeming the reproach of Christ **greater riches** than the treasures in Egypt: for he had respect unto **the recompence of the reward***" (Hebrews 11:24-26).

Now, let's look at some final passages and parables of the Lord and pull together everything we have seen thus far, seeing the connection with the five-day period begun by the blowing of that great trumpet. Here Christ will reward the remnant of Israel and give them their new name. He will also have gathered before Him all nations—much like Adam had every beast of the field and fowl of the air brought unto him—and there give them a name—either sheep or goat.

The main issue for members of the remnant, however, is whether they will be faithful or wicked, wise or foolish. If they are foolish and neglect the salvation to which they have been called, they will have no chance of escaping the coming purge. If they let slip the words of the Lord and of His apostles spoken unto them, the results will be disastrous. They will still be justified members of the remnant, but they will not receive the same great recompence of reward.

It is this issue, as applied to the saints, that will clothe that great city which has yet to descend. "*And to her was granted that she should be arrayed in fine linen, clean and white: for the fine linen is the righteousness of saints*" (Revelation 19:8).

Again, this does not represent the justification unto eternal life that they have before the Lord, which is in no way a reward. They could never have earned that no matter how hard they tried. This applies only to those who are already justified and have been given a garment. That justification can never be taken away. However, they can defile their garments and, therefore, lack when the time for rewards comes.

The issue for the remnant is similar to what faced the Shulamite woman in the Song of Solomon. Her beloved shepherd has already come and also "withdrawn" himself and is gone. He has left her his fragrance by which to remember him and she is to be constantly strengthened by keeping her mind stayed on the words that her beloved had spoken to her. She is to wait for his return and as she speaks of him and her great desire for his presence, she is abused and beaten by the watchmen of the city. They will not have his name even mentioned. She is to remain faithful to her beloved in the face of all the temptations that will be offered to her. In his absence, a king with a flattering tongue and speaking great things will come to her and attempt to get her to be unfaithful with him. He will offer the world and great riches to her if only she will join him and the virtual host of wives and concubines that he has already conquered. He will even attempt to imitate her beloved's return, but to the wise and discerning his true identity cannot be hid (Song of Solomon 3:6-11).

"Then if any man shall say unto you, Lo, here is Christ, or there; believe it not. For there shall arise false Christs, and false prophets, and shall shew signs and wonders; insomuch that, if it were possible, they shall deceive the very elect. Behold, I have told you before. Wherefore if they shall say unto you, Behold, he is in the desert; go not forth: behold, he is in the secret chambers; believe it not" (Matthew 24:23-26). But always before her mind is her beloved, His return and that glorious wedding in which she will finally be able to claim and enjoy *her* vineyard. At the end of the book she will be able to stand before Him and declare that she has kept herself for Him. In connection with this, you may want to search out the association of the number 666 with Solomon in his apostasy.

These are the works that are now in view, and the issue that the remnant is confronted with in the letters to the seven churches in Revelation and their candlesticks.

*"Rejoice and be exceeding glad for **great** is your **reward** in heaven: for so persecuted they the prophets which were before you. Ye are the salt of the earth: but if the salt have lost his savour, wherewith shall it be salted? It is thenceforth good for nothing, but to be cast out, and to be **trodden under foot** of men. Ye are the light of the world. A city that is set on an hill cannot be hid. Neither do men light a candle, and put it under a bushel, but on a candlestick; and it giveth light unto all that are in the house. Let your light so shine before men, that **they may see** your **good works**, and glorify your Father which is in heaven"* (Matthew 5:12-16).

*"Dearly beloved, I beseech you as strangers and pilgrims, abstain from fleshly lusts, which war against the soul; Having your conversation honest among the Gentiles: that, whereas they speak against you as evildoers, they may by your good works, which they shall behold, glorify God **in the day of visitation**"* (1 Peter 2:11,12).

*"I know **thy works**...because thou hast left thy first **love**. Remember therefore...To him that overcometh will I give...I will give unto every one of you according to your **works**...But that which ye have already hold fast till I come. And he that overcometh, and **keepeth** my **works** unto the end, **to him will I give** power over*

the nations...*for I have not found thy **works** perfect before God. Remember therefore how thou hast received and heard, and hold fast, and repent. Thou hast a few names even in Sardis which have not **defiled their garments;** and they shall walk with me in white: for they are **worthy**...Because thou hast kept the word of my patience, I also will keep thee from the hour of temptation, which shall come upon all the world, to try them that dwell upon the earth. Behold, I come quickly; hold that fast which thou hast, that no man **take** thy crown. Him that overcometh will I make...He that overcometh will I grant to sit with me in my throne...*" (Revelation 2:2,4,5,7,23,25,26; 3:2-4,10-12,21).

"*He brought me forth also into a large place; he delivered me, because he delighted in me. The LORD **rewarded** me **according to** my righteousness; according to the cleaness of my hands hath he **recompensed** me. For I have kept the ways of the LORD, and have not **wickedly** departed from my God. For all his judgements were before me, and I did not put away his statutes from me. I was also upright before him, and I kept myself from mine iniquity. **Therefore** hath the LORD **recompensed** me **according to** my righteousness, **according to** the cleaness of my hands in his eyesight. With the merciful thou wilt shew thyself merciful; with an upright man thou wilt shew thyself upright; With the pure thou wilt shew thyself pure; and with the froward thou wilt shew thyself froward*" (Psalm 18:19-26).

"*Whosoever therefore shall break one of these least commandments, and shall teach men so, he shall be called **least** in the kingdom of heaven: but whosoever shall do and teach them, the same shall be called **great** in the kingdom of heaven*" (Matthew 5:19).

"*Of his own will begat he us with the word of truth, **that we should** be a kind of firstfruits of his creatures. Wherefore, my beloved brethren, let every man be swift to hear, slow to speak, slow to wrath: For the wrath of man worketh not the **righteousness** of God. Wherefore lay apart all filthiness and superfluity of naughtiness, and receive with meekness the engrafted word, which **is able** to save **your** souls. But be ye doers of the word, and not hearers only, deceiving your own selves...But whoso looketh into the perfect law of liberty,* *and continueth therein, he being not a **forgetful** hearer, but a doer of the work, this man shall be **blessed** in his deed*" (James 1:18-22,25).

Please notice that these individuals already have justification before God and have already been begotten by the word of truth. However, the same thing that was set before the justified remnant in the Gospels is still the issue from Hebrews through Revelation.

"*LORD, **who** shall abide in thy tabernacle? **who** shall dwell in thy holy hill? **He that** walketh uprightly, and worketh righteousness, and speaketh the truth in his heart...**He that**...**He that**...**He that**...*" (Psalm 15). See also Psalm 24. The two places mentioned here, as well as in other places in the Scriptures, refer to specific places in that city which descends from above and will be on earth after Christ returns and sets up His kingdom. They are special positions of privilege and honor that will not be available to everyone.

This especially has to do with one's walk which is one of the reasons for the account in John 13. "*Peter saith unto him, Thou shalt never wash my feet. Jesus answered him, If I wash thee not, thou hast **no part with me**. Simon Peter saith unto him, Lord, not my feet only, but also my hands and my head. Jesus saith to him, He that is washed needeth not save to wash his feet, but is clean every whit: and ye are clean, but not all. For he knew who should betray him; therefore said he, Ye are not all clean*" (John 13:8-11).

Peter had already believed that gospel of the kingdom, was begotten by that word of truth and clean in the sight of God. This, however, would not guarantee a fullness of position with the Lord in His kingdom when He returns. "*If we say that we have fellowship with him, and walk in darkness, we lie, and do not the truth. But if we walk in the light, we have fellowship one with another, and the blood of Jesus Christ his Son cleanseth us from **all sin**. If we say that we have no **sin**, we deceive ourselves, and the truth is not in us. If we confess our sins, he is faithful and just to forgive us our sins, and to **cleanse** us from all **unrighteousness**...And he is the propitiation for **our** sins: and not for **ours** only, but also for the sins of the whole world. And hereby we do know that we know him, if we keep his commandments*" (1 John 1:6-9; 2:2,3).

Those addressed by John have that propitiation and have been cleansed in that fuller sense. But they, like David, are hardly without mistake. They are exhorted not to neglect that which has been spoken to them but to abide in Christ and His word and thereby perfect their righteousness in the practical sense. They are to *keep* their garments when their patience is tried. The issue is one of fruitfulness. (Revelation 2:26) *"For I have given unto them the words which thou gavest me; and they have received them, and have known surely that I came out from thee, and they have believed that thou didst send me...I pray not that thou shouldest take them out of the world, but that thou shouldest keep them from the evil. They are not of the world, even as I am not of the world. Sanctify them through thy truth: thy word is truth"* (John 17:8,15-17).

"The sinners in Zion are afraid; fearfulness hath surprised **the hypocrites. Who** *among us shall dwell with the devouring fire?* **who** *among us shall dwell with everlasting burnings?* **He that** *walketh righteously, and speaketh uprightly; he that despiseth the gain of oppressions, that shaketh his hands from holding of bribes, that stoppeth his ears from hearing of blood, and shutteth his eyes from seeing evil;* **He** *shall dwell on high:* **his** *place shall be the munitions of rocks: bread shall be given* **him;** **his** *waters shall be sure. Thine eyes shall see the king* **in his beauty:** *they shall behold the land that is very far off"* (Isaiah 33:14-17).

Simply put, if they are hypocrites, even though they are justified, they will not receive the deliverance they need in that evil day to stand before the Lord, neither will they obtain the great recompense of reward. *"***Brethren,** *if any of* **you** *do err from the truth, and one convert him; Let him know, that he which converteth the sinner from the error of his way shall save a soul from death, and shall hide a multitude of sins."* (Js 5:19,20).

Notice that there are those who may come under this category, even though James may rightfully call them "brethren." Simply because you are justified and a member of the remnant of Israel does not guarantee that you will endure to the end in the coming Day of the Lord. There will be no escape for those who neglect so great salvation. By the same token, there will also be special rewards for those who love not their lives unto death. For many, the time would come when they would have to resist unto death (Deuteronomy 32:35-43; John 16:1-6; Hebrews 12:4; James 5:6; Revelation 6:9).

"The law of the LORD is perfect, converting the soul: the testimony of the LORD is sure, making wise the simple" (Psalm 19:7).

"For thus saith the high and lofty One that inhabiteth eternity, whose name is Holy; I dwell in the high and holy place, with him also that is of a contrite and humble spirit, to revive the spirit of the humble, and revive the heart of the contrite ones. For I will not contend for ever, neither will I be always wroth: for the spirit should fail before me, and the souls which I have made" (Isaiah 57:15,16).

"But he that received seed into the good ground is he that heareth the word, and understandeth it; which also beareth fruit, and bringeth forth, some an hundredfold, some sixty, some thirty" (Matthew 13:23). Different people produce different amounts. I think it is also significant that these are in descending order. *"And shall not God avenge his own elect, which cry day and night unto him, though he bear long with them? I tell you that he will avenge speedily. Nevertheless when the Son of man cometh, shall he find faith on the earth?"* (Luke 18:7,8).

A very trying time will come upon this earth, the likes of which we have difficulty imagining.

"For then shall be great tribulation, such as was not since the beginning of the world to this time, no, nor ever shall be...if it were possible, they shall deceive the very elect" (Matthew 24:21,24).

"...And upon the earth distress of nations, with perplexity; the sea and waves roaring. Men's hearts failing them for fear, and for looking after those things which are coming on the earth: for the powers of heaven shall be shaken" (Luke 21:25,26).

There will be a premium on faithfulness. *"Whosoever therefore shall humble himself as this little child, the same is **greatest** in the kingdom of heaven"* (Matthew 18:4).

"...*She saith unto him, Grant that these my two sons may sit, the one on thy right hand, and the other on the left, in thy kingdom...And he saith unto them, Ye shall drink indeed of my cup, and be baptized with the baptism I am baptized with: but to sit on my right hand, and on my left, is not mine to give, but it shall be given to them for whom it is prepared of my Father...But Jesus called them unto him and said, Ye know that the princes of the Gentiles exercise dominion over them, and they that are great exercise authority upon them. But it shall not be so among you: but whosoever will be* **great** *among you, let him be your minister; And whosoever will be* **chief** *among you, let him be your servant: Even the Son of man came not to be ministered unto, but to minister, and to give his life a ransom for many*" (Matthew 20:21,23,25-28).

Again, those two particular positions are ones of special privilege, being especially close to the Lord in the inner circle of His government when He returns.

"*But he that is* **greatest** *among you shall be your servant. And whosoever shall exalt himself shall be abased; and he that shall humble himself shall be exalted*" (Matthew 23:11,12). "*Jesus said unto him, if thou wilt be perfect, go and sell that thou hast, and give to the poor, and thou shalt have treasure in heaven: and come and follow me*" (Matthew 19:21).

When we understand what will be happening during that coming time of trouble, we realize why the Lord says what He does about it being difficult for a rich man. This is no ancillary issue. This issue of selling all that you have is huge and is one of the commandments of the Lord to the remnant, which is why the little flock does what they do in the early chapters of Acts. Now I imagine *you* have not done this, and quite rightly. You are in no wise ungodly for not doing this. In fact, today "*If any provide not for his own, and specially for those of his own house, he hath denied the faith, and is worse than an infidel*" (1 Timothy 5:8). But the fact is that in God's program with Israel you *would* be ungodly for not doing so. The question is why? What has happened to change that? Read Paul's epistles and you'll find out.

Now, before we look at the parables I want to briefly expand upon the special position of the twelve.

"*Then answered Peter and said unto him, Behold, we have forsaken all, and followed thee; what shall we have therefore? And Jesus said unto them, Verily I say unto you, That ye which have followed me, in the regeneration when the Son of man shall sit in the throne of his glory, ye also shall sit upon twelve thrones, judging the twelve tribes of Israel. And every one that hath forsaken houses, or brethren, or sisters, or father, or mother, or wife, or children, or lands, for my name's sake, shall receive and hundredfold, and shall inherit everlasting life. But many that are first shall be last: and the last shall be first*"* (Matthew 19:27-30). We will touch upon this issue again with the parable of the wage earners that follows this passage.

To fully understand the special nature of the twelve, you need to have an appreciation for the doctrine of the remnant, or little flock, which was to be called out of the apostate nation. I hope you have a grasp of that issue by now. They are the firstfruits of the reborn righteous nation. We have already reviewed the book of Hosea dealing with the position of the nation from that point on and the promised future restoration. "*I am sought of them that asked not for me; I am found of them that sought me not: I said, Behold me, behold me, unto a nation that was not called by my name. I have spread out my hands all the day unto a rebellious people, which walketh in a way that was not good, after their own thoughts*" (Isaiah 65:1,2.).

This is not a reference to the Body of Christ and the Gentiles that make it up, or to any Gentiles in any program for that matter. We are the exact opposite of a nation. This is a description of what would be going on in the Gospels when He began to call the seed out of Jacob. The Hosea status of the nation did *not* take place at the cross nor was Israel's program suspended at that time.

In fact, the very opposite was the case as foretold by the Scriptures. "*A people that provoketh me to anger continually to my face; that sacrificeth in gardens, and burneth incense upon altars of brick; Which remain among graves, and lodge in the monuments, which eat swine's flesh, and broth of abominable things is in their vessels; Which say, Stand by thyself, come not near to me; for I am holier than thou. These are a smoke in my nose, a fire that burneth all the day"* (Isaiah 65:3-5).

Those are the ones that rule this people and they constantly provoked Him to His face when He was here on the earth. Notice also the connection between lodging in the graves and swine and compare with Matthew 8:28-34. But, as John had told them, *"When he saw many of the Pharisees and Sadducees come to his baptism, he said unto them, O generation of vipers, who hath warned you to flee from the wrath to come?"* (Matthew 3:7).

And so, *"Behold, it is written before me: I will not keep silence, but will recompense, even recompense into their bosom, Your iniquities, and the iniquities of your fathers together…therefore will I measure their former work into their bosom. Thus saith the LORD, As the new wine is found in the cluster, and one saith, Destroy it not; for a blessing is in it: so will I do **for my servants' sakes**, that I may not destroy them all. And I will bring forth a seed out of Jacob, and out of Judah an inheritor of my mountains: and mine elect shall inherit it, and my servants shall dwell there. And Sharon shall be a fold of flocks, and the valley of Achor a place for the herds to lie down in, for my people **that have sought me. But ye** are they that forsake the LORD, that forget my holy mountain, that **prepare a table** for that troop, and that furnish the drink offering unto **that number**. Therefore will I number you to the sword, and ye shall all bow down to the slaughter: because when I called, ye did not answer; when I spake, ye did not hear; but did evil before mine eyes, and did choose that wherein I delighted not"* (Isaiah 65:6-12).

They will prepare an offering for a particular number, the beast, and it is by their receiving of that number that they are destroyed.

"Search the scriptures; for in them ye think ye have eternal life: and they are they which testify of me. And ye will not come to me, that ye might have life. I receive not honour from men. But I know you, that ye have not the love of God in you. I am come in my

Father's name, and ye receive me not: if another shall come in his own name, him ye will receive...For had ye believed Moses, ye would have believed me: for he wrote of me. But if ye believe not his writings, how shall ye believe my words?" (John 5:39,43,46,47).

"Here is wisdom. Let him that hath understanding count the number of the beast: for it is the number of a man; and his number is Six hundred threescore and six" (Revelation 13:18).

*"Jesus saith unto them, Did ye never read in the scriptures, The stone which the builders rejected, the same is become the head of the corner: this is the Lord's doing, and it is marvelous in our eyes? Therefore say I unto you, The kingdom of God shall be **taken** from you, and given to **a nation** bringing forth the fruits thereof"* (Matthew 21:42,43).

Again, this is not the Body of Christ being referred to but the well-prophesied remnant of Israel that would be called by the name of the Lord and brought through the time of trouble. The twelve apostles would be instrumental in the Lord preparing what the nation of Israel is to be built upon for that coming kingdom.

*"But rather **seek** ye the kingdom of God; and all these things shall be added unto you. Fear not, little flock; for it is your Father's good pleasure to give you the kingdom. Sell that ye have, and give alms; provide yourselves bags which wax not old, a treasure in the heavens that faileth not, where no thief approacheth, neither moth corrupteth. For where your treasure is, there will your heart be also"* (Luke 12:31-34).

*"And he shall be for a sanctuary; but for a stone of stumbling and for a rock of offence to both the houses of Israel, for a gin and for a snare to the inhabitants of Jerusalem. And many among them shall stumble, and fall, and be broken, and be snared, and be taken. Bind up the testimony, seal the law among **my disciples**. And I will wait upon the LORD, that hideth his face from the house of Jacob, and I will look for him. Behold, I and the children whom the LORD hath given me are for signs and wonders in Israel"* (Isaiah 8:14-18).

This is the ministry of the Lord's disciples, especially as they lay the foundation and compile the Gospels and the circumcision epistles (Hebrews 2:1-4). And, as was promised, when He comes in His glory, they will sit upon twelve thrones judging the twelve tribes of Israel. "*Therefore saith the Lord, the LORD of hosts, the mighty One of Israel, Ah, I will ease me of mine adversaries, and avenge me of mine enemies. And I will turn my hand upon thee, and purely purge away thy dross, and take away all tin. And I will restore thy judges as at the first, and thy counselors as at the beginning: afterward thou shalt be called, The city of righteousness, the faithful city. Zion shall be redeemed with judgement, and her converts with righteousness*" (Isaiah 1:24-27).

It is no wonder then that when the Lord returns and when that city does finally descend out of heaven, something special about it is seen. "*And the wall of the city had twelve foundations, and in them the names of the twelve apostles of the Lamb*" (Revelation 21:14). Once again, they are going to be specially rewarded in the government of that coming kingdom.

Let's turn now to the parables. First of all, the Lord does not speak in parables to make things simple as is commonly taught nor did He speak in them from the beginning of His earthly ministry. The exact opposite is actually the case. "*And the disciples came, and said unto him, Why speakest thou unto them in parables? He answered and said unto them, Because it is given unto you to know the mysteries of the kingdom of heaven, but to them it is not given*" (Matthew 13:10,11).

He now leaves the blind to the blind and will focus His efforts on instructing His little flock and presenting new information on the lack of faith issue that will exist within the remnant as events progress into the time of Jacob's trouble. This is especially the case in Matthew 13. "*Then came Peter to him, and said, Lord, how oft shall my brother sin against me, and I forgive him? till seven times? Jesus saith unto him, I say not unto thee, Until seven times: but, Until seventy times seven...Therefore...*" (Matthew 18:21,22).

The Lord is here going to build upon several issues He has already set forth in His earthly ministry concerning being merciful and its impact on rewards or lack thereof. He has just finished giving power to the twelve to bind and loose, and talking to them about how the brethren in the church (Psalm 22:22, Hebrews 2:12) are to handle judgement and issues that arise among them according to the principles laid out in Proverbs and other places.

It is especially interesting to note the number the Lord uses here—seventy times seven—and while that is a rather large number, and for all practical purposes infinite, it is in fact finite. I submit that He didn't just pull this number out of thin air. Seventy times seven, or 490, is a very significant number in Israel's history and it bears a connection to the subject at hand. Israel went into the seventy-year Babylonian captivity because—among other things—they failed to keep the seventh year sabbath rest for the land, and had failed to keep it for 490 years. Therefore, God told them that they owed Him 70 years worth, not a year more and not a year less. Wouldn't you know that's how long Israel was in captivity under Babylon and out of the land. But when the seventy years was up, God told the king of Babylon that *his* time was up, took his kingdom and through Cyrus told Israel it was time to go back into the land and rebuild. The point, though, is that God waited seventy times seven before He took action. He is *long*-suffering, but He is not *forever*-suffering. There is an end to what He will put up with, and while long it does have an end.

*"The Lord is not slack concerning his promise, as some men count slackness; but is longsuffering to us-ward, not willing that any should perish, but that all should come to repentance. **But** the day of the Lord **will** come as a thief in the night; in the which the heavens shall pass away with a great noise, and the elements shall melt with fervent heat, the earth also and the works that are therein shall be burned up"* (2 Peter 3:9,10).

Likewise, you have Daniel's seventy weeks or seventy times seven. So when the Lord says this, it doesn't just come out of the blue; it has a direct parallel to the very patience of God Himself. Let's continue. *"Therefore is the kingdom of heaven likened unto a certain king, which would take account of **his servants**. And when he had begun to reckon, one was brought unto him, which owed him* ten thousand talents. But forasmuch as he had not to pay, his lord commanded him to be sold, and his wife, and children, and all that he had, and payment to be made. The servant therefore fell down, and worshipped him, saying, Lord, have patience with me, and I will pay thee all. Then the lord of that servant had compassion, and loosed him, and forgave him the debt. But the same servant went out, and found one of his **fellowservants**, which owed him an hundred pence: and he **laid hands** on him, and took him by the throat, saying, Pay me that thou owest. And his fellowservant fell down at his feet, and besought him, saying, Have patience with me, and I will pay thee all. And he would not: but went and cast him into prison, till he should pay the debt. So when his fellow servants saw what was done, they were very sorry, and came and told unto their lord all that was done. Then his lord, after that he had called him, said unto him, O thou wicked **servant**, I forgave thee all that debt, because thou desiredst me: Shouldest not thou also have had compassion on thy **fellowservant**, even as I had pity on thee? And **His lord** was wroth, and delivered him to the tormentors, till he should pay all that was due unto him. So likewise shall my heavenly Father do also unto you, if ye from your hearts forgive not every one **his brother** their trespasses" (Matthew 18:23-35).

This illustrates what the Lord had already told them in the Sermon on the Mount and what is sitting back in the prophets concerning rewards. It should be noticed that while he is wicked, he is still a servant, he belongs to the Lord and is a *fellow*-servant of the other individual mentioned. "*For if ye forgive men their trespasses, your heavenly Father will also forgive you: But if ye forgive not men their trespasses, neither will your Father forgive your trespasses*" (Matthew 6:14,15).

These individuals already have God as their Father. They are already justified having believed that gospel of the kingdom, but there is still the issue of rewards in that kingdom and whether or not things will be counted against them when portions are to be decided. "*So speak ye, and so do, as they that shall be judged by the law of liberty. For he shall have judgement without mercy, that hath shewed no mercy; and mercy rejoiceth against judgement"* (James 2:12,13).

"But many that are first shall be last; and the last shall be first. For the kingdom of heaven is like unto a man that is an householder, which went out **early in the morning** *to hire labourers into his vineyard. And when he had agreed with the labourers for a penny a day, he sent them into his vineyard. And he went out about the third hour, and saw others standing idle in the marketplace, And said unto them; Go ye also into the vineyard, and whatsoever is right I will give you. And they went their way. Again he went out about the* **sixth and ninth hour,** *and did likewise. And about the eleventh hour he went out, and found others standing idle, and saith unto them, Why stand ye here all the day idle? The say unto him, Because no man hath hired us. He saith unto them, Go ye also into the vineyard; and whatsoever is right, that shall ye receive. So when even was come, the lord of the vineyard saith unto his steward, Call the labourers, and give them their hire, beginning from the last unto the first. And when they came that were hired about the* **eleventh hour,** *they received a penny. But when the first came, they supposed that they should have received more; and they likewise received every man a penny. And when they had received it, they murmured against the goodman of the house, Saying, these last have wrought but* **one hour,** *and thou hast made them equal unto us, which have borne the burden and heat of the day. But he answered one of them, and said, Friend, I do thee no wrong: didst not thou agree with me for a penny? Take that thine is, and go thy way: I will give unto this last, even as unto thee. Is it not lawful for me to do what I will with mine own? Is thine eye evil, because I am good? So the last shall be first, and the first last: for many be called, but few chosen"* (Matthew 20:1-16).

Once again the issue is rewards not justification. He gives these people what they have earned for their labor. It is the exact opposite with justification which could never be earned or merited by anyone but the Lord Jesus Christ. There is a particular hour mentioned here and I believe it is the same hour of temptation that will come upon all the world (Revelation 3:10). The Lord began calling laborers at the beginning of His earthly ministry and would continue to do so into the Day of the Lord. Because of the conditions that will exist at that time, it will be substantially more difficult to join the remnant and be faithful to the Lord. And, many of those that would start out well while things were relatively calm would begin to falter and not remain faithful as they caved to the fear and pressure of the temptations of that time. "*Lead us not into temptation*" (Matthew 6:13). But the main point here is that there will be a very high price for being faithful and laboring for the Lord at that time. The lesson here is that it is never too late to turn to the Lord for today is the day of salvation.

"*Who then is a **faithful** and **wise** servant; whom his lord hath made ruler over his household, to give them meat in due season? Blessed is that servant, whom his lord when he cometh shall find so doing. Verily I say unto you, That he shall make him ruler over all his goods. But and if that evil servant shall say in his heart, My lord delayeth his coming; And shall begin to smite his fellow servants, and to eat and drink with the drunken; The lord of that servant shall come in a day when he looketh not for him, and in an hour that he is not aware of, And shall appoint him his portion with the hypocrites: there shall be weeping and gnashing of teeth*" (Matthew 24:45-51).

Many of the same observations from before apply here. Members of the remnant are exhorted to be faithful and wise rather than wicked and foolish, but they are still servants. Also, the weeping and gnashing of teeth is not synonymous with hell or the lake of fire, although it is certainly present there as well. The unfaithful servants are going to feel extreme regret when they realize just what a mistake they have made and see the rewards received by those who were wise, knowing that they themselves could have enjoyed the very same things. (See also Psalm 35 and Isaiah 33).

"*Then shall the kingdom of heaven be likened unto **ten** virgins, which took their lamps, and went forth to meet the bridegroom. And **five** of them were wise, and **five** were foolish. They that were foolish took their lamps, and took no oil with them: But the wise took oil in* *their vessels with their lamps. While the bridegroom tarried, they all slumbered and slept. And at midnight there was a cry made, Behold, the bridegroom cometh; go ye out to meet him. Then all those virgins arose, and trimmed their lamps. And the **foolish** said unto the **wise**, Give us of your oil; for our lamps are gone out. But the wise answered, saying, Not so; lest there be not enough for us and you: but go ye rather to them that sell, and buy for yourselves. And while they went to buy, the bridegroom came; and they that were ready went in with him to the marriage: and the door was shut. Afterward came also the other virgins, saying, Lord, Lord, open to us. But he answered and said, Verily I say unto you, I know you not. Watch therefore, for **ye** know neither the day nor the hour wherein the Son of man cometh"* (Matthew 25:1-13).

"There is treasure to be desired and oil in the dwelling of the wise; but a foolish man spendeth it up" (Proverbs 21:20).

*"And it came to pass about **ten** days after, that the LORD smote Nabal, that he died. And when David heard that Nabal was dead, he said, Blessed be the LORD, that hath pleaded the cause of my reproach from the hand of Nabal, and hath kept his servant from evil: for the LORD hath returned the wickedness of Nabal upon his own head. And David sent and communed with Abigail, to take her to him to wife. And when the servants of David were come to Abigail to Carmel, they spake unto her, saying, David sent us unto thee, to take thee to him to wife. And she arose, and bowed herself on her face to the earth, and said, Behold, let thy handmaid be a servant to wash the feet of the servants of my lord. And Abigail hasted, and arose, and rode upon an ass, with **five** damsels of hers that went after her; and she went after the messengers of David, and became his wife"* (1 Samuel 25:38-42).

The Lord will also expand upon this in the next parable and amplify the idea of *"Whosoever hath, to him shall be given, and he shall have more abundance: but whosoever hath not, from him shall be taken away even that he hath"* (Matthew 13:12). But here, once again, they are all virgins. The issue is whether they will be wise or foolish. If you are foolish, even though a virgin, you will miss out when it comes time for that great wedding celebration. The Lord is speaking to His own. He tells *them* to be watchful and to lay up treasures in heaven so that they are not ashamed when He returns. The unbelievers in Israel aren't even in the picture. The ones in view here are not among those to whom the Lord will say I *never knew you*. But they have left their first love and will not receive what they could have if they had been wise.

This marriage and the supper associated with it are a huge issue in Israel's program. The Lord has already illustrated this by a parable in Matthew 22 (which we will look at in our discussion of Succot). I will simply say here that it is inextricably tied up with that coming city and the receiving of the promises.

In the Gospels, the Lord begins to woo Israel just as was foretold by the scriptures in Hosea and other places. "*He that hath the bride is the bridegroom: but the friend of the bridegroom, which standeth and heareth him, rejoiceth greatly because of the bridegroom's voice: this my joy therefore is fulfilled*" (John 3:29).

He has already told them that many that are first shall be last. There are going to be those who will not be granted immediate entrance into that kingdom.

"*For I say unto you, That except your righteousness shall exceed the righteousness of the scribes and Pharisees, ye shall in no case* **enter into** *the kingdom of heaven*" (Matthew 5:20).

"*Wherefore* **my beloved brethren,** *let every man be swift to hear, slow to speak, slow to wrath: For the wrath of man worketh not the righteousness of God.* **Wherefore** *lay apart...and receive the* **engrafted** *word, which is able to save* **your** *souls...Be patient therefore,* **brethren,** *unto the coming of the Lord. Behold, the husbandman waiteth for the precious fruit of the earth, and hath long patience for it, until he receive the early and latter rain. Be ye also patient; stablish your hearts: for the coming of the Lord draweth nigh. Grudge not one against another, brethren,* **lest ye be condemned:** *behold, the judge standeth before the door*" (James 1:19-21; 5:7-9).

It is the believers whom James calls brethren that, even though justified, may very well be condemned in some sense when the

Lord returns. This should be no surprise given the doctrinal information presented in the prophets and the Gospels up until this point. If they have denied Him, they will be denied some things in that kingdom. It should also be noted that this is referring to the time when the Lord is *standing* at the door as the judge, when He has His Day of Wrath. He is currently seated at the Father's right hand and will continue to do so until the time comes and he is ready to resume His program with Israel.

"*For if these things be in you, and abound, they make you that ye shall neither be barren nor unfruitful in the knowledge of our Lord Jesus Christ. But he that lacketh these things is blind, and cannot see afar off, and hath **forgotten** that he **was purged** from his old sins. Wherefore the rather, brethren, give diligence to make your calling and election sure: for if ye do these things, ye shall never fall: For so **an entrance** shall be ministered unto you **abundantly** into the everlasting kingdom of our Lord and Saviour Jesus Christ*" (1 Peter 1:8-11).

"*For the kingdom of heaven is as a man travelling into a far country, who called **his own servants**, and delivered unto them his goods. And unto one he gave **five** talents, to another two, and to another one; to every man according to his several ability; and straightway took his journey. Then he that had received five talents went and traded with the same, and made them other five talents. And likewise he that had received two, he also gained other two. But he that had received one went and digged in the earth, and hid his lord's money. After a long time the lord of those servants cometh, and reckoneth with them. And so he that had received five talents came and brought other five talents, saying, Lord, thou deliveredst unto me five talents: behold, I have gained beside them five talents more. His lord said unto him, Well done, thou **good** and **faithful** servant: thou hast been **faithful** over a few things, I will make thee **ruler** over many things: enter thou into the joy of thy lord…then he which had received the one talent came and said, Lord, I knew thee that thou art an hard man, reaping where thou hast not sown, and gathering where thou hast not strawed: and I was afraid, and went and hid thy talent in the earth: lo, there thou hast that is thine. His lord answered* *and said unto him, Thou **wicked** and **slothful** servant, thou knewest that I reap where I sowed not, and gather where I have not strawed: Thou oughtest therefore to have put my money to the exchangers, and then at my coming I should have received mine own with usury. Take therefore the talent from him, and give it unto him which hath ten talents. For unto every one that hath shall be given, and he shall have **abundance**: but from him that hath not shall be taken away even that which he hath. And cast ye the unprofitable servant into outer darkness: there shall be weeping and gnashing of teeth"* (Matthew 25:14-30).

"The slothful man saith, There is a lion without, I shall be slain in the streets" (Proverbs 22:13).

Again, this individual is still a servant. But he is wicked, slothful and unprofitable. He has been given something by the Lord and the question is, what has he done with it. He is cast into *outer* darkness. This is not hell or the lake of fire. Why is it dark? What is it outside of? Understand either one and you can understand the other. There are many passages that deal with the light that will exist where the Lamb dwells here on earth. It is present with Him now in heaven and will come with Him when He returns. That coming city, while indeed humongous, does not encompass the entire earth as we have already seen. It will occupy only a certain piece of real estate on planet Earth. You still have the rest of the nations, however, and He will be sending out His messengers and these nations will be coming up to the house of prayer to worship.

*"And I will set a sign among them, and I will send those **that escape** of them unto the nations, to Tarshish, Pul, and Lud, that draw the bow, to Tubal and Javan, to the isles afar off, that have not heard my fame, neither have seen my glory; and they shall declare my glory among the Gentiles"* (Isaiah 66:19).

This will be the ultimate fulfillment of the great commission and the preaching of the gospel of the kingdom. *"And the inhabitants of one city shall go to another, saying, Let us go speedily to pray before the LORD, and to seek the LORD of hosts: I will go also. Yea, many people and strong nations shall come to seek the LORD of* hosts in Jerusalem, and to pray before the LORD. Thus saith the LORD of hosts; In those days it shall come to pass, that ten men shall take hold out of all languages of the nations, even shall take hold of the skirt of him that is a Jew, saying, We will go with you: for we have heard that God is with you" (Zechariah 8:21-23).

He will truly rule with a rod of iron and if any nation gives Him guff, they will feel the effects—no rain, etc. "And *the city* had no need of the sun, neither of the moon, to shine *in it*: for the glory of God did lighten *it*, and the Lamb is the light thereof. And the nations of them *which are saved* shall walk in the *light of it*. And the gates of it shall not be shut at all by day: for there shall be no night *there*. And they shall bring the glory and honour of the nations into it. And there shall in no wise enter into it any thing that defileth, neither whatsoever worketh abomination, or maketh a lie: but they which are written in the Lamb's book of life.…And behold, I come quickly; and my reward is with me, to give every man according as his work shall be. I am Alpha and Omega, the beginning and the end, the first and the last. Blessed are they that do his commandments, that they may have right to the tree of life, and may enter in through the gates into the city. For *without* are dogs, and sorcerers, and whoremongers, and murderers, and idolaters, and whosoever loveth and maketh a lie" (Revelation 21:23-27; 22:12-16).

The city has no need of the sun or moon but the rest of the world does. These ordinances are forever. "*If those ordinances depart from before me, saith the LORD, then the seed of Israel also shall cease from being a nation before me for ever.*" (Jeremiah 31:36). The lake of fire will also be present outside the city, along with some other tourist attractions that will stand as a testimony to those that pass by during that thousand years. The Beast and his false prophet will be in the lake of fire serving as the firstfruits of the second resurrection, the second death, yet to come at the end of the thousand years. Be careful of trying to counterfeit Christ.

The parable in Luke 19 is very similar to the one we have just looked at in Matthew 25. The main difference is that in Luke we also have unbelievers in view. "*And as they heard these things, he* *added and spake a parable, because he was nigh to Jerusalem, and because they thought that the kingdom of God should **immediately** appear*" (Luke 19:1). If they were familiar with the prophetic program, they would not have thought such a thing. They would have realized that He was going to go back to the Father and they were going to have to wait and have patience and endure the coming time of trouble and wrath until He returned. This much was spelled out in the prophets. The Lord Himself instructs them more clearly on it so they will know exactly what they need to understand in His absence. Actually, the kingdom was not, and could not be, "offered" until the work of Christ on the cross was successfully accomplished. It was preached as "at hand" while the Lord was on earth, and is offered only when He departs and all things are declared to be "ready."

It is interesting that many believers also think today that the kingdom should have appeared immediately, or that it already had appeared as the Lord speaks these words. The kingdom is *not* a spiritual reign in your heart or about going to heaven. It is about heaven coming here. That spiritual reign in the heart was present long before the Lord came on the scene in Israel. However, the signs of the coming kingdom were being manifested in Israel at that time as the king was in their midst. As was prophesied, He proved that He was who He said He was and that it was, in fact, the climactic stage in Israel's program. They would be given the opportunity to repent and respond to what was being manifested in Israel in light of the coming kingdom. The nation would also be given the chance to respond after the cross as that would not be held against them (more on that later). But then the purging fire would come and only then would He return and set up that glorious and promised kingdom. Back to the parable.

"*He said therefore, A certain nobleman went into a far country to receive for himself a kingdom, and to return. And he called his ten **servants**, and delivered them ten pounds, and said unto them, Occupy till I come. But his **citizens** hated him, and sent a message after him, saying, We will not have this man to reign over us. And it*

came to pass that when he was returned, having received the king-
dom, then he commanded these servants to be called unto him, to
whom he had given the money, that he might know how much every
man had gained by trading…Then came the first, saying, Lord, thy
pound hath gained **ten** *pounds. And he said unto him, Well, thou*
good servant: because thou hast been faithful in a very little, have
thou authority over **ten cities**…**five** *pounds…**five cities**…For I say*
unto every one which hath shall be given; and from him that hath
not, even that he hath shall be taken away from him. **But those** *mine*
enemies, *which would not that I should reign over them, bring*
hither, and **slay** *them before me"* (Luke 19:12-19,26,27).

The message sent from the citizens refers to the stoning of
Stephen told about in Acts 7 which we will examine later. For now,
notice that here the Lord goes beyond the remnant of Israel. He
deals also here with those that have not repented and are therefore
not members of the remnant. The issue for them is not one of
rewards. They are not servants and not numbered among them
whom the Lord can call *friend.* No, these are the Lord's *enemies*
spoken of in Psalm 110 and have quite a different fate.

We will now look at the Lord's teaching that acts as a capping
off to the parables that have gone just before it. It is here that the
Lord deals with the issue we saw earlier of the nations being
blessed in that coming kingdom.

"When the Son of man shall come in **his glory,** *and* **all** *the holy*
angels with him, **then** *shall he sit upon the throne of his glory: And*
before him shall be gathered all nations: and he shall separate them
one from another, as a shepherd divideth **his** *sheep from* **the goats:**
And he shall set the sheep on **his right** *hand, but the* **goats** *on* **the left.**
Then shall the King say unto them on **his right** *hand, Come, ye*
blessed *of my Father, inherit the kingdom* **prepared** *for you* **from** *the*
foundation of the world: For I was hungred, and ye gave me meat: I
was thirsty, and ye gave me drink: I was a stranger, and ye took me
in: Naked, and ye clothed me: I was sick, and ye visited me: I was in
prison, and ye came unto me. Then shall the righteous answer him,
saying, Lord, when saw we thee an hungred, and fed thee? or thirsty,

and gave thee drink? When saw we thee a stranger, and took thee in? or naked, and clothed thee? Or when saw we thee sick, or in prison, and came unto thee? And the King shall answer and say unto them, Verily I say unto you, Inasmuch as ye have done it unto one of the least of these **my brethren**, ye have done it unto me. Then shall he say also unto them on the left hand, Depart from me, ye **cursed**, into everlasting fire, prepared for the devil and his angels: For I was an hungred, and ye gave me no meat…Then shall they also answer him saying, Lord, when saw we thee an hungred…Then shall he answer them, saying, Verily I say unto you, Inasmuch as ye did it not to one of the least of these, ye did not to me. And these shall go away into everlasting punishment: but the righteous into life eternal" (Matthew 25:31-46. See also Matthew 10:40-42 and Psalm 79).

"And the beast was taken, and with him the false prophet that wrought miracles before him, with which he deceived them that had received the mark of the beast, and them that worshipped his image. These both were cast alive into a lake of fire burning with brimstone. And the remnant were slain with the sword of him that sat upon the horse, which sword proceeded out of his mouth: and all the fowls were filled with their flesh…And I saw thrones, and they sat upon them, and judgement was given unto them: and I saw the souls of them that were beheaded for the witness of Jesus, and for the word of God, and which had not worshipped the beast, neither his image, neither had received his mark upon their foreheads, or in their hands; and they lived and reigned with Christ a thousand years. But **the rest of the dead** lived not again until the thousand years were finished. This is the first resurrection. Blessed and holy is he that hath part in the first resurrection: on such the second death hath no power, but they shall be priests of God and of Christ, and shall reign with him a thousand years…But the fearful, and unbelieving, and the abominable, and murderers, and whoremongers, and sorcerers, and idolaters, and all liars, shall have their part in the lake which burneth with fire and brimstone: which is the second death…And the city had no need of the sun, neither of the moon, to shine in it: for the glory of God did lighten it, and the Lamb is the light thereof.

And the nations of them which are saved shall walk in the light of it: and the kings of the earth do bring their glory into it" (Revelation 19:20,21; 20:4-6; 21:8,23,24).

Again, it is my contention that these events will begin with the blowing of the great trumpet on Yom Kippur and continue during the five-day period until Succot. It seems interesting to me that the issues of being on the right and left, the number five and ten divided into two parts and the connection with the molten sea, and so on, are all pulled together when the time comes for rewards, division of the land and deciding the portion of the Gentiles. Also, not only do goats play a large role in the observance of Yom Kippur, but something else is mentioned in connection with this feast. *"And the bullock for the sin offering, and the goat for the sin offering, whose blood was brought in to make atonement in the holy place, shall one carry forth **without the camp**; and they shall **burn** in the **fire** their **skins**, and their **flesh**, and their **dung**. And he that burneth them shall wash his clothes, and bathe his flesh in water, and afterward he shall come into the camp"* (Leviticus 16:27,28).

Finally, it is interesting that when Abraham negotiated with the Lord to spare the Gentile cities for the sake of the righteous who might be in it, he decreases each number by five and ten.

*"That be far from thee to do after this manner, to slay the righteous with the wicked: and that the righteous should be as the wicked, that be far from thee: Shall not the **Judge of all the** earth do right? And the Lord said, If I find in Sodom fifty righteous within the city, then will I spare all the place for their sakes. And Abraham answered...Peradventure there shall lack five of the fifty righteous...forty...thirty...twenty...ten...And he said, I will not destroy it for ten's sake"* (Genesis 18:25-33).

Unfortunately, there were not even ten righteous people in that wicked city, but God did deliver righteous Lot. The connection with Abraham is also significant because the judgement of the sheep and goat nations is the fulfillment of the Abrahamic covenant. *"I will make of thee a **great** nation, and I will **bless thee**,* *and make thy name **great**; and thou shalt be a **blessing**. And I will bless them that **bless** thee, and **curse** him that **curseth** thee: and in thee shall all **families** of the earth be **blessed**"* (Genesis 12:2,3).

This kingdom has been *prepared from* the foundation of the world. *"The LORD hath prepared his throne in the heavens; and his kingdom ruleth over all. Bless the LORD, ye his angels, that excel in strength, that do his commandments, hearkening to the voice of his word. Bless ye the LORD, all his hosts; ye ministers of his, that do his pleasure. Bless the LORD, all his works in all places of his dominion: bless the LORD, O my soul"* (Psalm 103:19-22).

This is what the Lord had intended for planet Earth from the beginning and it will finally be realized when He rules as king of all the earth. *"And Melchizedek **king of Salem** brought forth bread and wine: and he was the priest of the most high God. And he blessed him, and said, Blessed be Abram of the most high God, **possessor of heaven and earth**"* (Genesis 14:18,19).

I do not believe it is any accident that the Lord mentions the things He does as He pulls together the teaching on this subject. So, even though I think you would be able to determine when the rewards issue will take place, given what we know about the prophetic scenario, I also believe that the little details that are scattered about clinch the matter and are all utilized by God to alert you to the seemingly minor importance of a five-day period on His calendar. I reiterate, however, if He has gone through the trouble of delineating a particular five days on His calendar for His appointed times, it *must* be important. That leaves us with one feast remaining, Succot.

— Chapter Nine —

Succot

The Wedding
&
The Marriage Supper of the Lamb

W e have now come to the end of the extra 45-day period given in Daniel chapter 12, the 1,335th day. *"Blessed is he that waiteth and cometh to the thousand three hundred and five and thirty days. But go thou thy way till the end be: for thou shalt rest, and stand in thy lot at the end of the days"* (Daniel 12:12,13).

We have completed the entire Season of Teshuvah beginning with the month of Elul. Rosh HaShanah and the ten Days of Awe have been fulfilled with the return of the Lord Jesus Christ to do battle in the Great and Terrible Day of the Lord. Yom Kippur has been fulfilled as the great trumpet has been blown and the scattered remnant gathered into the land for restoration and rebirth of the nation under the New Covenant and the fulfillment of the Abrahamic Covenant with all of the blessings associated with it.

During the five-day period following that great feast, the Lord has divided the portion and inheritance of the kingdom among His people. He has returned with the treasures they have been

189

accumulating in heaven and has given his remnant their rewards according to their faithfulness, wisdom and fruitfulness. But now, it is time to enter into that great celebration of joy. The Lord has taken this earth back and the government shall now rest upon His shoulders. Righteous judgement will issue forth from that great city, New Jerusalem; healing waters will flow from that great house and bring life and restoration to a planet that has so long been ravaged by the effects of ungodliness. My friends, it is time for Succot and the marriage supper of the Lamb. Let the celebration begin!

But first things first. Those who are left of the remnant of Israel are not the only ones who are to enjoy this great feast. All those who have been justified in God's program with this earth are to be resurrected so that they too may enjoy this glorious kingdom that has been prepared from the foundation of the world.

*"For I know that my **redeemer** liveth, and that he shall stand at the latter day upon the earth: And though after my skin worms destroy this body, yet in my flesh shall I see God: Whom I shall see for myself, and mine eyes shall behold, and not another; though my reigns be consumed within me"* (Job 19:25-27).

*"...Verily I say unto you, I have not found so great faith, no, not in Israel. And I say unto you, that many shall come from the east and west, and shall sit down **with Abraham**, and **Isaac**, and **Jacob**, in the kingdom of heaven"* (Matthew 8:10,11).

The eleventh chapter of Hebrews with its hall of faith also has much to say about this subject. *"...For he hath prepared for them a city...By faith Joseph, when he died, made mention of the departing of the children of Israel; and gave commandment concerning his bones...By faith the harlot Rahab perished not with them that believed not, when she had received the spies with peace...Women received their dead raised to life again: and others were tortured, not accepting deliverance; that they might obtain a **better** resurrection...And these all, having obtained a good report through faith, received not the promise: God having provided some better thing for us, that they without us should not be made perfect"* (Hebrews 11:16,22,31,35,39,40).

They too will be able to partake in the joy of that kingdom because of the blood of the Lord Jesus Christ and the New Covenant. *"But ye are come unto mount Sion, and unto **the city of the living God, the heavenly Jerusalem,** and to an innumerable company of angels, To the general assembly and church of the firstborn, which are written in heaven, and to God the Judge of all, and to **the spirits of just men made perfect,** And to Jesus the mediator of the new covenant, and to the blood of sprinkling, that speaketh **better** things than that of Abel"* (Hebrews 12:22-24. See also Psalm 22).

The blood of bulls and goats could never make the one who brought it perfect. So, while all these various Old Testament saints were justified in God's sight by faith, they could not be made perfect until the blood of the holy Lamb was shed. This is why at His death, the Lord descends into the heart of the earth to take the keys of hell and death, proclaim His victory to the angels chained in darkness who would now have no hope of escape or victory, and open the gates to Abraham's bosom that had held the spirits of just men for so long. He emptied that place out, led captivity captive and brought them up to the third heaven where they could now dwell, having been made perfect.

*"And I say also unto thee, That thou art Peter, and upon this rock I will build my church; and the **gates** of hell shall not prevail against it"* (Matthew 16:18).

"I am he that liveth, and was dead; and, behold, I am alive for evermore, Amen; and have the keys of hell and of death" (Revelation 1:18).

The reason the Lord has keys—plural—is because there are gates—plural—in the heart of the earth. Yes, in the heart of the earth. The only thing we know for sure about the inner chambers of the earth is that it's pretty hot down there, in part anyway, and the Bible already told you that. We also know from Revelation that there are some creatures waiting there to be loosed in the Lord's Day. Christ's power extends over them as well and He will be able to protect His remnant from their torment at that time. But that is what the Lord was referring to when He talked about the gates of hell. He was the one who would have the power over death, hell and the grave and He has the keys to prove it. Needless to say, the enemy is not at all happy about having lost this once great and terror-filled power of his.

"*Forasmuch then as the children are partakers of flesh and blood, he also himself likewise took part of the same; that through death he might destroy* **him that had** *the power of death, that is, the devil. And deliver them* **who through fear** *of death were all their lifetime* **subject to bondage**" (Hebrews 2:14,15).

Those who belong to Christ have the promise of resurrection, and death can in no way hinder the plans God has for those called by His name.

"*Then said Jesus again unto them, I go my way, and ye shall seek me, and shall die in your sins: whither I go,* **ye cannot come**" (John 8:21).

"*Jesus said unto her, I am the resurrection and the life: he that believeth in me, though he were dead, yet shall he live: And whosoever liveth and believeth in me shall never die. Believest thou this?*" (John 11:25,26).

"*And Jesus answered them, saying, The hour is come, that the Son of man should be glorified. Verily, verily, I say unto you, Except a corn of wheat fall into the ground and die, it abideth alone: but if it die, it bringeth forth much fruit. He that loveth his life shall lose it; and he that hateth his life in this world shall keep it unto life eternal. If any man serve me, let him follow me; and* **where I am, there shall also my servant be***: if any man serve me, him will my Father honour*"(John 23-27).

"*And we indeed justly; for we receive the due reward of our deeds: but this man hath done nothing amiss. And he said unto Jesus, Lord, remember me when thou comest into thy kingdom. And Jesus said unto him, Verily I say unto thee, To day shalt* **thou be with me** *in paradise*" (Luke 23:41-43).

"*Blessed be the God and Father of our Lord Jesus Christ, which according to his abundant mercy hath begotten us again unto* **a lively hope** *by the resurrection of Jesus Christ from the dead, To an inheritance incorruptible, and undefiled, and that fadeth not away,* reserved in heaven for you, Who are **kept** by the power of God through faith **unto salvation** ready to be revealed in **the last time.** Wherein ye greatly rejoice, though for a season, if need be, ye are in heaviness through manifold temptations: That the trial of your faith, being much more precious than of gold that perisheth, though it be tried by fire, might be found unto the praise and honour and glory at the appearing of Jesus Christ...Receiving the end of your faith, **even the salvation of your souls.** Of **which salvation** the prophets have enquired and searched diligently, **who prophesied of** the grace that should come unto you." (IPet 1:3-5,9,10). Compare this with the unsearchable riches of Christ of which we are partakers in accordance with the revelation of the mystery.

"And when he had opened the fifth seal, I saw **under the altar** the souls of them that were slain for the word of God, and for the testimony which they held: And they cried with a loud voice, saying, How long, O Lord, holy and true, dost thou not judge and avenge our blood on them that dwell on the earth. And white robes were given unto every one of them, that they should rest yet for a little season, until their fellowservants also and their brethren, that should be killed as they were, should be fulfilled" (Revelation 6:9-11).

Praise God that the one who was the king of terrors no longer has power over us (Job 18:14; 24:17; Psalm 55:4).

The Lord had the power to willingly lay down His life. But having fully finished the work of propitiation before He gave up the ghost, He descended into the lower parts of the earth as the only man that death and hell could claim no right over. He alone in this world had power to take up His own life again and be that glorious firstfruit. He did not give up the ghost until He was able to say "it is finished." Only the eternal Son of God could fully satisfy the righteous judgement of sins committed against the eternal God in a matter of three hours.

"Whom God hath raised up, having loosed the pains of death: because it was not possible that he should be holden of it....Because thou wilt not leave **my** soul in hell, **neither** wilt thou suffer **thine Holy One** to see corruption...Therefore being a prophet, and knowing that

God had sworn with an oath to him, that of the fruit of his loins, according to the flesh, he would raise up Christ to sit on his throne; He seeing this before spake of the resurrection of Christ, that his soul was not left in hell, neither his flesh did see corruption This Jesus hath God raised up, whereof we all are witnesses" (Acts 2:24,27,30-32).

Both of the above promises apply to Christ whose body would be transformed with that resurrection power and newness of life after only three days and three nights. But David also said that *his* soul would not be left in hell, though his body would see corruption. Well, David's soul is no longer in hell and when the day comes, he will be resurrected just as the firstfruits promises. *"The chariots of God are twenty thousand, even thousands of angels: **the Lord** is among them, as in Sinai, in the holy place. **Thou** hast ascended on high, **thou** hast led captivity captive: thou hast received gifts for men; yea, for the rebellious also, **that the LORD God** might dwell among them. Blessed be **the Lord**, who daily loadeth us with benefits, even the God of our salvation. Selah. He that is our God is the God of salvation; and unto **God the Lord** belong the issues from death"* (Psalm 68:17-20).

Various members of the godhead are referred to here as well as throughout the Scriptures but, needless to say, some things belong uniquely to Christ in light of His successful cross-work. *"Wherefore seeing we also are **compassed about** with so great a **cloud of witnesses**, let us lay aside every weight, and the sin which doth so easily beset us, and let us run with patience the race that is set before us, Looking unto Jesus the author and finisher of our faith; who for the joy that was set before him endured the cross, despising the shame, and is set down at the right hand of God"* (Hebrews 12:1,2).

This is the time for the seven-day celebration of the marriage supper of the Lamb which follows the restoration of the adulterous city under the New Covenant and God marrying the land. This is not a mystery issue dealing with the Body of Christ and the Body of Christ is *not* the "bride of Christ." In fact, this phrase is nowhere found in Scripture although the concept is there. I hesitate even addressing this subject here as it deserves a full treatment in its own right to deal with the valid objections or concerns that would rightly arise in the mind of any close student of Scripture. I will simply say that it is inextricably tied up with the true nature of the Body of Christ and what is and is not going on today in the purposes and plans that God has for both the heavenly places and the earthly places, namely gathering together *all* things in Christ. Perhaps verses such as Ephesians 5:22-33—that I believe are not fully appreciated in connection with this—can be dealt with in a later work.

But for now, I will state that the wedding has not taken place seven years earlier at the beginning of the tribulation, with a honeymoon lasting the duration of the tribulation and then a seven-day supper after the seven-year honeymoon. Much less does the marriage supper take place during the seven years of tribulation. I realize that may fit nicely with little rapture schemes and certain ideas of ecclesiology, but I do not believe it is in keeping with the clear testimony of Scripture. I myself believe that the Body of Christ is to be caught away before God resumes His program with Israel, in accordance with the mystery revelation committed unto the apostle Paul, but it is not for a wedding. That wedding is a huge part of the prophetic program, and when and with whom it takes place is clear.

Actually, even with Israel, individual justified Israelites are not considered the bride. Rather, they are children, guests bidden to the wedding, etc. See how many times throughout the Scriptures the Lord speaks directly to the city of Jerusalem. The wedding is really about the Lord being married to—and in union with—the land as that great city, New Jerusalem, comes down and rests upon the beams of the chambers that were laid in Genesis 1:2.

Sure enough, following the destruction of that great whore of Babylon—the city which was queen to the Antichrist—just as the Lord is about to rend the heavens and come down to earth with His city and treasures, the scripture declares, "*And I heard as it were the voice of a great multitude, and as the voice of many waters, and as the voice of mighty thunderings, saying, Alleluia: for the Lord*

195

God omnipotent reigneth. Let us be glad and rejoice, and give honour to him: for the marriage of the Lamb is come, and his wife hath made herself ready. And to **her** *was granted that* **she** *should be arrayed in fine linen, clean and white: for the fine linen is the righteousness of saints"* (Revelation 19:6-8).

Given our examination of the rewards issue I hope it is clear to you what is going on here—what the Lord had repeatedly instructed His remnant about in the Gospels and through the circumcision epistles. This is His return that they were to wait for with all patience, faithfulness, wisdom and fruitfulness so they would have a great reward in that coming kingdom and its city. Those saints will adorn and fill that city which had been prepared from the foundation of the world and will now finally descend from heaven and rest upon its beams. And, in keeping with the prophetic program, *"He saith unto me, Write, Blessed are they which are called unto the marriage supper of the Lamb. And he saith unto me, These are the true sayings of God. And I fell at his feet to worship him. And he said unto me, See thou do it not: I am thy fellowservant, and of thy brethren that have the testimony of Jesus: worship God: for the testimony of Jesus is the spirit of prophecy"* (Revelation 19:9,10).

I want you to keep in mind the cycling concept we looked at back in our examination of Daniel. This issue of going back and filling in details of a period of time that has already been given is, not surprisingly, also to be found in Revelation chapter 21 where you cycle back to the beginning of the thousand years mentioned in Revelation 20:4-15.

If you have been following the scriptures up to this point, it should be no surprise when you read, *"And I saw a new heaven and a new earth: for the first heaven and the first earth were passed away; and there was no more sea. And I John saw the holy city, new Jerusalem, coming down from God out of heaven, prepared as a bride* **adorned** *for* **her** *husband. And I heard a great voice out of heaven saying, Behold, the tabernacle of God is with men, and he will dwell with them, and they shall be his people, and God himself* *shall be with them, and be their God. And God shall wipe away all tears from their eyes; and there shall be no more death, neither sorrow, nor crying, neither shall there be any more pain: for the former things are passed away. And he that sat upon the throne said, Behold, I make all things new. And he said unto me, Write: for these words are true and faithful. And he said unto me, It is done. I am Alpha and Omega, the beginning and the end. I will give unto him that is athirst of the fountain of the water of life freely…And there came unto me one of the seven angels which had the seven vials full of the seven last plagues, and talked with me, saying, Come hither, I will shew thee the bride, the Lamb's wife. And he carried me away in the spirit to a great and high mountain, and shewed me that great city, the holy Jerusalem, descending out of heaven from God"* (Revelation 21:1-6,9,10).

This is the same thing Ezekiel saw, except it was given to him only to see the frame of the city upon which it will rest, along with the healing waters and river of life that will issue forth from it. If my understanding is correct, these purifying waters of regeneration that usher in the age of God making all things new, will begin to flow in connection with the seven day marriage supper celebration and the eighth day or 22nd of Tishrei when the kingdom will officially get under way. *"In **the last day**, that **great day** of the feast, Jesus stood and cried, saying, if any man thirst, let him come unto me, and drink. He that believeth on me, as the scriptures hath said, out of his belly shall flow rivers of living water"* (John 7:37,38).

The Lord here is directly speaking of the giving of the Spirit that would commence on Shavuot (Pentecost) which is stated in John 7:39. But this also points forward to another event that will take place. The event of Shavuot is a prelude to the events that will follow with the arrival of the fall feasts. More will be said about this later but the ministry of the Holy Spirit during the Lord's absence was to be one of empowering the remnant and enabling them to endure till the end through the prophesied time of trouble. His role was also going to include bringing the Lord's words to their remembrance that they were to abide in, and the wisdom associated with it as they separated themselves more and more from that apostate nation.

"*When the wicked cometh, then cometh also contempt, and with ignominy reproach. The words of a man's mouth are as deep waters, and the wellspring of wisdom as a flowing brook…The **name of the LORD** is a strong tower: the righteous runneth into it, and is safe…The spirit of a man will sustain his infirmity; but a wounded spirit who can bear? The heart of the prudent getteth knowledge; and the ear of the wise seeketh knowledge…A man's belly shall be satisfied with the fruit of his mouth; and with the increase of his lips shall he be filled. Death and life are in the power of the tongue: and they that love it shall eat the fruit thereof. Whoso findeth a wife findeth a good thing, and obtaineth favour of the LORD…A man that hath friends must shew himself friendly: and there is a friend that sticketh closer than a brother*" (Proverbs 18:3,4,10,14,15,20-22,24).

This will all be built upon by the circumcision epistles, especially James, but notice how much it lines up with what we are looking at in Revelation. The Lord did not include this verse about the wife for no reason. He knew perfectly well what He was saying and what the end of the book was going to say about the Lamb's wife and the living waters. But now is the time for this closest friend to show himself friendly in that great marriage supper.

"*And **in that day** thou shalt say, O LORD, I will praise thee: though thou wast angry with me, thine anger is turned away, and thou comfortedst me. Behold, God is my salvation; I will trust, and not be afraid: for the LORD **JEHOVAH** is my strength and my song; he also is become my salvation. Therefore with joy shall ye draw water out of the wells of salvation. And in that day shall ye say, Praise the LORD, call upon his name, declare his doings among the people, make mention that **his name** is exalted. Sing unto the LORD; for he hath done excellent things: this is known in all the earth. Cry out and shout, thou inhabitant of Zion: for great is the Holy One of Israel in the midst of thee*" (Isaiah 12:1-6).

"*And he shewed me a pure river of water of life, clear as crystal, proceeding out of the throne of God and of the Lamb. In the midst of* *the street of it, and on either side of the river, was there the tree of life, which bear twelve manner of fruits, and yielded her fruit every month: and the leaves of the tree were for the **healing** of the nations. And there shall be no more curse: but the throne of God and of the Lamb shall be in it; and **his servants shall serve him:** And **they** shall see his face; and **his name** shall be in their foreheads. And there shall be no night **there;** and **they** need no candle, neither light of the sun; for the Lord God giveth **them** light: and **they** shall **reign** for ever and ever"* (Revelation 22:1-5).

Everything goes back to the garden and what God had purposed for this earth from the very beginning. It is the promised and long-awaited regeneration that will come upon this earth. This final seven day period of Scripture matches almost exactly that first seven day week of creation. God had planned for seasons even back then and, sure enough, there will yet be months for the trees and fruit, days and years as the nations are to observe some things. Even the issue of light is brought up as it played a significant role at the time of creation. There are some significant differences as well but that is another discussion altogether. God began His work with seven days and it should be no surprise that He will end it with seven days as well.

*"And he that sat upon the throne said, Behold, I make all things new. And he said unto me, Write: for these words are true and faithful. And he said unto me, **It is done.** I am Alpha and Omega, the **beginning** and the **end.** I will give unto him that is athirst of the fountain of the water of life freely"* (Revelation 21:5,6).

"He which testifieth of these things saith, Surely I come quickly. Amen. Even so, come, Lord Jesus" (Revelation 22:20).

This is the long awaited *"times of restitution of all things."* (Acts 3:21) The events of the tribulation have prepared the earth geographically for the kingdom with mountains being made low, valleys exalted, etc. The reversal of the bondage of corruption *begins* with, and in, the New Jerusalem. God *begins* to make all things new with these first seven days of this glorious new age. However, while it starts here there will be no end. It will "increase" and consume the whole earth and last forever. And just as God officially got His creation "under way" after the first seven days of Genesis, so too will the eighth day mark the "first day" of the "world to come"(2 Peter 2:5)

The ark has been brought through the judgement and the time has come for the knowledge of the Lord to fill the earth as He brings to pass that which He had purposed for it from the beginning. *"And God blessed them, and God said unto them, Be fruitful, and multiply, and replenish the earth, and **subdue** it: and have **dominion**…"*(Genesis 1:28)

"For he must reign, till he hath put all enemies under his feet. The last enemy that shall be destroyed is death…And when all things shall be subdued unto him, then shall the Son also himself be subject unto him that put all things under him, that God may be all in all"(1 Corinthians 15:25,26,28).

*"And he shall reign over the house of Jacob **for ever**; and of his kingdom there shall be **no end**"*(Luke 1:33. See also 2 Samuel 7:12; Isaiah 9:7 and Dan 2, 7, 8).

Finally, we come to the role of Gentiles in Israel's program. The Gentiles play a huge role in God's program with Israel and the earth. In fact, the Abrahamic Covenant is all about God's name being hallowed and a praise in all the earth. The instrumentality through which this will happen is the restoration of that adulterous Jerusalem in the great marriage that will take place. I strongly encourage you to study Ezekiel 16 in connection with this. Who is the bride of Revelation? The Scriptures are crystal clear on the matter and don't waiver. *"I speak as to wise men; judge ye what I say."* (1 Corinthians 10:15).

*"Awake, awake; put on strength, O Zion; put on **thy beautiful garments**, O **Jerusalem**, the holy city: for henceforth there shall no more come into thee the uncircumcised and the unclean. Shake thyself from the dust; arise, and sit down, O **Jerusalem**: loose thyself from the bands of thy neck, O captive daughter of Zion. For thus saith the LORD, Ye have sold yourselves for nought; and ye shall be **redeemed** without money…Therefore my people shall know my*

name: therefore they shall know in that day that I am he that doth speak: behold, it is I...Thy watchmen shall lift up the voice; with the voice together shall they sing: for they shall see eye to eye, when the LORD shall bring again Zion. Break forth into joy, sing together, ye waste places of Jerusalem: for the LORD hath comforted his people, he hath **redeemed** Jerusalem. The LORD hath made bare **his holy arm** in the eyes of all the nations; and all the ends of the earth shall see the salvation of our God" (Isaiah 52:1-3,6,8-10).

"For Zion's sake will I not hold my peace, and for **Jerusalem's** sake I will not rest, until the righteousness thereof go forth as brightness, and the salvation thereof as a lamp that burneth. And the Gentiles shall see **thy** righteousness, and all kings **thy** glory: and **thou** shalt be called by a new name, which the mouth of the LORD shall name. **Thou** shalt also be a crown of glory in the hand of the LORD, and a royal diadem in the hand of thy God. **Thou** shalt no more be termed Forsaken; neither shall **thy land** any more be termed Desolate: but **thou** shalt be called Hephzibah, and **thy land** Beulah: for the LORD delighteth in **thee**, and **thy land** shall be **married**. For as a young man marrieth a virgin, so shall **thy sons** marry thee: and as the bridegroom rejoiceth over the bride, so shall thy God rejoice over thee...And give him no rest, till he establish, and till he make **Jerusalem** a praise in the earth...But they that have gathered it shall eat it, and praise the LORD; and they that have brought it together shall drink it in the courts of my holiness. Go through, go through the gates; prepare ye the way of the people; cast up the highway; gather out the stones; lift up a standard for the people. Behold, thy salvation cometh; behold, his reward is with him, and his work before him. And they shall call **them**, The holy people, The redeemed of the LORD: and **thou** shalt be called, Sought out, A **city** not forsaken" (Isaiah 62:1-5,7,9-12).

That city has children but she is the one being spoken to. "O Jerusalem, Jerusalem, thou that killest the prophets, and stonest them which are sent unto thee, how often would I have gathered thy children together, even as a hen gathereth her chickens under her wings, and ye would not! Behold, your house is left unto you desolate" (Matthew 23:37,38).

"*Even unto them will I give in mine house and within my walls a place and a name better than of sons and of daughters: I will give them an everlasting name, that shall not be cut off. Also the sons of the stranger, that join themselves to the LORD, to serve him, and to love the name of the LORD, to be his servants, every one that keepeth the sabbath from polluting it, and taketh hold of my covenant; Even them will I bring to my holy mountain, and make them joyful in my house of prayer: their burnt offerings and their sacrifices shall be acceptable upon mine altar; for mine house shall be called an house of prayer for all people. The Lord GOD, which gathereth the outcasts of Israel saith, Yet will I gather others to him, beside those that are gathered unto him*" (Isaiah 56:5-8).

The above is what will be available for Gentiles who remain such in the prophetic program. There will, of course, be the everlasting gospel which will be preached during Daniel's seventieth week as stated in Revelation 14:6-8. This message focuses on God as Creator and the bare minimum of what is expected of the nations in general. It is also, not by accident, the main subject of Ecclesiastes. "*Remember now thy Creator in the days of thy youth, while the evil days come not, nor the years draw nigh, when thou shalt say, I have no pleasure in them; While the sun, or light, or moon, or the stars, be not darkened, nor the clouds return after the rain...Let us hear the conclusion of the matter: Fear God, and keep his commandments: for this is the whole duty of man. For God shall bring every work into judgement, with every secret thing, whether it be good, or whether it be evil*" (Ecclesiastes 12:1,2,13,14).

The gospel of the kingdom will also be preached to the nations in view of the coming kingdom, and those who have responded positively to the former message will be prepared for the latter. "*But he that shall endure unto the end, the same shall be saved. And **this gospel** of the kingdom shall be preached in all the world for a witness unto all nations; and then shall the end come*" (Matthew 24:13,14).

This is the same gospel that the Lord will commission His twelve apostles with as He sends them out just days later in accordance with the prophetic program. "*And Jesus came and spake unto them, saying, All power is given unto me in heaven and in earth. Go ye therefore, and teach all nations, baptizing them in the name of the Father, and of the Son, and of the Holy Ghost: Teaching them to observe all things whatsoever I have commanded you: and, lo, I am with you alway, even unto the end of the world. Amen*" (Matthew 28:18-20).

Now I'm sorry, but *you* don't follow that. You may think you do but you are only deceiving yourself. Some groups teach men to observe more commandments of the Lord than others, but virtually every one of these groups miss the mark when it comes to these commissions for the same reason as when Paul was on the earth. Men refuse to accept what Paul has to say about what God has done and is doing in connection with the revelation of the mystery which was not made known in generations and ages past. Until the time Paul is raised up as a new apostle, everything is going along in perfect agreement with what was spoken before by the prophets. You need to ask yourself why, though this ministry to the nations was committed to the twelve, they will later hand the Gentiles over to Paul when they find out what was revealed to him. They will confine their ministry and continue to minister the gospel of the circumcision which deals with those prophetic things in Israel's program. And if you think that every time it says "gospel" it must mean the same thing, you have some serious problems on your hands.

The twelve were preaching the gospel of the kingdom for the better part of the Lord's ministry, and only towards the end does He begin to speak of His death about which they know and understand nothing. They quite obviously are not preaching the same gospel of the grace of God that you and I preach today. Why is it that Paul can say, "*For Christ sent me not to baptize, but to preach the gospel: not with wisdom of words, lest the cross of Christ should be made of none effect*" (1 Corinthians 1:17)? The twelve in a million years could never say anything like that.

Getting back to the prophetic program, Israel has a role to fulfill in the kingdom and it involves the nations. But there is also special privilege available to those who join themselves to Israel. This again is in perfect keeping with the prophetic program. They will also have a special inheritance in that redeemed city and land just as is laid out in the book of redemption, the book of Ruth.

It is through Israel that the Gentiles are to be blessed in the prophetic program, but there is a huge difference between Jew and Gentile in that program. They are not on the same level by any means. Israel is the one His covenant is with. Israel is the one He has chosen. Israel is to be the head and not the tail. The Gentiles as such are cut off from God's dealings. The believing Israelite in that program is to be blessed as a believing member of that nation. The Gentile woman in Matthew 15 receives the blessing from the Lord only when she takes her place as a Gentile dog. "*But he answered her not a word. And his disciples came and besought him, saying, Send her away; for she crieth after us*" (Matthew 15:23).

Interestingly, there are three rejections of this woman in the actual passage. First the Lord ignores her. Then He declares He is not sent but unto the lost sheep of the house of Israel. Thirdly, He tells her that as a Gentile dog she has no right to the children's bread. But all three times she would not relent. She continued steadfastly after Him and worshipped Him. Acknowledging that she was indeed a dog as far as the program was concerned, she asked for the crumbs that fall from the master's table. "*Then Jesus answered and said unto her, O woman, great is thy faith: be it unto thee even as thou wilt. And her daughter was made whole from that very hour*" (Matthew 15:28).

The same concept is also true with the centurion that the Lord encountered. "*And when Jesus was entered into Capernaum, there came unto him a centurion, beseeching him…The centurion answered and said, Lord, I am not worthy that thou shouldest come under my roof: but speak the word only, and my servant shall be healed…And I say unto you, That many shall come from the east and west, and shall sit down with Abraham, and Isaac, and Jacob, in the kingdom of heaven*" (Matthew 8:5,8,11)

But getting back to the Gentile woman, it should be noted Ruth was also rejected three times when she sought to remain with her mother-in-law Naomi. The other daughter-in-law left after the second time Naomi tried to send them away, but Ruth would not let go. *"And they lifted up their voice, and wept again: and Orpah kissed her mother in law; but Ruth clave unto her. And she said, Behold, thy sister in law is gone back unto her people, and unto her gods: return thou after thy sister in law. And Ruth said, Intreat me not to leave thee, or to return from following after thee: for whither thou goest, I will go; and where thou lodgest, I will lodge: thy people shall be my people, and thy God my God. Where thou diest, will I die, and there will I be buried: the LORD do so to me, and more also, if ought but death part thee and me. When she saw that she was steadfastly minded to go with her, then she left speaking unto her"* (Ruth 1:14-18).

Much yet remains for the Gentiles in Israel's program, but it will come only when God has finished His whole work upon Zion. Israel is the key that will unlock the door of blessings for planet Earth and the nations. *"For if the casting away of them be the reconciling of the world, what shall the receiving of them be, but life from the dead?"* (Romans 11:15).

Today, God is doing something very different and unnatural with Jew and Gentile quite apart from Israel's program. Today, they all are on the same level. But be not highminded, this situation is only temporary as God works out some specific things according to the mystery of His will (Ephesians 1:9). He is zealous to resume and fulfill His purposes for Israel and earth.

In connection with all of this, Israel is called to be a holy nation and kingdom of priests which they will be enabled to do under the new covenant.

"Now therefore, if ye will obey my voice indeed, and keep my covenant, then ye shall be a peculiar treasure unto me above all people: for all the earth is mine: And ye shall be unto me a kingdom of priests, and an holy nation. These are the words which thou shalt speak unto the children of Israel" (Exodus 19:5,6).

"*For thou art an holy people unto the LORD thy God: the LORD thy God hath chosen thee to be a special people unto himself, above all people that are upon the face of the earth. The Lord did not set his love upon you, nor choose you, because ye were more in number than any people; for ye were the fewest of all people: But because the LORD loved you, and because he would keep the oath which he had sworn unto your father's, hath the LORD brought you out with a mighty hand, and redeemed you out of the house of bondmen, from the hand of Pharaoh king of Egypt. Know therefore that the LORD thy God, he is God, the faithful God, which keepeth covenant and mercy with them that love him and keep his commandments to a thousand generations*" (Deuteronomy 7:6-9).

"*For thou art an holy people unto the LORD thy God, and the LORD hath chosen thee to himself, above all nations that are upon the earth*" (Deut 14:2). "*And the LORD hath avouched thee this day to be his peculiar people, as he hath promised thee, and that thou shouldest keep all his commandments; And to make thee high above all nations which he hath made, in praise, and in name, and in honour; and that thou mayest be an holy people unto the LORD thy God, as he hath spoken*" (Deuteronomy 26:18,19).

How some could say that Israel was supposed to be a special nation without being a special *nation* or that somehow you and I are fulfilling this today is beyond me. We *are* a peculiar people and holy as well but it is part of a very different program to accomplish some very different things. The whole issue with us is that we are *not* a nation. There is no way that God could do what He is doing with you and me as Gentiles today in that program. In the one program, there *is* a difference between Jew and Gentile and in the other program there is not. In one program the difference is there intentionally and by design and is instrumental in God's plans with the earth.

The national relationship that exists with planet Earth is fundamental as are many other earthly elements and rudiments of the world that exist in God's program with Israel. This is what we are about to turn to. But as you study the role of Gentiles and nations in the kingdom of heaven it should be quite clear that we who believe today, whether Jew or Gentile, are being made spiritually fit by God to fulfil a very different role. That is exactly what the apostle Paul tells us in his epistles. We are not spiritual Israel. We are not today the fulfillers of her program. The reason that there is neither Jew nor Gentile is *not* because we are all Jews. We are something altogether different with a completely different program according to a completely different purpose, although the two programs are most definitely related.

That prophetic program has been *temporarily* suspended so God can accomplish something He purposed within Himself but had said nothing about. He is today forming one new man, the Body of Christ, to fulfill that purpose. Until He is finished, Israel will remain blinded and will not see her program fulfilled. It is interesting that Paul when writing to us as members of the Body of Christ never once says we are a kingdom of priests. We would think that something as important as that would get at least a brief mention from him, but no such luck. The reason is that we are *not* that. That is Israel's role in accordance with their ministry to the nations in the kingdom of heaven. When we understand what our destiny and future role is, it is clear why we are not that nation and priesthood.

We do, however, have the position of sonship or adoption. This is a glorious position and at the very heart and soul of the edification process today. It is this privilege that I believe most believers are referring to when they speak of the priesthood of all believers. And this is unfortunate because too often it results in not really appreciating what the biblical doctrine of adoption is all about. This is not the place to expound upon it but a bare bones synopsis of it is that we are not under the tutors and governors of the law. Israel will also enjoy that position in the coming kingdom, as it is tied to their role as priests. Let us just note that once you return to the prophetic program you again encounter all the elements you expect to see.

Peter, ministering the gospel of the circumcision and continuing the ministry the Lord had on earth as that minister of the circumcision, declares to the scattered remnant in Asia, "*But ye are a chosen generation, a royal priesthood, an holy nation, a peculiar people; that ye should shew forth the praises of him who hath called you out of darkness into his marvellous light"* (1 Peter 2:9. See also Zechariah 13:7).

Interestingly enough, Peter writes from Babylon, and between the scattered remnant in Asia, Babylon and Jerusalem as found in the circumcision epistles we have the major groupings of where the remnant is to be found in the Lord's Day of Wrath. There are the seven churches in Asia, there are those who are to flee from Jerusalem and the Lord will call for His people to come out of the city of Babylon before its destruction. *"And from Jesus Christ, who is the faithful witness, and the first begotten of the dead, and the prince of the kings of the earth. Unto him that loved us, and washed us from our sins in his own blood, And hath made us kings and priests unto God and his Father"* (Revelation 1:5).

"And they sung a new song, saying, Thou art worthy to take the book, and to open the seals thereof: for thou wast slain, and hast redeemed us to God by thy blood out of every kindred, and tongue, and people, and nation; And hast made us unto our God kings and priests: and we shall reign on the earth" (Revelation 5:9,10).

Israel has quite a role to fulfill in that kingdom with the nations. It is concerning this function that there will be a system of sacrifices in the coming kingdom as laid out in Ezekiel and other books. Israel will not be under the tutors and governors of the Law but the nations will. It is all about education and instruction. I encourage you to study this issue on your own but, simply stated, they will be functioning as priests and offering up various things on behalf of the nations that come up to Jerusalem and the Lord's house. We have no need to offer up anything on anyone else's behalf as priests.

Today, Gentiles are privileged to hear the message of reconciliation. It is Paul's gospel that is preached to them, whereby they are told that God has broken down the middle wall of separation and has committed to the Apostle of the Gentiles a special dispensation of His grace for the Gentiles as He forms His one new man. As long as God is forming His one new man, He will continue to have this message preached. Any person saved today is a member of the church of the mystery and will be a partaker of its hope and glory (Ephesians 2:11–3:11).

But God has a system for dealing with the nations as such in the prophetic program. You and I are told not to let anyone judge us when it comes to the keeping of feasts or any such ordinances. While people may enjoy celebrating various festivals, they have nothing to do with spirituality today and we are in no way called upon to observe them. There are those who believe it is wrong therefore to in any way celebrate various feasts for any reason other than educational or teaching purposes, but I personally am of the persuasion that freedom means freedom.

It seems to me that some of those who are most critical in these kinds of matters are just as bad as those they criticize. They cry legalism but hold forth Sunday as being the day uniquely set apart by the Lord for worship. The fact is, those who are the most critical and demanding are really the ones bordering on ungodliness because they are interfering with the sonship of the believer and the work of God in his life.

*"Him that is weak in the faith receive ye, but not to doubtful disputations. For one believeth that he may eat all things: another, who is weak, eateth herbs. Let not him that eateth despise him that eateth not; and let not him which eateth not judge him that eateth: for God hath received him. Who art thou that judgest another man's servant? To his own master he standeth or falleth. Yea, he shall be holden up: for God is able to make him stand. One man **esteemeth one day above another**: another esteemeth every day alike. Let every man be fully persuaded in his own mind. He that regardeth the day, regardeth it unto the Lord; and he that regardeth not the day, to the Lord he doth not regard it. He that eateth, eateth to the Lord, for he giveth God thanks; and he that eateth not, to the Lord he eateth not, and giveth God thanks…For meat destroy not the work of God"* (Romans 14:1-6, 20).

Paul also has some harsh words concerning observing days for the judaizers in Galatians 4. But again, it all focuses on our position as adopted full-grown sons. The lesson: Don't try to put fellow believers under the tutors and governor system, regardless of what side you are on. Even if you are completely right, that other believer needs to grow naturally according to the way God has designed His word to work in that individual's inner man. We are supposed to be *renewed* in knowledge. Paul will tell you the things you are to know in order to be like God in accordance with what He is doing today. There is, of course, always the danger that by regarding certain days, etc, your true identity in Christ will be lost or clouded. But brother, *"Who art thou that judgest another man's servant?...Let us not therefore judge one another any more: but judge this rather, that no man put a stumblingblock or an occasion to fall in his brother's way"* (Romans 14:4,13)

All the judaizers were trying to do was pull believers back into another program in which they may very well have been godly. But God had made a change and they needed to acknowledge and accept that what Paul was saying was true, rather than despising his apostleship. Knowing who you are today—and why—is important when it comes to the issue of godliness. This is true in God's program with Israel and the same is true in His program with us. There is freedom, friends, and quite frankly the yoke of bondage can work either way.

However, in God's program with Israel and this earth, godliness *will* be measured quite differently for the nations. One of the names that Succot is known by is the "feast of the nations." As we have seen, the nations are very much in view in the prophetic program. *"And there was given him dominion, and glory, and a kingdom, that all people, nations, and languages, should serve him: his dominion is an everlasting dominion, which shall not pass away, and his kingdom that which shall not be destroyed"* (Daniel 7:14).

He will rule over this earth from a particular place. It is the place of the commanded blessing.

"Why leap ye, ye high hills? this is the hill which God desireth to dwell in; yea, the LORD will dwell in it for ever" (Psalm 68:16).

"Behold, how good and how pleasant it is for brethren to dwell together in unity! It is like the precious ointment upon the head, that

ran down upon the beard, even Aaron's beard: that went down to the skirts of his garments. As the dew of Hermon, and as the dew that descended upon the mountains of Zion: for there the LORD commanded the blessing, even life for evermore. Behold, bless ye the LORD, all ye servants of the LORD, which by night stand in the house of the LORD. Lift up your hands in the sanctuary, and bless the LORD. The LORD that made heaven and earth bless thee out of Zion" (Psalm 133, 134). They will only get that blessing, however, because the precious blood first ran down the head of Messiah.

One of the most prominent features of the celebration of Succot is the use of branches and leaves and dwelling in tabernacles. *"And ye shall take you on the first day the boughs of goodly trees, branches of palm trees, and the boughs of thick trees, and willows of the brook; and ye shall rejoice before the LORD your God seven days"* (Leviticus 23:41).

When this feast finds its ultimate fulfillment it will mean more than just the people praising Him and rejoicing.

*"For ye shall go out with joy, and be led forth with peace: the mountains and the hills shall break forth before you into singing, and **all the trees of the field will clap their hands.** Instead of the thorn shall come up the fir tree, and instead of the briar shall come up the myrtle tree: and it shall be to the LORD for a name, for an everlasting sign that shall not be cut off"* (Isaiah 55:12,13).

*"And it shall come to pass, that **every one that is left of all nations** which came against Jerusalem shall even go up from year to year to worship the King, the LORD of hosts, and to **keep the feast of tabernacles.** And it shall be, that whoso will not come up of all the **families** of the earth unto Jerusalem to worship the King, the LORD of hosts, even upon them shall be no rain. And if the family of Egypt go not up, and come not, that have no rain; there shall be the plague, wherewith the LORD will smite the heathen that come not up to keep the feast of tabernacles. In that day shall there be upon the bells of the horses, HOLINESS UNTO THE LORD; and the pots in **the LORD's house** shall be like the bowls before the altar"* (Zechariah 14:16-20).

Unless you are one who is inclined to spiritualize this passage and completely ignore the prophetic program as God clearly makes it to be understood, it is obvious that this does not refer to the position Gentiles enjoy today before God. This *is* how He works, however, when He is dealing with Israel, the earth and the nations as such.

So, once again, when we are back in the prophetic program and taken into the Lord's Day, it should come as no surprise when we read, "*After this I beheld, and, lo, a great multitude, which no man could number, of all nations, and kindreds, and people, and tongues, stood before the Lamb, clothed with white robes, and **palms in their hands**. And cried with a loud voice, saying, Salvation to our God which sitteth upon the throne, and unto the Lamb…And one of the elders answered, saying unto me, What are these which are arrayed in white robes? And whence came they? And I said unto him, Sir, thou knowest. And he said to me, These are they which **came out of great tribulation**, and have washed their robes, and made them white in the blood of the Lamb. Therefore are they before the throne of God, and serve him day and night in his temple: and he that sitteth on the throne shall **dwell** among them*" (Revelation 7:9,10,13-15).

"*Also in the fifteenth day of the seventh month, when ye have **gathered in the fruit of the land**, ye shall keep a feast unto the LORD seven days: on the first day shall be a sabbath, and on the eighth day shall be a sabbath…Ye shall **dwell** in booths seven days; all that are Israelites born shall **dwell** in booths; That your generations may know that I made the children of Israel to **dwell** in booths, when I brought them out of the land of Egypt: I am the LORD your God*" (Leviticus 23:39,42-44).

"*In that day shall the **branch** of the LORD be beautiful and glorious, and **the fruit of the earth** shall be excellent and comely for them that are **escaped of Israel**. And it shall come to pass, that he that is **left in Zion**, and he that **remaineth in Jerusalem**, shall be called holy, even every one that is **written among the living** in Jerusalem: When the Lord shall have washed away the filth of the* *daughters of Zion, and shall have purged the blood of Jerusalem from the midst thereof by the spirit of judgement, and by the spirit of burning. And the LORD will create upon **every dwelling place** of mount Zion, and upon her assemblies, a cloud and smoke by day, and the shining of a flaming fire by night: for upon all the glory shall be a defence. And there shall be a **tabernacle** for a shadow in the daytime from the heat, and for a place of refuge, and for a covert from storm and rain"* (Isaiah 4:2-6).

This is what all of history is moving toward. We have an appointment with destiny and God intends to keep it. We can rest assured that, based on His track record, the Lord will bring these things to pass. The wonderful thing is that He wants you on His side and even now extends the opportunity to avoid the lot of those that take their stand against Him.

"Have I any pleasure at all that the wicked should die? saith the Lord GOD: and not that he should return from his ways, and live?" (Ezekiel 8:23).

"The Lord is not slack concerning his promise, as some men count slackness; but is longsuffering to us-ward, not willing that any should perish, but that all should come to repentance" (2 Peter 3:9).

The time will come, however, when this offer will be taken off the table. And, dear friend, if you don't believe now when God has made it so easy, what on earth makes you think that you will trust and believe Him when spiritual deception and persecution will exist like has never been known on this planet. *"Even him, whose coming is after the working of Satan with **all** power and signs and lying wonders, And with **all** deceivableness of unrighteousness in them that perish; because they received not the love of the truth, that they might be saved. And for this cause God shall send them **strong delusion, that** they should believe a lie: **That** they all might be damned who believed not the truth, but had pleasure in unrighteousness"* (2 Thessalonians 2:9-12).

Yes, it's possible you **might** believe once that time came, but I wouldn't count on it. Chances are you wouldn't even know what was going on around you and would think those strange Jews carrying the testimony of Jesus Christ and going around talking about the kingdom of heaven were kooks. You would probably join in on the persecution against them to remove the thorn that they would be in your side—that is, if you even live that long. But you are not even guaranteed tomorrow and once death clasps its cold hands around you it will be too late.

God could not have demonstrated His concern and love for you in any greater way than the sacrifice of Calvary. He offers you the benefits of that shed blood today and it means nothing less than full reconciliation with God. The choice is yours. In the meantime, God has marked His calendar. He has an appointment, and though longsuffering, He is eager to keep it.

Virtually every time the Lord speaks of the rain in Scripture, He talks about the former rain (fall rain) and latter rain (spring rain) in that order. Yet, when He speaks of His appointment to meet with Israel we read, "*His going forth is prepared as the morning; and he shall come unto us as the rain, as the latter and former rain unto the earth*" (Hosea 6:3). He would first come to them as their King during the spring rain, then the fall rain after that.

There are two triumphal entries into Jerusalem, one during the spring feasts (latter rain) and one during the fall feasts (former rain). All during His ministry, Messiah said His hour had not yet come. He refused to be thrust into the position of kingship until that time came. Then, when everything had been carefully "prepared," He entered Jerusalem and Israel was told to behold her humble king coming unto her. "*Behold, thy King cometh unto thee: he is just, and having salvation; lowly, and riding upon an ass, and upon a colt the foal of an ass*" (Zechariah 9:9).

But she refused Him as King and responded with "we will not have this man to reign over us" "*Pilate saith unto them, Shall I crucify your King? The chief priests answered, We have no king but Caesar*" (John 19:15). And so, the Lord declares to His people, "*Ye shall not see me henceforth, till ye shall say, Blessed is he that cometh in the name of the Lord*" (Matthew 23:39). Because she refused Him when He offered Himself freely to her, Israel will only see

Him again when she acknowledges her offence, seeks Him and declares, "Come thou and reign over us." It is only then that He will come to her and give her that long promised salvation. It is at that time that Israel will behold her formerly rejected King as He comes to her triumphantly and fulfills those three remaining fall feasts. *"And it shall come to pass in that day, that I will seek to destroy all the nations that come against Jerusalem. And I will pour upon the house of David, and upon the inhabitants of Jerusalem, the spirit of grace and supplications: and they shall look upon* **me** *whom they have* **pierced***, and they shall mourn for* **him***, as one mourneth for his only son, and shall be in bitterness for him, as one that is in bitterness for his firstborn"* (Zechariah 12:9,10). There have been many preparations made for these appointments. You can rest assured that when the time comes, He will be ready and right on time.

"And the LORD spake unto Moses, saying, Speak unto the children of Israel, and say unto them, Concerning the **feasts of the LORD***, which ye shall proclaim to be holy* **convocations***, even these are* **my feasts***...And Moses declared unto the children of Israel the* **feasts of the LORD"** (Leviticus 23:2,44).

— Chapter Ten —

But in the meantime...

The Mystery of Christ
&
The Dispensation of Gentile Grace

I n the meantime are Paul's epistles, Romans through Philemon, along with something that God had never said anything about in ages and generations past. The Lord Jesus Christ was very much a part of what God had revealed. Indeed, the volume of the book is all about Him (Psalm 47; Hebrews 10:7). The righteousness that He would provide to His people through that great sacrifice of Calvary was also very much spoken of by the prophets. Even the issue of Gentile salvation was laid out in the Scriptures and, as we have seen, the nations as such are to play a huge role in that coming kingdom as Christ rules over the earth from the New Jerusalem.

But then there is something called the mystery of Christ. This is what Paul's apostleship is all about. It is for this cause that God raised him up as a new apostle and separated him from the twelve whose role was to minister the things that pertain to Israel's program. God was ushering in a new dispensation and program about which He had said absolutely nothing before in His Word. This had been very deliberate on His part and was done so that He might once again take the wise one in his own craftiness (1 Corinthians 2:6-8). He first made known the revelation of the mystery unto Paul, revealing to him that He was *temporarily* suspending the prophetic program with Israel and earth so He might accomplish something He had purposed within Himself before the foundation of the world.

For this formerly secret purpose, God would form "one new man" out of both Jew and Gentile. With the suspension of Israel's program, the Jews were removed from the place of special privilege in God's dealings and put on the same level as the Gentiles. They were thoroughly and specially put on notice of this fact by the apostle Paul in the book of Acts. The temporary setting aside of the nation did *not* take place at the cross. I will discuss this further in the appendix but, simply put, that act was not held against them. It was also not a mystery. You will have problems with this only if you fail to understand the role and ministry of the twelve in the prophetic program.

What you find in the Gospels, early chapters of Acts and Hebrews through Revelation is exactly what you should expect if you have been following the Bible up to that point. The change begins with the raising up of Paul in Acts. The twelve have been ministering to the little flock, the remnant of Israel, which is keeping the testimony and commandments of Jesus Christ as they await the Lord to arise from the Father's right hand in heaven and have His prophesied Day of Wrath. He has thoroughly prepared them for what is going to transpire on earth and they have detailed instructions on how they are to conduct themselves in His absence. After certain events have transpired, they will know that His arrival is near and that at any time He will burst through the darkness in His brilliance and wage war against the nations. He brings that prophesied city with Him, along with His rewards, and they receive those treasures they had been storing up there. At that time God's name will be hallowed in all the earth as had been spoken by the prophets, and His will shall be finally done on earth as it is in heaven. This truly is the kingdom of heaven.

The little flock—or as some describe it, the kingdom church—is that long prophesied remnant of Israel. Their program is Israel's and there is nothing out of kilter with it in the Gospels or the early chapters of Acts. In that program, the opportunity for Gentiles is just what we have seen up to this point. The nations are very much involved and are to be dealt with in due time. They may join Israel, but there is still a huge difference between the two and the Lord Himself recognizes them positionally in their national status to be dogs.

Unfortunately, all too often Pauline truth is read back into the Gospels and Acts but his message is that *that* program has been put on hold. The little flock is not some distinct entity separate from Israel's program and national future. They do not make up this new thing that the Lord was doing on earth. He was doing with them exactly what the Scriptures and program called for Him to do with the nation. *"Now I say that Jesus Christ* **was a minister of the circumcision for the truth of God, to confirm the promises** *made unto the fathers"* (Romans 15:8).

That is not what the Lord is now doing in accordance with the mystery of Christ. The twelve apostles are to sit on twelve thrones judging the twelve tribes of Israel. Their names will be on that coming city with the names of the twelve tribes. Paul's name is not there. There are twelve apostles for the twelve tribes of Israel in the prophetic program. The future glory that is associated with them in Israel's program fulfills a particular purpose in God's plans for earth. There is one apostle for the one body of Christ in the mystery program. The future glory associated with that body also fulfills a particular purpose in God's plans, but not for earth.

Today, if you have trusted in the Lord Jesus Christ and His sacrifice for the remission of your sins and salvation from the penalty of your sins, then you have been forever forgiven and reconciled to God. You can have perfect peace knowing that having accepted His offer and received His precious gift, the punishment you so rightly deserved was laid upon Christ at that awful cross. He was forsaken so you wouldn't have to be. You died with Christ on that cross and were raised with Him and it is in Him that your identity is to be found. In other words, you have justification in God's sight. You have been made spiritually fit by God and sanctified by Him and He desires to use you in accordance with what He is doing today. You have not been saved in a vacuum. We often focus on our inheritance in the Lord, but we often fail to realize that He has an inheritance in us. He also receives something by saving us.

As a believer today, either as a Jew or Gentile, you are not saved according to Israel's program. He has an inheritance in Israel too and they have an inheritance in Him. It is that issue which we have been examining all throughout this book. The Gentiles are also to be saved in Israel's program. But there, it is through the instrumentality of Israel. Today, you are saved in spite of Israel and *because* of their fall. God has saved you in accordance with another purpose of His.

There are things which have been ordained for our glory. Israel has been promised a glorious position in Christ with respect to His plans for earth. But He is also forming a brand new entity, the Body of Christ. As members of that body, we have been given a glorious position in Christ, but for a different purpose. This is the mystery of God's will. There is an aspect of His will about which He had said nothing. There is something He purposed in Himself to accomplish which He kept secret.

What is it? "*Blessed be the God and Father of our Lord Jesus Christ, who hath blessed us with all spiritual blessings in heavenly places in Christ…In whom we have redemption through his blood, the forgiveness of sins, according to the riches of his grace; Wherein he hath abounded toward us in all wisdom and prudence; Having made known unto us the mystery of his will, according to his good pleasure which he hath purposed in himself*" (Ephesians 1:3,7-9).

Here the apostle Paul reviews the issue of our having been made spiritually fit to be used by God. Notice, however, that this is not according to the promises, or covenants or any such thing. That is because God's prophetic program never called for what is going on with Jews and Gentiles today. It is truly an unnatural situation just as Paul describes it in Romans 11. No, there is something else going on, something which requires you to **rightly** *divide* the word of truth (2 Timothy 2:15).

So what is it that God has made us fit for? Paul goes on. *"That in the dispensation of the fulness of times he might gather together in one **all** things in Christ, **both** which are in **heaven, and** which are on earth; even in him."* (Eph 1:10).

It is by Christ that *all* things were created. It is perfectly fitting therefore to learn that God intends to reconcile *all* things back to Himself in Christ. Indeed, it would have to be in Christ if it was ever going to happen. This issue is extremely important and is one of the primary reasons that God has ushered in this dispensation of Gentile grace in order to form that one *new* man, the Body of Christ. He had made known from the beginning His intention to take back this earth and contend with Satan over it. We are well aware of the rebellion and wickedness that Satan has conducted with man on this planet. But friends, there is much more to creation than just this earth. There are heavenly places and *things* associated with them. Satan began his traffic in rebelliousness and wickedness in those heavenly places among the angelic beings that fill those ranks. That is their domain and where they function. You are introduced to some of these characters not too long after the events of the Garden of Eden when the sons of God make an appearance.

Earth was not the only sphere that had experienced defilement in connection with Satan's activities. But man, as such, has *his* place. It is here on earth. This is where He is designed to function and this is where his authority is to be. This is where He was given dominion, and this is where that dominion will be restored to man under the headship of the Lord Jesus Christ.

*"And God said, Let us make man in our image, after our likeness: and let them have **dominion over** the fish of the sea, and **over** the fowl of the air, and **over** the cattle, and **over** all the earth, and **over** every creeping thing that creepeth upon the earth…and **subdue** it: and have **dominion over**…"* (Genesis 1:26,28).

"*When I consider thy heavens, the work of thy fingers, the moon and the stars, which thou hast ordained; What is man, that thou art mindful of him? and the son of man, that thou visitest him? For thou hast made him a little lower than the angels, and hast crowned him with glory and honour. Thou madest him to have dominion over the works of thy hands; thou hast put all things under his feet: All* **sheep** *and* **oxen**, *yea, and the* **beasts of the field**; *The* **fowl of the air**, *and the* **fish of the sea**, *and whatsoever passeth through the paths of the seas. O LORD our Lord, how excellent is thy name in all* **the earth**." (Psalm 8:3-9).

"*Thou hast put all things in subjection under his feet. For in that he put all in subjection under him, he left nothing that is not put under him. But now we see not yet all things put under him.*" (Hebrews 2:8).

This was always the destiny of man from the very beginning and God has been working, with Israel being instrumental to it, to bring that which He had purposed from the beginning to pass. That is what the prophetic program is all about.

But who has dominion in those heavenly places? It isn't man. That is not what he was created for nor was that the dominion committed unto him. That, my friends, is where the Body of Christ and the mystery of Christ comes in. If God wants to reconcile those heavenly places back to Himself and fill them accordingly, He will need a *new* creation. That is what the Body of Christ is, one *new* man. This is a part of God's will that He had never before revealed until He raised up Paul and commissioned him to minister the truth concerning His mystery program.

This is why Satan and his minions despise the Body of Christ and seek to deceive concerning the truth of it. They try to hide and cover the identity that has been given to those that the Lord is currently pouring His grace upon. This dispensation is the height of embarrassment for this most prideful of beings who was taken as a fool by the Lord at the cross. "*Behold, thou art wiser than Daniel; there is no secret that they can hide from thee.*" (Ezekiel 28:3).

This is what Satan said to himself. But glory of glories, the Lord would provide for the complete and total destruction of Satan's entire plan of evil by doing something as simple as keeping a secret. This most brilliant of beings is infuriated by the prospect that God is going to take some of these pathetic jars of clay on planet Earth and use them to replace and fill the positions that he and his minions now possess in the heavenly places. He hates this truth and fights tooth and nail to keep the mystery just that, a mystery.

"*And having spoiled principalities and powers, he made a shew of them openly, triumphing over them in it. Let no man therefore judge you in meat, or in drink, or in respect of an holy day, or of the new moon, or of the sabbath days: Which **are** a shadow of things **to come**.*" (Col 2:15-17).

They don't concern us or the program of which we are a part. They are, however, an integral part of the program that was interrupted by the mystery program and will resume when God is finished with His present purpose. We are not under the elements and ordinances of the world that are utilized by God with a particular nation in a particular land for *earthly* purposes.

The Gentiles in Israel's program most certainly are subject to such things as is abundantly clear from the prophetic program. Those are all perfectly compatible with God's plans for earth as it relates especially to the Abrahamic Covenant. Israel is to be the head and not the tail. There is of course opportunity for the Gentiles just as there has always been, but there is most certainly a difference between Jew and Gentile. Earth is where Israel is to have her impact, especially on the nations and, as such this is what her future in Christ is related to. We, however, in accordance with the mystery of Christ, currently have an impact on the angelic realm. Our conduct as ambassadors here on earth is directly related to that impact. The heavenly places are what our future in Christ is related to.

In Israel's program, the angels have a prominent ministry to those on earth. Read Paul's epistles and I think you will find that the exact opposite is the case with us. We are the ones who even now minister to that angelic realm in ways which constantly hold before them that all-encompassing wisdom of God that was manifested at the cross of Calvary. The fullness of God's genius is to be put on display before all. "*For we wrestle not against flesh and blood, but against principalities, against powers, against the rulers of the darkness of this world, against spiritual wickedness in high places*" (Eph 6:12). How can we be anything but full of praise and thanksgiving in the face of such a mighty grace and privilege which has come unto us.

"*All things were made by him; and without him was not any thing made that was made*" (Jn 1:3). What we have been discussing is the true doctrine of universal reconciliation. Such a doctrine is indeed taught in the Bible, as we have seen, but not in the way many would define it. There are those who believe that everyone will be reconciled to God in the end, even Satan. To me, this is nonsense and I don't understand how any student of the Scripture could come to such a conclusion. It is unfortunate obviously for a host of different reasons, not the least being that it causes a lack of appreciation for the real doctrine.

The Lord is concerned about reconciling some particular *things* to himself, not people. The *people* that are reconciled to him are indeed used by Him to fill those things. He makes them spiritually fit so He can use them according to His purpose. The issue is not getting back every person on earth, although He would certainly like nothing better. The issue is getting those earthly places back to Himself especially as it relates to dominion. "*But is long-suffering to us-ward, not willing that any should perish, but that all should come to repentance*" (2 Peter 3:9).

He does not desire that any should perish, but that is their choice. He has made full provision available for them *if they are willing* to humble themselves and take advantage of what God offers them. There is no excuse. He could not have done anything more to provide a way out for man. But it is up to man to choose whether he will take God up on His most gracious offer—namely, the gift of salvation through His Son—or if he will reject the bloody payment that has been made and trust in his own righteousness to save him. When he finds himself in hell it will be his own choice. But regardless of what man chooses, in the end *all* things *will* be under the headship of the Lord Jesus Christ.

"*In whom we have redemption through his blood, even the for-giveness of sins: Who is the image of the invisible God, the firstborn of every creature: For by him were all things created, that are in heaven, and that are in earth, visible and invisible, whether they be thrones, or dominions, or principalities, or powers: all things were created by him, and for him: And he is before all things, and by him all things consist. And he is the head of the body, the church: who is the beginning, the firstborn from the dead; that in all things he might have the preeminence. For it pleased the Father that in him should all fulness dwell; And, having made peace through the blood of his cross, by him to reconcile all things unto himself; by him, I say, whether they be things in earth, or things in heaven.*" (Col 1:15-20).

And so in accordance with this fullness of Christ, God has revealed the mystery of Christ and ushered in the program associated with it to accomplish His present purpose for the heavenly places. God's Word follows the outworking of His plan. Genesis through Acts 7 follows the earthly program with Israel and the five Courses of Punishment that come upon the nation. As you reach the end of the Gospels, you will see that Israel will be given a chance to respond to the stumbling stone that has been laid, then the Lord will arise and have His Day of Wrath.

As Peter declared to the nation, the last days in the program had arrived. With the final act of rebellion in the stoning of Stephen, it was officially declared to the apostate rulers that the Son of man was *standing* at the right hand of the Father in heaven. To any Jew who knew his Old Testament that meant only one thing, the time had arrived for the Day of the Lord to come upon this earth.

That fifth and final installment in the Fifth Course of Punishment in Israel's program that would see the arrival of Antichrist and the great tribulation, and end with Christ's return and the setting up of the kingdom was finally here. But the Lord's Day of Wrath did not come. Instead, completely unexpectedly and not according to the program, the Lord returns from heaven and appears to Paul. He raises him up as a new apostle and makes known to Him the mystery, revealing to him that He is temporarily suspending His program with Israel, putting them on the same level as the Gentiles, and is going to make of both Jew and Gentile one *new* man, the Body of Christ.

This entity would be formed in accordance with His purposes and plans for the heavenly places. The fullness of His grace would be seen as He did this very unnatural thing among the Gentiles. But, this situation is temporary. Just as this program was ushered in, so shall it be ushered out. God has no more forsaken His program with Israel than He has His plans and purposes for earth. In accordance with this mystery Paul, as our apostle, ministers the truths that concern our identity and therefore future. When you understand the nature of the change that has taken place, you understand better the naturalness of the things Paul will tell you as a member of the Body of Christ.

As long as God is engaged in what He is doing today, that prophesied Day of His Wrath will not come. In Israel's program He explicitly instructed them that He would not return until the very end of that great tribulation. And indeed, according to the prophetic program He is not to return until that time. But in accordance with the ushering in of this dispensation and the revelation of the mystery, He has and will return before that time. We, as part of that mystery program and part of that one new man, have nothing to do with those things that will come upon the earth when He resumes His program with Israel. In fact, they cannot transpire until He has finished what He is doing today and ends this current program with the Body of Christ.

In accordance with this, we have been promised a coming of the Lord for us for the express purpose of delivering us from the wrath to come. This is *not* to come to take His bride. This is to come to take His own body, the one *new* man—the event we look for. This coming is part of the mystery and not a part of the prophetic program. And much like the Lord unexpectedly returned from heaven and appeared to Paul, interrupting and suspending the prophetic program, so will He do in coming for us and thereby resume that prophetic program and fulfill the remaining events on the calendar. When He returns for us, He will do so with all the instruments with which to have His Day. Our departure marks the resumption of that prophetic program.

"*There are also **celestial bodies**, and **bodies terrestrial**: but the **glory of** the celestial is one, and the **glory of** the terrestrial is another…And as we have borne the image of the earthy, **we shall also** bear the image of the heavenly…Behold, I shew you a **mystery**; we shall not all sleep, but we shall be changed…*" (1 Corinthians 15:40,49,51).

"*And ye became **followers of us, and** of the Lord, having received the word in much affliction, with joy of the Holy Ghost: So that ye were **ensamples** to all that believe…For they themselves shew of us what manner of entering in **we had** unto you, and how ye turned to God from idols to serve the living and true God; And to wait for His Son from heaven, whom he raised from the dead, even Jesus, **which delivered us from the wrath to come**"* (1 Thessalonians 1:6,7,9,10).

"*For the Lord himself shall descend from heaven with a shout, with the voice of **the archangel**, and with **the trump** of God: for the dead in Christ shall rise first: Then we which are alive and remain shall be caught up together with them in the clouds, to meet the Lord in the air: and so shall we ever be with the Lord. Wherefore comfort one another with these words. But of the times and the seasons, brethren, **ye have no need** that I write unto you. For yourselves know perfectly that the day of the Lord so cometh as a thief in the night…For God **hath not appointed us** to wrath, but to obtain salvation by our Lord Jesus Christ. Who died for us, that, whether we wake or sleep, we should live together with him*" (1 Thessalonians 4:16–5:2,9,10).

"*If any man think himself to be a prophet, or spiritual, let him acknowledge that **the things that I write** unto you **are** the commandments **of the Lord**"* (1 Corinthians 14:37).

It is not Paul versus Jesus. The ascended Christ has spoken from heaven and revealed something you need to listen to because it is this revelation that has enabled you to be a member of the Body of Christ in the first place. As participants in this mystery program of God we are not appointed unto the wrath to come. This is a special promise the Lord made to the Body of Christ. It is incredibly important and is one example of why it is necessary to rightly divide the word of truth. Paul did not preach the gospel of the kingdom nor did he preach Jesus Christ according to that program.

"*Now to him that is of power to stablish* **you according to my gospel**, *and the preaching of Jesus Christ,* **according to the revelation of the mystery,** *which was kept secret since the world began,* **But now** *is made manifest, and by the scriptures of the prophets, according to the commandment of the everlasting God, made known to all nations for the obedience of faith: To God only wise, be glory through Jesus Christ for ever. Amen*" (Romans 16:25-27).

These particular scriptures have been given to you as a member of the Body of Christ to accomplish a specific work in the edification of your soul. Many believe the rapture of the Body of Christ takes place in Revelation 4:1, but that is dealing with the prophetic program and does not even constitute a rapture in Israel's program as they are to endure till the end and only then will He return.

John is an apostle of the circumcision and ministers that gospel. When you are in the book of Revelation, along with those seven churches, you have already been taken into the Lord's Day of Wrath. The rapture of the Body of Christ has taken place much earlier than Revelation. The one new man has been caught away with the ending of Paul's epistles in Philemon.

In accordance with the outworking of God's plans, the interruption that took place back in Acts 9 with the raising up of Paul has ended. The wild branches have been broken off and God once again re-orients you to the prophetic program and the gospel of the circumcision with the arrival of the book to the Hebrews. Then, just as you have already been prepared by Galatians 2, you will be introduced to the apostles of the circumcision ministering the gospel of the circumcision.

*"But of these who seemed to be somewhat, (whatsoever they were, it maketh no matter to me: God accepteth no man's person:) for they who seemed to be somewhat in conference added nothing to me: But contrariwise, when they saw that the gospel of the uncircumcision was committed unto me, as the gospel of the circumcision was unto Peter; (For he that wrought effectually in Peter to the the apostleship of the circumcision, the same was mighty in me toward the Gentiles:) And when **James, Cephas,** and **John,** who seemed to be pillars, perceived the grace that was given unto me, they gave to me and Barnabus the right hands of fellowship; that we should go unto the heathen, and they unto the circumcision. Only they would that we should remember the poor; the same which I also was forward to do"* (Galatians 2:6-10).

After you have resumed the prophetic program with Hebrews, picking up where Acts 7 left off, you then will come upon the apostles of the circumcision ministering that gospel of the kingdom in this order: James, 1 and 2 Peter, 1, 2, and 3 John. They do indeed speak of Jesus Christ, but it is according to the prophetic program and the gospel of the kingdom. *Their* fellowship is the fellowship of prophecy (1 John 1:1-10). Paul preaches Jesus Christ according to the revelation of the mystery which is what *our* fellowship is all about.

"If ye have heard of the dispensation of the grace of God which is given me to you-ward…Whereby when ye read, ye may **understand** *my knowledge in the mystery of Christ…And to make all men see what is* **the fellowship** *of the mystery, which from the beginning of the world hath been hid in God, who created all things by Jesus Christ:* **To the intent** *that now unto the principalities and powers in heavenly places might be known by the church the manifold wisdom of God,* **According to the eternal purpose** *which he purposed in Christ Jesus our Lord"* (Ephesians 3:2,4,9-11).

For this reason, God tells you to rightly divide His word in order to appreciate and understand it. *"Study to shew thyself approved unto God, a workman that needeth not to be ashamed, rightly dividing the word of truth"* (2 Timothy 2:15).

But don't even think of becoming conceited about what is happening today. This will not last forever. This situation is only temporary. The time will come, as it must if He is ever to resume His program with Israel, when the current dealings of God with the Gentiles will end. Genesis through Acts 7 is the "time past" of God's dealings; Romans through Philemon is the "but now" of God's dealings; and Hebrews through Revelation is the "to come" of God's dealings. All of the Scriptures are for us and are to be studied and appreciated, but not all Scripture is written *to* us and *about* us. The natural branches will once again be grafted back into their own tree and enjoy the place of privilege and special dealings by God. They will understand at that time that the promises had not been fulfilled because of the revelation made known to Paul (2 Peter 3:15).

God does not despise His program with Israel as unfortunately too many believers do. He suspended it temporarily but only to fulfill His mystery purpose—God is eager and zealous to return to His dealings with them and wrap things up so to speak. We can be thankful God is longsuffering. The events in Acts did not catch Him by surprise. In fact all was going exactly according to the program as laid out in the Scriptures. The current program of God was not some kind of back-up plan as I hope is abundantly clear by this point. Quite the contrary, He knew exactly what was going to happen, but he had intentionally been keeping it a secret all along.

*"I say then, Hath God cast away his people? God forbid. For I also am an Israelite, of the seed of Abraham, of the tribe of Bejamin. God hath not cast away his people **which he foreknew…**"* (Romans 11:1,2).

When God ushered in this dispensation of His grace to the Gentiles it was a deliberate and purposeful act on His part which is the way He always conducts His business. But don't for a minute think that this is all there ever is to be. The idea that God is glad to be done with Israel, and that what is going on today is the only thing that He is or ever has been concerned with, is completely inconsistent with what God thinks and has revealed about the matter. But it is this thinking that is precisely what He said the tendency among believers would be and, hence, He will give warnings about that very issue. It is different, yes. But Israel is God's key in His program with this earth just as the Body of Christ is His chosen vessel for the heavenly places.

When you slander God's program with Israel, you slander Him. They are the apple of His eye, engraven on His palms and precious in His sight. You desire to have the heart of God! He wept for His people that they might enter into the blessedness that is rightfully theirs which He Himself had purposed for them. You desire to be Pauline!

"*I say the truth in Christ, I lie not, my conscience also bearing me witness in the Holy Ghost, That I have great heaviness and continual sorrow in my heart. For I could wish that myself were accursed from Christ for my brethren, my kinsmen according to the flesh: Who are Israelites; **to whom pertaineth** the adoption, and the glory, and the covenants, and the giving of the law, and the service of God, and the promises; Whose are the fathers, and of whom as concerning the flesh Christ came, who is over all, God blessed forever. Amen*" (Romans 9:1-5).

The Dispensation of Gentile grace is a marvelous part of God's will, but it is only a part. The position you and I enjoy today, especially as Gentiles, is a glorious one and ought to be appreciated as such. But our standing is purely by the mercy of God *according to the riches* of His grace. The time will come when He will end this purpose of His with the Gentiles. He will return for His body, the one *new* man, meet him in the air in accordance with his vocation and take him up into the heavenly places where He will cast out the current rebellious occupants and fill those places with the members of His body. When He removes that one new man, He will end His current dealings with the Gentiles. The wild branches will be broken off and that current message of reconciliation, the gospel of the grace of God, will be withdrawn.

"And all things are of God, who hath reconciled us to himself by Jesus Christ, and hath given to us the ministry of reconciliation; To wit, that God was in Christ, reconciling the world unto himself, not imputing their trespasses unto them; and hath committed unto us the word of reconciliation. Now then we are ambassadors for Christ, as though God did beseech you by us: we pray you in Christ's stead, be ye reconciled to God" (2 Corinthians 5:18-20).

A unique opportunity is available today. But the Lord is going to call His ambassadors home and will then formally declare war. The program will resume, that Man of Sin will arise and the times and seasons will once again take their place in the prophetic program for planet Earth.

*"For I would not, brethren, that ye should be ignorant of this mystery, lest ye should be wise in your own conceits, that blindness **in part** is happened to Israel, **until** the fulness of the Gentiles be come in. And so all Israel shall be saved: **as it is written,** There shall come out of Sion the Deliverer, and shall turn away ungodliness from Jacob: For this is my covenant unto them, when I shall take away their sins. As concerning the gospel, they are enemies for your sakes: but as touching the election, they are beloved for the father's sakes. For the gifts and calling of God **are without repentance.** For as ye in **times past** have not believed God, yet have now obtained mercy through their unbelief: Even so have these also now not believed, that through your mercy they also may obtain mercy. For God hath concluded them all in unbelief, that he might have mercy upon all. O the depth of the riches both of the wisdom and knowledge of God! how **unsearchable** are his judgements and his ways past finding out! For who hath known **the mind** of the Lord? or who hath been his counsellor? Or who hath first given to him, and it shall be recompensed unto him again? For of him, and through him, and to him, are **all** things: to whom be glory for ever. Amen"* (Romans 11:25-36).

God has much to say through the apostle Paul about this most important of subjects. It is something He wants you to understand and appreciate. Do yourself a favor and read all about it. You need to know who you are in Christ and be nourished in the things necessary for growth. *"Hold fast the form of sound words, which thou hast heard of me, in faith and love which is in Christ Jesus"* (2 Timothy 1:13).

Chapter Eleven

Biblical Evolution & Man's Condition

The Creator, Ecclesiastes,
The Vanity of Man's Wisdom
&
The Trends of Ungodliness

A s we lurch back to Babylon we will continue to see the erosion of national sovereignty as it is offered upon the altar of international will and the collective good. These are the days of the global community and the advances in transportation and communications has made this progression inescapable. How quickly this metamorphosis will take place depends on how much cooperation there is on the part of our leaders but even there it will serve only to delay the process.

Pressure will continue to increase and it is going to seem only right and proper that this one world of ours should have some form of one government that, unlike the UN, is actually relevant and effective. This was the case in the formation of our own federal government and even then it was only after the Civil War, a time of great crisis and internal struggle, that the United States took its current form. There will indeed be great shows of force when the time of the beast arrives and, undoubtedly, there will be great conflict before then as well.

However, the forces that lead us on up to that time will most likely be far more subtle in their influences. They come as angels of light shrouded in positivism and fanciful dreams of utopia created by man. It is the same thinking that believes man is inherently good and if we would only pick up our signs of peace and love, then surely those tanks will stop and we will enjoy peace on earth and goodwill toward men. There is of course no place for the Prince of peace in these imaginations and they deny what the Creator says is the reality of this sin-cursed world of ours and the depravity of man.

But the masterful and wise ones know how to appeal to man. They know what he desires and the way he wants to obtain it. The god of this world will continue to obfuscate the truth and manipulate what God has said about the environment that man has been placed in. It all goes back to that infamous garden, only now man is in the lap of that wicked one and will eat whatever the serpent feeds him.

"*Now the serpent was more subtil than any beast of the field which the LORD God had made. And he said unto the woman, Yea, hath God said, Ye will not eat of every tree of the garden?...And the serpent said unto the woman, Ye shall not surely die: For God doth know that in the day ye eat thereof, then your eyes shall be opened, and ye shall be as gods, knowing good and evil. And when the woman saw that the tree was good for food, and that it was pleasant to the eyes, and a tree to be desired to make one wise, she took of the fruit thereof, and did eat, and gave also unto her husband with her; and he did eat. And the eyes of them both were opened, and they knew that they were naked; and they sewed fig leaves together, and made themselves aprons*" (Genesis 3:1,3-7).

Notice that God doesn't say that it wasn't good for food or pleasant to the eyes. He simply said it was off limits but we still insist on following the god of this world. We want it and that's all there is to it. Why not? Why shouldn't I do it? I enjoy it so much. God wouldn't have made it so good if it was wrong for me to have it. It's what I want and desire, therefore God couldn't possibly have a problem with it. And if He does, well then, He must be pretty rotten and oppressive.

Having already been made in God's likeness, man then sets out on a long history of vainly seeking godliness in the most ungodly of ways. Man's history has amply demonstrated that he is now made in the likeness of his father Adam rather than God. If God says "ye shall surely die" then we in our vanity and self deception will follow the response that "ye shall not surely die."

This outworking of man's rebelliousness will be seen later as we look at some of the specific manifestations of ungodliness, but it should also be noted that the serpent is subtle and one of his favorite areas to work in is the religious and spiritual realm. It is easy for him to exploit man's various lusts and physical appetites. But don't forget that Satan himself is inherently a spiritual being, filled with pride and superiority. This is especially the case when it comes to this unworthy and pathetic race that God has seen fit to create on planet Earth. The devil is a consummate counterfeit and has no problem with appealing to man's "better" side. As long as he can increase darkness and deception to tighten his grip, secure his possessions and spoil what belongs to God, he will.

Satan does not spend all his time coming up with scripts for potential horror flicks. No doubt he reviews them, but quite frankly he is far more sophisticated than that. If you saw him in all his glory you would probably fall down and worship him. And don't forget that he was the father of many of the religious leaders in Israel. Satan wants to be like the Most High and loves to speak in His name and misrepresent Him. For all the bad things that are often said about them, the fact is that the Pharisees' morality would put most of this world to shame. Nevertheless, Satan was running the show in Israel when Christ came on the scene and the serpent continued his seductive tactics when faced with new challenges. The "church" was fairly easy for Satan to get control of and he had accomplished much of his work before the apostle Paul had even gone off the scene. Read what Paul says in his epistles and it should come as no surprise that Christendom took the course that it did.

"*Would to God ye would bear with me a little in my folly: and indeed bear with me. For I am jealous over you with godly jealousy: for I have espoused you to one husband, that I may present you as a chaste virgin to Christ. But I fear, lest **by any means**, as the serpent beguiled Eve through his subtilty, so your **minds** should be corrupted from the simplicity that is in Christ. For if he that cometh **preacheth another Jesus**, whom we have not preached, or if ye receive **another spirit**, which ye have not received, or **another gospel**, which ye have not accepted, ye might well bear with him…For such are false apostles, deceitful workers, transforming themselves into the apostles of Christ. And no marvel; for Satan himself is transformed into an angel of light. Therefore it is no great thing if his ministers also be transformed as the ministers of righteousness; whose end shall be according to their works*" (2 Corinthians 11:1-4, 13-15).

Beware, these characters lift up Jesus, have a spirit and preach the gospel. That is why they are seductive, my friends. You wouldn't go with a kidnapper if he looked like one.

"*Now we beseech you brethren, by the coming of our Lord Jesus Christ, and by **our** gathering unto him, That ye be not soon shaken in **mind**, or be troubled, neither **by spirit**, nor **by word**, nor **by letter as from us**, as that the day of Christ is at hand. Let no man **deceive you by any means**…*" (2 Thessalonians 2:2).

"*Let no man beguile you of your reward in a voluntary humility and worshipping of angels, intruding into those things which he hath not seen, vainly puffed up by his fleshly mind, And not holding the Head, from which all the body by joints and bands having nourishment ministered with the increase of God*" (Colossians 2:18,19).

"*That thou mightest charge some that they teach no other **doctrine**, Neither give heed to fables and endless genealogies, which minister questions, rather than godly edifying which is in faith: so do…From which some having swerved have turned aside unto **vain jangling**; Desiring to be **teachers of the law**; understanding neither what they say, nor whereof they affirm…Now the Spirit speaketh* *expressly, that in the latter times some shall depart from the faith, giving heed to **seducing** spirits, and **doctrines** of devils; Speaking lies in hypocrisy; having their conscience seared with a hot iron; Forbidding to marry, and commanding to abstain from meats, which God hath created to be received with thanksgiving of them which believe and know the truth...But refuse profane and old wives fables, and exercise thyself rather unto **godliness**...Perverse disputings of men of corrupt minds, and destitute of the truth, supposing that gain is **godliness**: from such withdraw thyself. O Timothy, keep that which is committed to thy trust, avoiding profane and **vain** babblings, and oppositions of science falsely so called: Which some professing have erred concerning the faith*" (1 Timothy 1:3,4,6,7; 4:1-4,7; 6:5,20,21).

If you look at just the above list alone you will find almost everything that has plagued the various systems that name the name of Christ. "*Study to shew thyself approved unto God, a workman that needeth not to be ashamed, rightly dividing the word of truth. But shun profane and vain babblings: for they will increase unto more ungodliness. And their word will eat as doth a canker...*" (2 Timothy 2:15,16).

It is important not to be ignorant of Satan's devices and not be puffed up in spiritual things. A simple pursuit of things spiritual, especially in the Christian context, is not enough to protect and inoculate you from the deception and destruction that the serpent wants to bring to your walk of faith. Be very careful, because his desire is for you to think that you are being godly while ungodliness is on the throne and he takes you captive at his will. It is as simple as erring from the truth and a refusal to follow God's instructions on the matter. I recommend that you read 2 Timothy 2:15 again very carefully and try to understand why that injunction has been given for your protection in the pursuit of godliness.

God makes very sure to place that verse where He does for a reason. "*Hold fast the form of sound words, which thou hast heard of me, in faith and love which is in Christ Jesus...This thou knowest, that **all** they which are in Asia be turned away from me...*" (2 Timothy 1:13,15).

They didn't turn away from Christ or the Scriptures or a host of things that can be found in the Bible. They turned away from Paul and the unique apostleship and message that he had to defend at every turn. They failed to rightly divide the word of truth.

All this should be kept in mind as we look later at the general ungodliness of the world against the Creator. There should by no means be an attitude of self-righteousness or holier-than-thou sentiments felt as we examine these issues. It is simply a matter of agreeing with what God has said and not fooling ourselves and justifying our wickedness as we continue our rebellion as a race. We need to examine *ourselves* first and foremost.

However, there are most certainly trends that will consume this globe as we approach our appointment and we need to be aware of them. Above all I want you to understand that this is a battle of the mind. Man's thinking has been corrupted and is diseased.

"*And be not conformed to this world: but be ye transformed by the **renewing of your mind**, that ye may prove what is that good, and acceptable, and perfect, will of God.*" (Romans 12:2).

"*Mortify therefore your members which are upon the earth; fornication, uncleaness, inordinate affection, evil concupiscence, and covetousness, which is idolatry: For which things' sake the wrath of God cometh on the children of disobedience: In the which ye also walked some time, when ye lived in them. But now ye also put off all these; anger, wrath, malice, blasphemy, filthy communication out of your mouth. Lie not one to another, seeing that ye have put off the old man with his deeds; And have put on the new man, which is **renewed in knowledge** after the image of him that created him*" (Colossians 3:5-10).

I simply desire to point out this situation and recognize that this sin-cursed world is following a certain course. This is something that needs to be dealt with honestly so that there is at least some hope of personally avoiding the danger ahead. How many would have been saved on the Titanic if only they had their thinking straight and the right information, namely the truth? Far more people would have used the available lifeboats and been spared. Unfortunately, far too many thought everything would be fine and went on partying. By the time they realized something was amiss, it was too late. Even though the lifeboats were there and available, they did absolutely no good for those who chose not to use them but rather to remain on the great supposedly unsinkable ship.

Friend, I don't condemn you as I have absolutely no right or place to do so. *"For God sent not his Son into the world to condemn the world; but that the world through him might be saved. He that believeth on him is not condemned: but he that believeth not is condemned already, because he hath not believed in the name of the only begotten Son of God. And this is the condemnation, that light is come into the world, and men loved darkness rather than light, because their deeds were evil. For every one that doeth evil hateth the light, neither cometh to the light, lest his deeds should be reproved"* (John 3:17-20).

I simply stand in Christ and urge you to come in before it is too late and the ship you currently stand on sinks. *"I exhort therefore, that, first of all, supplications, prayers, intercessions, and giving of thanks, be made for all men...For this is good and acceptable in the sight of God our Saviour; Who will have all men to be saved, and to come unto the knowledge of the truth. For there is one God, and one mediator between God and men, the man Christ Jesus; Who gave himself a ransom for all, to be testified in due time. Whereunto I am ordained a preacher, and an apostle, (I speak the truth in Christ, and lie not;) a teacher of the Gentiles in faith and verity"* (1 Timothy 2:1,3-7). This lifeboat is more than big enough for all but I can't force you. The choice is yours.

But the fact is that the more this ship sinks into the great deep, the more it will begin to take on a certain form as it is seen from the murky distance of time. Just how long it will take belongs to God alone but eventually it will be consumed by the waters, or should I say fire (2 Peter 3:12). And as this global transformation takes place, the prideful one will continue to steer the ship—all the while convincing man in his vanity that he is really at the helm. The serpent comes as the great liberator and urges you to cut the lifeboat away so that the ship may yet survive and no longer be troubled by the messages of those pessimistic passengers. Ah yes brother, he cares. He comes to set you free. What's your pleasure? He wants to open your eyes to a whole new experience. Don't you know that ye shall be as gods. If only ye believe. Believe what you say? It makes no difference, brother, just as long as you ignore those pesky passengers and stay on the ship. I am here to tell you that he is nothing but a murdering liar.

"*Jesus said unto them, If God were your Father, ye would love me: for I proceeded forth and came from God; neither came I of myself, but he sent me. Why do ye not understand my speech? Even because ye cannot hear my word. Ye are of your father the devil, and the lusts of your father ye will do. He was a murderer from the beginning, and abode not in the truth, because there is no truth in him. When he speaketh a lie, he speaketh of his own: for he is a liar, and the father of it. And because I tell you the truth, ye believe me not. Which of you convinceth me of sin? And if I say the truth, why do ye not believe me? He that is of God heareth God's words: ye therefore hear them not, because ye are not of God. Then answered the Jews, and said unto him, Say we not well that thou art a Samaritan, and hast a devil*" (John 8:42-48).

It never fails. When that old devil is confronted, he will work in his children and rise up in righteous indignation and declare the Lord himself to be the ungodly one. He must have a devil! Well, he's a slick one and he will move us towards the sands of Shinar without too much persuasion. This is a new world and calls for new international measures. The dragon has a fiery bronze hand but he clothes it in a velvet glove. He is the god of this world and it will continue to follow the course he sets. He will continue to corrupt true tolerance and mold it to his ends. Sensitivity and its companion—conformity—will continue to tighten the grip of the state. Not to worry though, tolerant and enlightened people will lead the way as we reach for the full potential of mankind...I mean *person*-kind. You see, they have had their eyes opened, they know better than to think that what the Creator has said is true. "Yea, hath God said…Ye shall **not** surely die."

The fullness of civilization will ever seem to be at hand. The power and achievements of man will evidently rise higher and higher as he is evermore puffed up by the wisdom of this world. His quest is the conquering of the unknown and every inconvenient and debilitating thing that stands in his way. However, his lot is a state of blindness as to the root causes of the situation he faces. The more he discovers of the creation of which he is a part, the more blinded and puffed up he will become in his thinking. The more man explores that which manifestly declares the handiwork of the One who is responsible for him being here, the more man will deny the Creator and His rightful place as such.

The force responsible for man being here must *at least* be as personal as man. The intelligence and intellectual capacity present in the human brain must be in an even greater degree present in that personal force responsible for man being here. The creativity, diversity, rationality, sense of self, search for significance and meaning, desire for order and purpose are all reflective of the being who brought us about in the first place. The intricacy and complexity of all the mechanisms in the universe are universal in their testimony of a designer of some kind. Simply put, the force responsible for us being here must of necessity have at least those qualities that we ourselves possess.

Actually, in some measure He must possess these qualities to a greater extent and must of necessity excel in power in order to bring it about. The thing created will always be in some sense "less" than the one who created it. But at the same time it will reflect the intelligence, ability, purpose and design of the creator. Of course, even if the creator makes the object perfectly according to his specifications, it is quite possible that something will affect the usefulness of that particular vessel.

It should be obvious that whoever is responsible for us being here possesses at least the qualities that you and I exhibit (except where we as a vessel have of our own will departed and become *unlike* Him). The God of the Bible claims that He is that someone. "*And God said, Let us make man in our image, after our likeness...So God created man in his own image, in the image of God created he him, male and female created he them.*" (Genesis 1:26,27).

God alone is the one with creative power; Satan is nothing more than a counterfeit. His desire is to be *like* God, but not in His character and essence. Rather, Satan's desire is to be like Him in His ruling power and dominion. Without being a creator himself, he wants to usurp the position of Creator and have his *will* be supreme. "*How art thou fallen from heaven, O Lucifer...For thou hast said in thine heart, I will ascend into heaven, I will exalt my throne above the stars of God: I will sit also upon the mount of the congregation, in the sides of the north: I will ascend above the heights of the clouds; I will be like the most High.*" (Isaiah 14:13,14). I will, I will, I will.

Thus, when God creates man in His image and likeness and gives him dominion to rule on His behalf, you can imagine that Lucifer would be just a little bit interested in the situation. He is the father of rebellion and a counterfeiter, that is all. Powerful yes, but nothing more. All he can do is mar the image of God as it is reflected throughout the universe. Murder is nothing less than an attack on this image. "*Whoso sheddeth man's blood, by man shall his blood be shed: for in the image of God made he man.*" (Genesis 9:6).

There is nothing wrong with anger or jealousy. The problem is with **ungodly** anger and jealousy. There are many horrible things that one should be righteously angry about, and the Creator Himself possesses these qualities. "*I am jealous over you with godly jealousy...*" (2 Corinthians 11:2; see also 1 Corinthians 10:22).

But rebellion raises its head and desires to take that which God has given and use it in an ungodly manner. All Satan can do is corrupt and misuse what God has given to be appreciated and enjoyed in the way He made it.

"*Wherefore God also gave them up to uncleaness through the lusts of their own hearts, to dishonour their own bodies between* *themselves: Who changed **the truth** of God into a lie, and worshipped the creature more than the Creator, who is blessed for ever. Amen. For this cause God **gave them up** unto vile affections: for even their women did change the **natural use** into that which is against nature: And likewise also the men, leaving the **natural use** of the woman, burned in their lust one toward another; men with men working that which is unseemly, and receiving in themselves that recompence of their error which was meet. And even as they did not **like** to **retain** God in their knowledge, God **gave them over** to a reprobate mind, to do those things which are not convenient; Being filled with all unrighteousness, fornication, wickedness, covetousness, maliciousness; full of envy, murder, debate, deceit, malignity; whisperers, Backbiters, haters of God, despiteful, proud, boasters, inventors of evil things, disobedient to parents, **Without understanding**, covenantbreakers, without **natural** affection, implacable, unmerciful: Who knowing the judgement of God, that they which commit **such things** are worthy of death, not only do the same, but have pleasure in them that do them."* (Romans 1:24-32).

I'm sure you haven't committed *any* of the above things so you'll be just fine when you stand before the judgement. *"Therefore thou art inexcusable, O man, whosoever thou art that judgest: for wherein thou judgest another, thou condemnest thyself; for thou that judgest doest the same things. But we are sure that the judgement of God is according to truth against them which commit such things. And thinkest thou this, O man, that judgest them which do such things, and doest the same, that thou shalt escape the judgement of God? Or despisest thou the riches of his goodness and forbearance and longsuffering; not knowing that the goodness of God leadeth thee to repentance? But after thy hardness and impenitent heart treasurest up unto thyself wrath against the day of wrath and revelation of the righteous judgement of God."* (Romans 2:1-5).

Now just imagine if you were an artist and someone took one of your paintings and began to add to it or mutilate it in some way, say by painting a mustache on it or some such thing. How would that make you feel? Or what if someone took your sculpture and began to desecrate it and use it for things it was never intended. Would you care? Why? Let's say for some strange reason this beautiful image you created to be appreciated and enjoyed began to be popularly used for whacking people over the head or some vile act. Yes strange, I know. Not only that, but eventually it forever becomes identified with this foul, offensive, hurtful and repugnant act. Would you have some feelings about the matter? Well, this is what has happened to what God has created as man in his rebelliousness and ungodliness has misused and abused His artwork. He is not amused and fully intends to bring an action against this desecration. (I hope you have a good attorney.)

There is one fundamental force behind all of this. Pride, rebellion and the lifting up of the will against God. Man has the knowledge of his Creator planted deep within him and his conscience bears him witness. He knows things are not the way they are supposed to be in the universe. But why? If there is no God, if all is just an accident, then he shouldn't know any better. There should be no concept of what things *should* be like if there really is no Creator. Man knows instinctively that in some sense the world around him is not the way God created it.

It just so happens that is exactly what God says. Something entered into His creation and has been working at marring His image and likeness from that time on. Now there is a lot you wouldn't know unless He told you and that is exactly what He has done in His Word, the Bible. He has made known His intention to contend with this rebelliousness and utterly defeat it through the seed of the woman, the Lord Jesus Christ.

Man knows there is a right and wrong. But without God, all his thinking on the subject is utter vanity. Without God you cannot say that anything is really wrong or immoral. Absolutely nothing. Maybe inconvenient, maybe counterproductive, but not wrong. Certainly not immoral. The holocaust? Not wrong, not immoral. "But they massacred millions of people!" So what? Who says that is wrong or immoral? "Well, I wouldn't want someone to do that to me." So what? Who says *that* is wrong? Child molestation? Not wrong, not immoral. And besides, that's a loaded characterization—"molestation." Why, it's just a wonderful expression of diversity, the human body, the love between...blah, blah, blah. "Well, as long as it is between two consenting adults." Oh there you go pushing your morality down my throat. First of all, who are you to limit this wonderful experience to two? Or to adults? And furthermore, where did you get this business about having to be consenting?

You have just set up one morality for another that is more in keeping with your liking. Well, what if I say that as long as they are consenting and not mentally deficient? That's a nice practical rule, isn't it. After all, we don't want to further the production of more mentally deficient people in society. Oh, you don't like that. Well, who are you to push your morality on me. And while we are at it, why don't we permit only people who are tolerant, understanding and enlightened to procreate. But who's defining all this? And what about when they come to silence me because my work is classified as intolerant, unenlightened and harmful to the self-esteem of man. Lord knows we certainly can't have that. We need to feel better about ourselves. We need to sear our conscience so that it no longer troubles us. God forbid that we should be plagued by that evil bondage of guilt. No, we need validation. We must tell ourselves that what we are doing is really okay. In fact, we need to pursue more of it so we can achieve fulfillment, happiness and satisfaction with self. There, doesn't that feel better?

Man will always try to set up moral systems and he recognizes that certain things such as the holocaust are truly immoral because he holds the truth within himself. But, in his rebelliousness, he holds it in unrighteousness. Again, if there is no God, if evolution is true, then I fail to see how social Darwinism—especially as applied to the atrocities of Hitler's Germany—can credibly be condemned. It may be incorrect in its application but immoral? Men will of course condemn it because they *know* it is wrong, they hold the truth. But in his rebellion, in his denial of the rights of the Creator, man is doomed to vanity in his thinking. Without God, appealing to something being "wrong" or "immoral" is nothing but blind faith.

"*For the wrath of God is revealed from heaven against all ungodliness and unrighteousness of men, who hold the truth in unrighteousness; Because that which may be known of God is manifest in them; for God hath shewed it unto them. For the invisible things of him from the creation of the world are clearly seen, being understood by the things that are made, even his eternal power and Godhead; so that they are without excuse: Because that, when they knew God, they glorified him not as God, neither were thankful; but became **vain** in their imaginations, and their **foolish** heart was **darkened**. Professing themselves to be wise, they became **fools**, And changed the glory of the uncorruptible God into an image made like to corruptible man, and to birds, and fourfooted beasts, and creeping things*" (Romans 1:18-23).

This is all the vanity of the book of Ecclesiastes. This is the vanity of all godless systems, beliefs and philosophies that refuse to acknowledge the Creator and His rights as such.

It is utterly amazing that what we so readily admit and see all around us, we will not grant and accept when it comes to the Creator. We care so much about our identity and reputation that we have causes of action at law concerning slander, misrepresentation and on and on the litigation goes. We consider it a moral duty that people get credit for the work they do and are properly recognized accordingly. There are possible consequences if you take someone's work, a painting for instance, and alter it in such a way that is not in keeping with what the artist intended for it. Man's own laws will condemn him. In an even greater sense, God has the copyright, patent and trademark rights on His creation. It is His intellectual property.

"*For as many as have sinned without law shall also perish without law: and as many as have sinned in the law shall be judged by the law; (For not the hearers of the law are just before God, but the doers of the law shall be justified. For when the Gentiles which have not the law, do by nature the things contained in the law, these, having not the law, are a law unto themselves: which shew the work of the law written in their hearts, their conscience also bearing witness, and their thoughts the mean while accusing or else excusing one another;) In the day when God shall judge the secrets of men by Jesus Christ according to my gospel"* (Romans 2:12-16).

Many people have pets. Now as much as you may love your pet, there is an inherent understanding of the difference in the relationship. You expect the animal to understand its role and, over time you expect certain responses and conduct from that animal. Now you had absolutely nothing to do with bringing that animal into existence. That creature has life, is in many respects like you, and in some ways may even be more intelligent.

God, however, is infinitely superior in His very essence and every part of His being. He *is* responsible for you being here. He knows you inside and out. He made man in His image. All He asks of you is to take part in the great privilege of being *like* Him— godly. Man, because of the entrance of sin, is naturally unfit as a vessel to be utilized by God in His plans and purposes. This is a problem, because the time is coming when He is going to do a great housecleaning, wanting to salvage as many vessels as He can. He does this in the face of one who desires to *keep* them in his service and have them follow him when he is cast out. These vessels are inherently corrupt and only by the work of the Creator can they be restored and made acceptable for use.

A disease is eating away at the universe. As I once heard it said, "Man is S.I.N. positive." Eventually God is going to perform an operation and cut this cancer off. He has made it clear to man what his condition is and that he is in need of the cure.

"Have I any pleasure at all that the wicked should die? saith the Lord GOD: and not that he should return from his ways, and live?" (Ezekiel 18:23).

"Who will have all men to be saved, and to come unto the knowledge of the truth" (1 Timothy 2:4).

"The Lord is not slack concerning his promise, as some men count slackness; but is longsuffering to us-ward, not willing that any should perish, but that all should come to repentance" (2 Peter 3:9).

The first step is for man to believe what God has said about his condition. If a person denies that he does indeed have a diseased condition, he will not see his need for a cure and therefore perish. But having understood that he is indeed in a wretched state if something is not done, he then must choose what his response will be. He may deny he is sick in which case he is certainly lost.

You may say, "I am sick, but I will take my chances, everything will probably work out." When dealing with eternity, these are not good odds. You may say, "I am sick, but I would rather face the consequences than take that cure." So be it, your wish will be granted. You may say, "I am sick, but I will heal myself. I will take aspirin, cough medicine, leeches…etc. Everyone has their own way to healing you know. It's arrogant for you to think that this cure is the *only* answer for my condition. Besides, I have faith. I sincerely believe this aspirin will cure me. Isn't that enough."

No, and the leeches might serve only to make your condition worse. "*Jesus saith unto him, I am **the way, the truth,** and **the life:** no man cometh unto the Father, but by me.*" "*…By the name of Jesus Christ…Neither is their salvation in any other: for there is none other name under heaven given among men, whereby we must be saved*" (Acts 4:10,11).

You may say, "Well, I am not as sick as other people." Good for you, you will still die. I am only telling you what the Creator, not me, has said your condition is. He has given me the privilege of being His ambassador and offering you on His behalf the one and only cure for your condition.

You may give all of the responses above, but the absolute worst response is to not broach the subject at all. The desire to not even address the situation is a powerful one because the bringing up of the subject makes you reflect on what you know and are afraid to face. Don't continue to deceive yourself, the price in the end will be too much to pay (Romans 4:1-25; 6:17-23). God truly does want to make you fit to be used by Him in His plans and purposes. He is in the garden calling for you, "Adam, where are you?" Stop hiding from Him.

You are afraid to come out because you know you are naked, you have been disobedient. He wants to clothe you. He wants to call you by a new name, Christ. You think you can cover up your nakedness yourself. You can't. Those fig leaves of good works are nothing but filthy rags. They will eventually dry up and you will be exposed for the disobedient sinner you are. You need the covering that only God can provide you with. It requires the shedding of the blood of a substitute, one who has no sins of their own to pay for. It requires one who will give their life, their very soul, in your place.

"Dead man walking!" is the call that is heard as you continue down the path in your present condition. This is true in more ways than one. Eternal death awaits you, the second death. It will come for you after the first death and your fate will be sealed. *"And as it is appointed unto men once to die, but after this the judgement."* (Hebrews 9:27). You will await the second death and any prospect for enjoying the presence of God will be forever lost. Utter hopelessness will be your only lot. This, my friend, is *true* depression and anything that you think you know or have experienced on this earth does not even begin to compare to the mental anguish and torment of that time.

But you truly are a dead man walking. The second death will come for you because you are spiritually dead now. It is a wretched disease that is working in you even now. Functionally, you are dead to God. Anything you think you can offer Him is simply waste and refuse, but he wants to make you alive in Christ. Don't remain in Adam any longer. Adam recognized his inadequacy and you need to as well. As you walk down that green mile, there is One who offers you an unspeakable gift. He offers to take your place. That judgement you so rightly deserve, He will take upon Himself in your stead. You never have to see that dark dread judgement that awaits at the end of that long walk.

What will your response be? "No stranger, what was your name again? Oh yeah, Jesus. Well sir, I'm sure I'll be just fine. I've always taken care of myself. How bad could it really be? Besides, a call from the governor will come any minute now. I'll get a chance to make my case…the whole process was really unfair, you know. They will see that I am really not as bad as they think, I certainly don't deserve this. And besides, I have done so many good things in my life. I am really quite a nice and decent person. It was just one little mistake I made. If I hadn't been caught, well nobody would have cared. In fact, some might say I did a great service with that act of mine. He was a real *#*@%* anyway. The whole system's corrupt. They'll see. Everything will work out."

You are just deceiving yourself. What will your response be? Your little fig apron is already beginning to tear. Your covering might have more leaves on it than everyone else's on death row but that doesn't change where you are and why. And it won't make a difference at the end of that mile.

It needn't be so, however. You *should* have a healthy fear about what lies ahead, but you shouldn't fear coming out of hiding to the only one who can change your predicament. He gave all that He had, His only begotten Son, to make it possible for you to escape that awful judgement to come. That dark, bloody cross is where mercy met wrath. God can grant you forgiveness and at the same time not compromise the holy justice which the law demands. Someone must pay for the sins committed in society.

Christ has stepped up to meet the challenge, and in all that the perfect law demands, He paid the price. Will you believe that? Will you receive that free gift by trusting Christ and His finished work to reconcile you back to God. Or will you reject that free gift? Stop trusting in these ridiculous fig leaves of yours. Simply believe the message God has delivered to you and receive the free gift of His grace He offers you. Trust in His cross work, and *His* work alone, that your debts were paid for on that bloody tree. Believe that and you will stand justified before God.

Having truly believed that glorious message, you died with Christ on that tree and rose again out of the tomb the third day in newness of life. If you have trusted in His shed blood alone, then not only have the accounts between you and God been cleared, but a deposit has been made for you to draw on. You have been given a marvelous position in the Lord Jesus Christ. You not only have justification, but you also have sanctification. Having been made fit with the imputation of Christ's righteousness, you have been set apart by God for His use.

You can now begin to offer something *acceptable* to Him for His glory. He wants to accomplish some fantastic things as we work with Him in what He is doing according to His plans and purposes. If you are interested in what God has to tell you about all He wants to do with you, I strongly urge you to read Paul's epistles, Romans through Philemon. It is a truly awesome and marvelous message. Don't remain in the darkness and vanity of your thinking any longer (2 Corinthians 4:1-6). What will your response be?

For all that God has said to us, there still remain things that belong solely to Him. For instance, why? Why has He allowed any of it at all. Why didn't He just destroy everything at the very beginning and be done with it. The real question is why has He allowed wicked and rebellious man to continue as long as He has? God does address this subject in part. Much of what we have seen already concerning His plans and purposes for earth touch upon this. He has not abandoned this planet. He intends to rectify the situation and reconcile it all back to Himself.

There are also lessons being learned at this time and things that are and will be put on display in the time to come. The universe is being put through an education, both man and the angelic realm. Once He has completely finished with His work, what happened in the past will never happen again. In the end, God will be completely exonerated and justified before all. There will no longer be any mystery as to the place of God in this world. The darkness will be dissipated and the vanity removed. As for timing, well that all belongs to the One who dwells in eternity. *"But beloved, be not ignorant of this one thing, that one day is with the Lord as a thousand years, and a thousand years as one day"* (2 Peter 3:8).

Apparently God thought that it was all worth it and He ultimately will be successful in getting it all back. The awesome question that exists is, why would God allow a situation to arise whereby the only remedy was the sacrifice of His Son? The only way to rectify the plague that would come upon mankind in his rebellion was for the second member of the godhead to take on human flesh.

The eternal, immortal One becomes one of His creatures. He hungers, thirsts, aches and tires like any man. He is reviled, scorned, mocked and hated. He is publicly humiliated and stripped. Being without flaw and blameless He is unjustly accused and numbered as a common criminal. His beard is torn out and His flesh is stripped from His body as the Roman whips tear into Him exposing His organs. His brow will be punctured with the very emblem of the curse that He has come to take upon Himself, the crown of thorns. He is forced to carry the instrument of His death up the long path of Golgotha's hill where He will be erected for all to see.

Even there, in that hour, He will be mocked and slandered on either side by two thieves. "*And one of the malefactors which were hanged railed on him, saying, If thou be Christ, save thyself and us.*" (Lk 23:39).

Thou fools, for Him to come down off that cross would mean utter hopelessness for those gathered there and for all mankind. It was for this very purpose He came into the world. The ugly cross was His mission and destiny. The single most important event in history occurred on a wooden cross with a little known Jew in the land of Israel. But all of heaven and earth will know that name.

"*Let this mind be in you, which was also in Christ Jesus: Who, being in the form of God, thought it not robbery to be equal with God: But made himself of no reputation, and took upon him the form of a servant, and was made in the likeness of men: And being found in fashion as a man, he humbled himself, and became obedient unto death, even the death of the cross. Wherefore God also hath highly exalted him, and given him a name which is above every name: That at the name of Jesus every knee should bow, of things in heaven, and things in earth, and things under the earth; And that every tongue should confess that Jesus Christ is Lord, to the glory of God the Father"* (Philippians 2:5-11).

There are two kinds of people in this world. Both of them are on crosses condemned to die. Both of them must respond to this crucified Lord who hangs in their midst.

*"For **the preaching of the cross** is to them that perish foolishness; but unto us which are saved it is the power of God. For it is written, I will destroy the wisdom of the wise, and will bring to nothing the understanding of the prudent. Where is the wise? Where is the scribe? Where is the disputer of this world? For after that in the wisdom of God the world by wisdom knew not God, it pleased God by the foolishness of preaching to save them **that believe**. For the Jews require a sign, and the Greeks seek after wisdom: But we preach Christ crucified, unto the Jews a stumbling block, and unto the Greeks foolishness; But unto them which are called, both Jews and Greeks, Christ the power of God, and the wisdom of God. Because **the foolishness of God** is wiser than men; and **the weakness of God** is stronger than men…But God hath chosen the foolish things of the world to confound the wise; and God hath chosen the weak things of the world to confound the things that are mighty…that no flesh should glory in his presence. But of him are ye **in Christ Jesus**, who of God **is made** unto us **wisdom**, and **righteousness**, and **sanctification**, and **redemption**: That according as it is written, He that glorieth, let him glory in the Lord"* (1 Corinthians 1:18-25,27,29-31).

Both condemned men begin in the same place at separation from Christ and often an attitude of scorn and mocking, an attitude that places you and Christ on the same level. But what pride, for He does not deserve to be there. You do. But ah, perchance, a ray of light breaks through the darkness of our thinking and hardened hearts.

*"The other answering rebuked him saying, Dost not thou fear God, seeing thou art in the same condemnation? And we indeed **justly**; for we receive **the due reward** of our deeds: but this man hath*

*done nothing amiss. And he said unto Jesus, **Lord**, remember me when thou comest into thy kingdom. And Jesus said unto him, Verily I say unto thee, To day shalt thou be with me in paradise"* (Luke 23:40-43).

As long as you are able to hold breath in that dying body of yours, the mercy of God is extended to you and the light of hope still flickers. You say, "But I have done horrible things." Naturally, that's why you're hanging on that cross. *"But when Jesus heard that, he said unto them, They that be whole need not a physician, but they that are sick. But go ye and learn what that meaneth, I will have mercy and not sacrifice: for I am not come to call the righteous, but sinners to repentance."* (Matthew 9:12,13).

Christ does not deserve to be there, and yet there He is. He cannot save Himself *and* save you. He has come to save you and that's why He won't come down off that cross until "it is finished." Oh, this is the glorious message of the gospel of the grace of God, and this is the glorious God of the Bible. What unfathomable love, such a love that I cannot even begin to comprehend it. What kind of God would allow His Son to endure such things, even willingly, for us. That is a kind of love that makes me stop and look in awesome fear. That is a love that overwhelms me and stops me dead in my tracks. What kind of love is this? I had better not deal with that cross lightly.

*"What shall we then say to these things? If God be for us, who can be against us? He that spared not his own Son, but delivered him up for us all, how shall he not **with him** also freely give us all things?"* (Romans 8:31,32).

If you are in Christ, you have a glorious and secure position. His love demonstrates what He was willing to go through to deliver you from a dreadful fate. So, if you refuse the provision God has made for you, then He that spared not His only, righteous, holy and spotless Son can in no wise spare you. He did not do this for good and obedient creatures that had nothing but praise and worship for Him since they drew their first breath that He had given to them. No, He did this for a people who have rebelled against Him, mocked Him, criticized, ridiculed and killed His messengers, cursed His very name, denied His place in their lives, slanderously attributed words and actions in His name, refused to credit Him for His handiwork and masterpieces, and in many instances, denied His very existence.

*"And hope maketh not ashamed; because the love of God is shed abroad in our hearts by the Holy Ghost which is given unto us. For when we were yet **without strength**, in due time Christ died for **the ungodly**. For scarcely for a righteous man will one die: yet peradventure for a good man some would even dare to die. But God commendeth his love toward us, in that, **while we were yet sinners**, Christ died for us"* (Romans 5:5-8).

If you are one who has acknowledged your nakedness before Him and has accepted the righteousness that only He can provide through the shed blood of His perfect Lamb, then even greater and more glorious communion with the Creator awaits you. *"**Much more** then, **being** now justified by his blood, we shall be saved from wrath through him. For if, **when we were** enemies, we were reconciled to God by the death of His Son, much more, **being reconciled**, we shall be saved by his life. And not only so, but we also joy in God through our Lord Jesus Christ, by whom we **have now received the atonement"*** (Romans 5:9-11).

The fact is, no other god even comes close to this awesome Being. No other religious system, philosophy, belief or spirituality even begins to compare to the God of the Bible. He is a God that sinful man would never come up with in his wildest imaginations. In all of his godless thinking, man does just what his parents did in the garden so long ago. He runs away from God and hides and seeks shelter in any vain imagination that will help him accomplish this. But be sure your sin will find you out. So will the love of Christ, if you will receive it. Hallelujah, what a Savior!

Well, these are the elements that have always been present in the world since the rebellion and are a part of all the general ungodliness that characterizes men. But this will all just continue to fill up until it simply overflows into the streets of that great golden city which will represent all that man can possibly achieve. As we find our roots, forces will inexplicably draw our focus back to the land of Shinar. The woman's daughters are even now at play preparing her home. All of the rebellious forces which are trying to dominate the culture today were all foretold in scripture.

We are nothing but dressed up pagans and everything from the drug culture to the revival of necromancy has been anticipated by God. These are not merely foreign ideas which existed far in the past but are forces that have always been at work and will continue to gain dominance with the cooperation of the wickedness of man. It all goes back to the exaltation of self and the prideful father of it as he continues to declare, "I will, I will, I will" (Isaiah 14:11-15). Self will continue to exalt itself against the Creator and reign supreme above all else.

"*This know also, that in the last days perilous times shall come. For men shall be lovers of their own selves, covetous, boasters, proud, blasphemers, disobedient to parents, unthankful, unholy, Without natural affection, trucebreakers, false accusers, incontinent, fierce, despisers of those that are good, Traitors, heady, highminded, lovers of pleasures more than lovers of God; Having a form of godliness, but denying the power thereof: from such turn away...Yea, and all that will live godly in Christ Jesus shall suffer persecution. But evil men and seducers shall wax worse and worse, deceiving and being deceived*" (2 Timothy 3:1-5,12,13).

So much for Christians spreading and/or bringing in the kingdom. The only one who will do that is the Lord Jesus Christ, and only after personally and forcibly taking over when the ungodliness of man has reached its absolute worst. Many of these trends were present in Paul's day and they were simply going to wax worse and worse as the longsuffering of God was extended and man became more "enlightened" and vain in his thinking. But these trends are to increase in a particular way. They will not simply exist *within* the culture as sin always has but they will *be* the culture and completely dominate the atmosphere and direction of society. When you think of a given country what do you naturally associate with it? That is how characteristic these various forms of ungodliness will be.

One of the very interesting trends of ungodliness is the erection by man of a system whereby he defines godliness in an ungodly way. This is to be a major issue as we draw ever closer to the appointed times for earth. He will use the Scriptures as a cloak for his sin and to justify his wickedness. He will speak a great deal of caring, tolerance and morality. "We desire a plurality and diversity of thought, beliefs and opinions." But woe unto the man who disagrees with us. Woe, woe unto the man who will actually stand up for the Creator. That simply will not be tolerated. It is *immoral* for you to express your morality in the law. After all, isn't there a verse that says "judge not."

Never mind how those verses tell you to apply that sentiment. I know, let's use "and they shall beat their swords into plowshares, and their spears into pruning hooks…" and engrave it on the U.N. Never mind the significance that it actually has for the people of earth and the utter destruction and judgement on the nations and world of the ungodly that has preceded it. And never mind that we actually despise the God who wrote it and what He stands for. And never mind that we as a body and institution have taken a hostile stand to the nation that will end up being exalted after the whole messy affair is over. Increasingly in society it is considered immoral to believe what God has said in His Word. Not just a matter of disagreeing mind you, but actually immoral. But of course we don't believe in "immorality"…except…. And on and on the vanity goes.

It used to be that while people in society might engage in all kinds of sinful behavior, there was still the acknowledgement by society that these things were wrong. That is, "I do it because I want to or can't help it but I still know that what I am doing is wrong." But we as a race cannot let this guilty conscience sit for too long. It is only a matter of time before we begin to exonerate ourselves and actually declare our behavior to be natural, virtuous and admirable. Moreover, those who would say that our behavior and conduct is immoral are actually the ones who are evil. They will continue to call good evil and evil good. If God has said that sex is to be enjoyed in the relationship of marriage between a man and a woman and that anything outside of this is immoral, then man will say there is absolutely nothing wrong with sex outside of marriage and will actually come up with a list of reasons why it is desirable and makes sense. The foremost reason, of course, being that he wants to.

When he faces the consequences of such behavior—disease, unwanted children, failing relationships and broken hearts, etc.—does he consider perhaps some of the obvious solutions that God had already declared? No, of course not. Our desire is to be more *ungodly*. Abstinence? Fidelity? You must be joking. No, we would much rather wear ribbons and feel better about ourselves as we fight this most holy and admirable crusade against the plight of AIDS and other sexually transmitted diseases because, after all, we just have to find some way to combat it, don't you know. It's the same game man has played since the beginning. How can I murder you and not get caught? How can I engage in whatever my heart desires and not suffer the consequences.

"*The heart is deceitful above all things, and desperately wicked: who can know it? I the LORD search the heart, I try the reins, even to give every man according to the fruit of his doings*" (Jeremiah 17:9,10).

Oh! There are possible consequences to my actions that might actually mean responsibility for *me*, and not just someone else? That's okay, I'm sure whatever gets in my way I can deal with it. A baby? Just kill it. Why not? Why is it wrong to kill it? Do you want to? Is it an inconvenience for you? Then do it, who cares. Why stop at three months or six months or two years or seven years? Hey, what about that teenager that's a real hassle for you? You don't think it's *wrong* or *immoral*, do you? Because we won't tolerate you pushing your morality on us. Not only that, let's stand up and fight for this most virtuous *right* of ours. To think, someone might actually feel that our actions are wrong. Those people are just downright immoral to try to push their morality on us.

I'm extremely glad we're so much more evolved and enlightened than those primitive peoples and sickening, laughable pagans with their child sacrifice, sexual religious practices and all that. It's so comforting to know that by rejecting and repudiating any idea that is corrupted by the Bible or God, we can achieve a society free from domination and tyranny. All we need is to liberate ourselves from the Creator and only embrace evolution, science, naturalism and humanism. Then we can finally achieve a utopian civilization like China and the Soviet Union. Oh, what a blessed thought! God forbid that we should have a nation founded upon even a semblance of biblical principles. God forbid that the Creator is even remotely acknowledged in the culture, even if it is in a watered down and non-offensive way. God forbid that we have the ten commandments working in the conscience of our children. If we did that, why they just might follow it. Wouldn't that be disastrous?

*"But the LORD of hosts shall be exalted in judgement, and God that is holy shall be sanctified in righteousness... Woe unto them that draw iniquity with cords of vanity, and sin as it were a cart rope: They say, Let him make speed, and hasten his work, that we may see it: and let the counsel of the Holy One of Israel draw nigh and come, that we may know it! Woe unto them that call evil good, and good evil; that put darkness for light, and light for darkness; that put bitter for sweet, and sweet for bitter! Woe unto them that are wise in their own eyes, and prudent in their own sight! Woe unto them that are mighty to drink wine, and men of strength to mingle strong drink: Which justify the wicked for reward, and take away the righteousness of the righteous from him! Therefore as the fire devoureth the stubble, and the flame consumeth the chaff, so their root shall be as rotteness, and their blossom shall go up as dust: because **they have cast away the law** of the LORD of hosts, **and despised** the word of the Holy One of Israel"* (Isaiah 5:16-24).

It is no surprise that evolution has come to the forefront of the culture in bed with all the forces that seek to reach ever higher into the heavens as man continues to move ever forward toward mastering his destiny and vainly seeking the answers to his origins. Why does he care so much? This alone ought to be some kind of clue to this deceived soul that he is more than an accident. Perhaps we will make contact with the beings out there and then finally we will have the answers we so desperately seek. Once again, we lurch closer and closer to Babylon of old and the great tower where that mystical woman's system of wisdom and idolatry began.

One of the defining features of the time before the flood was the contact man had with the space travelers who kept not their first estate. God declares that something akin to those days will make an appearance in the time to come. Man longs for that ancient Tower and even now is preparing the throne of the serpent who offers to satisfy his desires and grant him wisdom and knowledge so that he shall be as gods.

The radical homosexual agenda will continue to increase. It is one thing for a society to say that what goes on in an individual's castle is their own business and we don't want the all-powerful state regulating such matters. Aside from the horrific health consequences of such a lifestyle, many would simply say who cares. But it seems rather obvious that much more than that is being sought after.

One of the features characterizing the end times will be what was going on in Sodom and Gomorrah. Now you have had individuals engaging in unnatural conduct when it comes to their bodies ever since the rebellion, but something more was going on in that infamous area. Individuals were running the place on a homosexual agenda. It dominated the everyday lives of the citizens there and the account of what occurred with Lot should really be no surprise. I will not here delve into the psychological and sociological issues of deviancy as they relate to this topic, as they also do to all the various sexual forces which are sweeping over the land in ever greater tides. Nor do I mean to say that any one individual is more devious than another person who has a fancy for a different particular sin.

But there are deeper forces at work and when they work on the sexual level, there is understandably the capacity for some surprisingly beastly behavior. I am speaking here of a movement, a cultural phenomenon which always has an amplified and often strange impact. There is a definite agenda and you are kidding yourself if you think there isn't. There is a strategy and it is one that seeks to dominate the culture.

As an aside, one of the things said about the coming Antichrist leader is that he doesn't regard "...*the desire of women*" (Daniel 11:37). I must confess that I am not exactly sure of all this description entails. I do not think, as many do, that this is a reference to the Messiah as the desire of women. I have no doubt that this is a reference to Genesis 3:16. It does not, however, necessarily mean the Antichrist will be a homosexual, but it may be significant as to the major influences working at that time. Study it for yourself. It seems that among other things he will not be subject to the politics of his fathers as described in Daniel 11:1-20. Furthermore, it seems that this particular characteristic of his will stand out as he counterfeits Christ. However, the strongest connection seems to be to Solomon. His downfall was his insatiable appetite for and love of many strange women. The adoption and worship of their gods brought the utter corruption and downfall of Solomon and his kingdom. So, when this issue about the Antichrist is pointed out to us, it is in the following context. "*And the king shall do according to his will; and he shall exalt himself, and magnify himself above every god...Neither shall he regard the God of his fathers, nor the desire of women, nor regard any god: for he shall magnify himself above all.*" His downfall will not be that of Solomon's. Interestingly, it seems that it will be his opposite response that will ultimately bring about his ruin. There will only be two others that he will honor at that time and it will apparently get him into trouble with the "mingled" people and everyone else for that matter.

The current homosexual agenda—and I stress that is what I am addressing here, not individuals per se—is an agenda, a radical one. I realize that many would differ with the characterization of "radical" but that is because of the moral choice you have already made in your own mind concerning the matter. Gay marriages are permissible but polygamy is not, or whatever it is you choose to include and exclude in your circle of tolerance. After all, heterosexual marriage just perpetuates the patriarchal system of oppression. In fact, maybe we should just abolish this institution altogether. Oh, what freedom we would enjoy if we would just liberate ourselves from these archaic bondages of the past. Don't look now, but I smell a serpent.

This force will continue to expand and dominate the culture. It will in some measure be state sponsored as we continue to wipe out "discrimination." This is not tolerance, this is social engineering and it is where all the smart people play the game. It is not enough to simply kill someone. But if it was a "hate crime," oh my, now we're talking. That's really bad. Why? Well its *immoral* and…" Here we go again. This by the people who are constantly complaining about the imposition of morality. If you can control the education system, then you can control the adults and society of tomorrow. It's about fooling yourself into thinking that you are not making moral choices when that is all you are doing every step of the way. Not only is it good politics but it helps to perpetuate your vain deception of yourself. There is One, however, who truly judges the thoughts and intents of the heart and He is the One you will have to answer to, no matter who you may fool down here.

This is also true when it comes to radical feminism, especially as it relates to the emasculation and feminizing of men (effeminate). All of this is a big issue with God, and with Satan for that matter in his assault on God as *Creator*. But more for our purposes they are characteristics which will dominate the culture. It should be noted that the previous behaviors, while often joined, are not necessarily the same. One may engage in homosexual conduct and not be effeminate, and one may be effeminate and not engage in homosexual conduct. But they are all part of the same stream of rebelliousness against the Creator.

It all goes back to the natural use of what God has designed and created and what He says about the blurring of the sexual lines and identity. Forces are at play that are working very hard at exploiting this and they will only increase as we move ever closer to the time of judgement. The old female cults will continue to regain their spiritual control as never before and lead the culture on to enlightenment.

This force is the sister to radical environmentalism which, at its heart, is really religious. I do not speak here of those who desire to be good stewards of what is around them. But I will simply say that they are most likely ignorant of what lies behind the leadership of these movements—and that is just what is on the surface. Forces and beings are actually at work who have a very long history and much experience when it comes to these matters. All of these are nothing more than neo-paganism, the old cults revived and the worship of anything and everything except the one true God. At least there are some today in these movements who are honest enough to admit it, nay proud.

I find it interesting that these forces are almost always to be found together. If there is no connection between them, why are they invariably assembled with one another. These are not mere loose attachments but highly organized, rabid and angry movements that seek to push their agenda through any and all means at their disposal, especially intimidation. But of course it is for a "good" cause. The ferocity and radical fundamentalism of these groups as a whole easily rivals anything found by those on the anti-abortion sides and other opposition as a whole and, in my mind, far exceeds it. It is absolutely fascinating to observe the bed in which are gathered evolution, alien-ology, "new age," eastern mysticism, communism, the assorted tolerance movements and neo-evangelicalism. This is no accident. The same spirit animates all of them and I think it is getting pretty restless as its hour to arise and shine as never before approaches.

The battle is for the mind and for the youth. The agendas seek to shape people's thinking through domination of the culture.

These particular forces are often state sponsored and are introduced into the government, workplace and education system in a number of ways and all in the name of tolerance and enlightenment. A wide range of mediums are also available today by which a subtle numbing influence comes over the culture and is able to move the societal ship just a few degrees, but that is all it takes for the ship to get disastrously and hopelessly off course.

This is why I have nothing but praise for those involved in home-schooling. It is truly one of the last frontiers of liberty and freedom from statism, tyranny and mind control. The key is to be aware of what is going on in the culture and schools and take action. It is your responsibility as a parent to meet the challenge. It is not enough to complain. It is even worse to be blind. You are in large measure responsible for what becomes of your children. You are not supposed to be their buddy. You are their parent. Your job is to *train* them. And don't simply do the reverse of the pagan culture. Don't brainwash them with the truth. Train them to think. Train them to analyze for themselves. Show them *why* it is the truth and why the other is false. If you don't equip them, they will be nothing but fodder for the academic and cultural forces in the world. Teach them to be truly tolerant.

Whatever you do, don't buy into the ridiculous and nonsensical relativism of the new tolerance. This is a force that demands your approval, not just your tolerance; a force that demands you accept the belief that one way, system, lifestyle, and so on, is just as good as another—unless, of course, it has to do with the Creator and is at variance with the elites and keepers of wisdom. This is a force that declares it immoral to declare something immoral, unless of course it is something our great tolerant person finds offensive. This vanity will only increase to more ungodliness and you need to be on guard.

Man as a whole will continue to embrace all that is a fundamental repudiation of the Creator. It is no surprise that man runs to the system of evolution and moral relativism as it provides a justification and cloak for all kinds of sins against the absolutes set out by the Creator. But there is a problem—vanity. If there are no absolutes, then there are no absolutes. If all things are relative, then all things are relative. First of all, this statement is stupid and intellectually bankrupt. If there are no absolutes, then you can't make that absolute statement. The logic of this is just a reflection of the fact that there are absolutes. But furthermore, we hold this truth in ourselves. We may try to desensitize ourselves to that conscience but it is nevertheless present testifying to us.

"Now the Spirit speaketh expressly, that in the latter times some shall depart from the faith, giving heed to seducing spirits, and doctrines of devils; Speaking lies in hypocrisy; having their conscience seared with a hot iron" (1 Timothy 4:1,2).

"This I say therefore, and testify in the Lord, that ye walk not as other Gentiles walk, in the vanity of their mind, Having the understanding darkened, being alienated from the life of God through the ignorance that is in them, because of the blindness of their heart: Who being past feeling have given themselves over unto lasciviousness, to work all uncleaness with greediness" (Ephesians 4:17-19).

And, of course, our heart is deceitful above all else, so it is hardly an accurate and dependable guide. This is part of the unrighteousness we hold the truth in, so we try to apply and figure out this truth that we know according to our deceived and unrighteous ways. The result is the vanity of all the philosophies and systems man has erected. Man needs to receive godly counsel from the One who is perfect in holiness.

If everything is relative, then I will just shoot you right now simply because I feel like it. It isn't wrong. It may be inefficient or whatever for society as a whole but not wrong. There have even been arguments made in the past concerning murder that such action is desirable for the very reason that it *is* efficient and productive; i.e., bringing about a more advanced species. But the fact is that we know it's morally wrong. And the ones who cry the loudest about not imposing your morality on them are often the ones who support all kinds of agendas and issues that stand on absolutely nothing more than morality. "It is immoral not to allow certain people to engage in...You have no right to tell someone...I can do whatever I want with my body...." Aside from not being true anyway (laws concerning drugs, prostitution, etc.) it is a moral choice. "Intolerance is immoral." Where did that morality come from?

My only point is that you might believe the thoughts expressed above and buy into various agendas but they all express your morality. You want relativism in favor of your morality and are actually quite intolerant of those who dissent. True tolerance says that even though I think you are wrong, you still have the right to think and believe what you want, speak and debate. I recognize your inherent worth and value as an individual with a right to your own understanding of issues, but those whose cry is tolerance are the first ones to silence those whose views they find unacceptable. You are not even allowed to think certain things. This is why I personally find much of these movements to be dangerous. The Political Correctness police are the Gestapo for these movements and they desire to enforce compliance to the will of these various groups.

This "imposition of morality" complaint is nothing more than a political ploy. The law is all about imposing morality and setting codes. The question is *whose* morality. But, as all good propaganda, it is beneficial to your cause because it sets up a false situation and choice. Any system that attempts to dismantle the idea of morality is just nonsense and manifests the vanity of man's thinking because, in order to do so, it must itself stand on a superior moral foundation that somehow trumps the system it seeks to replace as the standard. It does not necessarily mean that the positions advanced are invalid, but the arguments and justifications used are often vacuous.

Greater forces are at work in the culture. Why is there such opposition on the part of some to parental consent concerning minors and abortions? In any other kind of serious operation or "medical procedure," parental consent is a given and not even remotely brought into question. Yet here there is opposition to the very idea of it. Why? There are values and principles being fought for at all costs. Those values are part of the larger trends, and part of the legs holding up the great animal-like force continuing to dominate the landscape.

The rise of the welfare state is just another example of the ungodliness of man as those in power will continue to exploit certain groups for their own political benefit and create an ever-growing reliance and dependency upon the government. Notice I said "welfare state," not charity. They are not the same and should not be confused. Charity is considered by God to be a great virtue and something He desires to overflow in the hearts of all believers. In fact we are exhorted, *"Let him that stole steal no more: but rather let him labour, working with his hands the thing which is good, that he may have to give him that needeth"* (Ephesians 4:28).

The welfare state, however, is nothing but legalized theft and the product of an entitlement philosophy. Forget about receiving from another's generosity, I'll just take it. Or, I can really feel better about myself and take it from you so I can give it to someone else. The fact that there is no longer shame attached to being on the public dole is no accident. There is such a thing as a healthy guilt and a healthy shame.

It used to be understood—even by those we were truly desirous to aid such as single mothers, widows, etc.—that they were being given the money someone else had worked hard for to provide for themselves and their family. They were often reluctant to accept help and most certainly there was not the deluded idea that they were somehow entitled to it. This country was built upon the idea that we have the right to *pursue* happiness. We are not entitled to happiness itself. But, as we strive for ungodliness, if God says there should be shame in connection with it, then we declare there should in no wise be shame associated with it.

"For yourselves know how ye ought to follow us: for we behaved not ourselves disorderly among you; Neither did we eat any man's bread for nought; but wrought with labor and travail night and day, that we might not be chargeable to any of you...For even when we

*were with you, this we commanded you, that if any would not work, neither should he eat. For we hear that there are some which walk among you disorderly, working not at all, but are busybodies. Now them that are such we command and exhort by our Lord Jesus Christ, that with quietness they work, and eat **their own** bread. But ye, brethren, be not weary in well doing. And if any man obey not our word by this epistle, note that man, and have no company with him, that he may be **ashamed**. Yet count him not as an enemy, but admonish him as a brother"* (2 Thessalonians 3:7,8,10-15).

This is just a sampling of some of the notable and significant trends of ungodliness as outlined in Scripture. They are not necessarily more important or more evil than other acts of rebelliousness but are characteristics that will surprisingly dominate the culture more and more as time passes. We could just as easily have surveyed the issue of interest in angels and the revival of spiritualism taking place on a whole new level or good old-fashioned fornication and the general culture of lasciviousness and escape which may hit home a little more for some. UFOs and alien-ology are also a very significant development for the days ahead.

But the trends we have seen generally need a helping hand, so to speak, from the state and therefore have a dominating *political* influence. The whole point is that they are not content to merely work on the private and personal ungodly level but instead often work in far more subtle ways through the political arena. For many involved in these movements everything is politics and the battle over conforming to certain policies will only heat up. They desire something more than just "tolerance" and have an agenda to accomplish it.

All of these are a part of man's ungodly culture, but these particular trends represent somewhat of a departure from generally accepted norms and therefore will employ the cooperation of the state to help force the culture in the "right" direction. They demand acceptance and validation from society and expect others to extol the virtues of such ideas and lifestyles. Anything less is intolerant and bigoted. They are set forth as the official policies of the government and therefore take on a whole new dimension in their manifestation of ungodliness. These ungodly trends can be summed up by man's preoccupation with and exaltation of self. Man has always been rebellious but something unique is to develop and flourish as we approach the end of this ungodliness. *"For men shall be lovers of their own selves...lovers of pleasures more than lovers of God"* (2 Timothy 3:1,4).

Everything listed in 2 Timothy 3 would not only be present as realities but would be gloried in by society as a whole. This is often the case in many of the subcultures that exist in our society but they are striving to *be the culture* and every indication is that they will eventually succeed to a large extent. God is to be cast away because we realize the restraining influence His presence has, even if He is only recognized in a general way. There is something we desire more than the truth because too often we don't like its implications.

We now have the phenomenon of a culture dominated by the idea of self and *self*-esteem. Everything revolves around *me*. Forget about the real and major problems that have faced the human race at various times throughout history. If I don't see my therapist at least once a week I just won't be able to go on. We are moving at such a pace that we have even named our ungodliness according to the Scripture magnifying the very word and idea of self. Should a murderer feel good about himself? If not, why? This is just bunk and is the height of man loving himself. Man's problem is not a lack of self-esteem, his problem is too much of it. He is consumed with his own person and the idea of finding himself. If he were more concerned about the truth and focusing on the One who has the answers rather than himself he might actually find relief.

Man really does like himself and that is why he cares so much. If you really hated yourself you wouldn't care and might even be glad. But of course after man has manifested his utter preoccupation with himself, he tries to cloak himself with the idea that he is really selfless and couldn't dislike himself more. "*And because iniquity shall abound, the love of many shall wax cold.*" (Matthew 24:12).

This is the exaltation of self which is the opposite of *agape* love, or charity, as it is described in the Bible. *Agape* love is *self*-less love or charity. "*If there be therefore any **consolation** in Christ, if any **comfort** of **love**, if any fellowship of the Spirit, if any bowels and **mercies**, Fulfill ye my joy, that ye be likeminded, having the same **love**, being of one accord, of one mind. Let nothing be done through strife or vainglory; but in lowliness of mind let each **esteem other** better than **themselves**. Look not every man on his own things, but every man also on the things of others*" (Philippians 2:1-4).

The more man focuses on self, the deeper he will make the hole he sought to climb out of in the first place. It should be no surprise that the industry of therapy that has perpetuated this preoccupation with self arose from the psychological philosophies and premises of individuals who identified man's problems as being the result of guilt. Well, we can't have that, we're special and we want to pursue all kinds of ungodliness unhindered. So, we continue to erect ideologies and philosophies that enthrone self as never before while, at the same time, systematically removing God and everything that might stand in our deceived and darkened way.

Why? Because iniquity shall abound. Because we *love* those things. We must convince ourselves that there really is no problem of sin dwelling in our innermost being. Anything we want or desire is perfectly okay and should be indulged. We worship ourselves and bow down to these idols that we devote ourselves to. They are usually beliefs and movements that are nothing more than fronts for our rebelliousness and the gods of wisdom and enlightenment that we seek to honor and thereby gain liberation.

Absolutely nothing has changed from that garden of long ago. We come up with as many justifications as we can to eat of the forbidden fruit. We would rather believe the serpent because he is willing to tell us whatever we want to hear. "*Then your eyes shall be opened, and ye shall be as gods, knowing good and evil*" (Genesis 3:5).

Man does not have a problem with self-esteem, he has a problem with self. His problem is a lack of *God*-esteem. In his rebelliousness he seeks enlightenment but all he will find is depravity and darkness. In his pursuit to be as gods he reaches nothing but the depths of *ungodliness*. "…*Heady, highminded, lovers of pleasures more than lovers of God*" (2 Timothy 3:4). These all go together and man only proves himself to be a fool in his denial of the One who gives him life, and through his sinful and disobedient conduct man demonstrates that he is indeed worthy of the judgment of God.

It is absolutely amazing when you track this ungodly evolution to see man follow the exact course that God said he would take. We keep moving "forward" and eventually we will come to the time when God will say enough is enough. His longsuffering will end and the record will be set straight. Everything will be revealed and man will discover that God really was telling the truth all along and the serpent was nothing but a liar. Unfortunately, by then it will be too late. "*For in the day that thou eatest thereof thou shalt surely die*" (Genesis 2:17).

Only the truth of God's word will protect us from the deceit of our own heart and rebelliousness. Only the living Word can renew our minds, transform our thinking and set us on the proper course. However, this world as a whole will continue down the course set for it. Never put your trust in an institution, nation or mere man. There are times when a nation, a leader and a culture should be praised. But blind allegiance is dangerous and the descent to tyranny is often a subtle one. The pressure to conform to the global community is only going to increase.

Our human systems, just as the very powerful forces in the universe, have the capacity for great good, but they are equally capable of great evil. The genius may be able to use his great ability to achieve truly wondrous things. But that also means that same genius may choose to use that power for diabolical purposes. Just ask Lucifer.

Democracy is no safeguard. Hitler was the people's choice. Never mind the fact that this nation was not begun as a pure democracy anyway nor was it meant to be. A people may use a truly admirable system in any way they want. Our American system has always rested on a very delicate balance.

The founders understood that the success of this nation rested with the people. What would *the people* do with the system they had been given? In connection with this, it is interesting to note the importance they placed on religion and its role in society and the virtues of the people who would control this nation and its institutions. "Our Constitution was made for a moral and religious people. It is wholly inadequate to the government of any other" (John Adams).

Success and plenty breed discontent. Without something to fight for and real danger in our midst we begin to lend our time and thinking to the most ridiculous things. We forget what is really important. We also forget the work that went into giving us the bounty in the first place. One of the results of this phenomenon is the victimization syndrome that has come upon us as a society. That is not the spirit that made this country great in the first place. Contrary to its declared compassionate intentions, it does nothing but pander to man's need to blame and perpetuate the cycle of dependency crippling those we wish to help, emboldening others to follow their course, and punishing those that produce and refuse to be victimized by all the well intentioned intelligentsia.

Remember, Lucifer tightens his grip by proclaiming liberty. He is just here to help and make you feel better. Especially if it means you will continue in the path of ungodliness. All the while, however, he is securing his position and weighing his victim down with even more shackles. He works very hard at employing helpers in these endeavors and training prophets and teachers who are able to go out and show forth "his ways" to the people. This makes his job easier and also gives him a sick sense of satisfaction as he continues to deceive and delude this race of earth dwellers, keeping them in darkness and bondage to him.

Often it is only by facing the consequences of our actions that we are forced to change and be saved from an even greater destruction down the road. When we coddle sin we do nothing but make ourselves feel better and increase the burden upon the other people in society who, though not perfect by any means, are at least working hard and doing their jobs. We make victims of the guilty and those who often simply need to "get a grip" and acquire some soberness of thinking. We do this while, at the same time, we blame those who are productive members of society or truly victims at the hands of criminals. There is always someone to blame, always some oppressor. We refuse to take responsibility and, when confronted, we not only deny responsibility but offer another in our place because we know that justice has been offended and must be pacified.

"And he said, Who told thee that thou wast naked? Hast thou eaten of the tree, whereof I commanded thee that thou shouldest not eat? And the man said, The woman whom thou gavest to be with me, she gave me of the tree, and I did eat" (Genesis 3:11,12).

Of course, it isn't my fault. I may have done it, but I can't really be held responsible. It's the powers that be. The system, the man, the ones in authority, the people around me. Yeah, everybody else, in fact the woman that "**thou** hast given me." Sure enough, God has to be blamed at some point for the choices we make. "That's just the way I am, God made me like that." "This mind altering substance is okay, God made it, it's natural." Well, I suppose you won't object to me taking over the world and sparing no one because that's how God made me, a psychopathic megalomaniac. And I suppose you won't object to me taking this rock and hitting you over the head with it because it's natural. God made it.

This is absurd but it's the kind of thinking that goes on in the vanity of man's darkened heart and mind as he seeks to justify his behavior. In his vanity, however, he fails to see the ludicrous nature of his justifications and their logical consequences and implications if followed through. He doesn't want to accept responsibility for what he has *chosen* to do with his will.

"Someone made me do it." Absolutely anyone is a candidate but me. "The devil made me do it." This does nothing but hide the truth of the matter. The devil is responsible for many ills, but this is the one area where he is unjustly accused. Where you pursue ungodliness he is *successful* to be sure. But you are the one who did it, you made the choice. You chose to follow him and he thereby gets the glory, as opposed to God, by having you submit your will to his. He didn't force Eve to do anything, He *beguiled* her. No doubt she thought she was in control the whole time. Boy, she was going to be as a god. "It's my life and I can do whatever I want with it. Look at me, I'm in charge." But when it's time to face the consequences of my actions, then I'm not such a big man anymore. All of sudden I wasn't *really* in control. Mercy, mercy judge! But even as Eve is confronted and she passes blame to the serpent, her burden isn't that she has broken the heart of the Creator who has given her everything she has in the first place; rather it's that "*the serpent beguiled me, and I did eat.*" (Genesis 3:13). He lied to me, how dare him. Actually he only told a *little* white lie, what's the harm? He just didn't tell her the *whole* story. He takes the truth and begins to shape it to foster discontent and appeal to man's selfishness and rebelliousness. He doesn't care, he got what he wanted. Friend, he has no concern for you and certainly wouldn't die on a cross for you. In fact, he finds it utterly confusing and incomprehensible that the spurned and rejected Creator would endure such humiliation and pain for such an unworthy and rebellious race as ours. But thank God that He "*so loved the world, that he gave his only begotten Son, that whosoever believeth in him should not perish, but have everlasting life.*" (Jn 3:16)

No, the devil can't make you do anything, that's part of the fight. But you most certainly can cooperate with him. And as we noted earlier, he likes to employ others in his service to carry out his work. He has many "useful idiots" in this world who are so deluded in their thinking that he is able to take them captive at his will. He taught Eve well and before long she was spreading the "good" word and teaching others these liberating ways. He really is a smart one. Eve was able to get Adam to do something that he might not otherwise have done if the serpent had approached him directly. He will use anything at his disposal to convince you to follow him. Different strokes for different folks. He may appeal to your sense of decency or spirituality, he may appeal to the depths of your depravity and debauchery. He may impugn the Bible and decry all things religious, he may extol the Word of God—as he did to Jesus in the wilderness—and offer to teach you from it. It really doesn't matter to him. As long as you end up taking his lead, he has achieved one more success.

"*But I fear, lest by any means, as the serpent beguiled Eve through his subtilty, so your minds should be corrupted from the simplicity that is in Christ*" (2 Corinthians 11:3).

He is a liar and the only protection is the truth. There must be soberness and renewal of thinking through the preservation of God's words in our mind. We must humble ourselves and believe what God has said, knowing that we can trust *Him*. If we choose to follow Him, we will in no wise end up being disappointed. "*...yea, let God be true, but every man a liar; as it is written, That thou mightest be justified in thy sayings, and mightest overcome when thou art judged.*" (Romans 3:4). But if we reject Him, reject His Word, and the truth, then that void is left to be filled with nothing but darkness and vanity. Without the preserving effect and power of the words of life, our minds and hearts are left to decay and corruption. As a junkie dependent on his dealer for a fix, this process can work in the heart of a rebellious one to such an extent that he will return time after time for the words of his pied piper. "*And the servant of the Lord must not strive; but be gentle unto all men, apt to teach, patient, In meekness instructing those that oppose themselves; if God peradventure will give them repentance to the acknowledging of the truth; And that they may recover themselves out of the snare of the devil, who are taken captive by him at his will*" (2 Timothy 2:24-26).

As long as old man Adam is around we will continue to play the blame game and search for victims. As applied to crime it means that innocent people are often victimized because of a lack of resolve in punishment and an "enlightened" understanding of the criminal's motivations. After all, can we really hold him responsible? In some way, aren't we all to blame for what he has done. Aren't we really the ones at fault for the criminal's activity?

"*Woe unto them that **draw iniquity with cords of vanity,** and sin as it were a cart rope…Woe unto them that call evil good and good evil; that put darkness for light, and light for darkness; that put bitter for sweet, and sweet for bitter! Woe unto them that are wise in their own eyes, and prudent in their own sight!…Which **justify the wicked** for reward, and **take away** the righteousness of the righteous from him!*" (Isaiah 5:18,20-23). As long as we are playing this blame game, who has committed the greater sin—the criminal or the coddler?

The point is that in relation to the governments and institutions of this world, a system is only as good as the keepers of it which is why we need to place our trust in God. Our own government has been an experiment in freedom with many successes through the years, and has made an impact in this world to be felt for many years to come. However, with freedom comes choice and with sinful man that choice is very likely to be the wrong one. No matter what forces seemingly work against each other, they are all working together and moving us forward to the time when man's ungodliness has overflowed and the wrath of God is poured out.

The Bible makes it clear that the rebellion against the Creator is only going to continue and actually increase as time marches on. These are modern trends but part of an old story as we reach unto the heavens. The stage is even now being set. The events of September 11 have taught us how quickly the world scene can change in an instant. We are once more being brought back to the Middle East and that ancient land. Israel will continue to be the focal point as the nations round about her continue to scheme for her annihilation.

"*The burden of the word of the LORD for Israel, saith the LORD, which stretcheth forth the heavens, and layeth the foundation of the earth, and formeth the spirit of man within him. Behold, I will make Jerusalem a cup of trembling unto all the people round about, when they shall be in siege both against Judah and against Jerusalem. And in that day will I make Jerusalem a burdensome stone for all people: all that burden themselves with it shall be cut in pieces, though all the people of the earth be gathered together against it"* (Zechariah 12:1-3).

Though the Arab world may be divided on a host of issues, one subject that brings them in unity to the table is the utter destruction of Israel from off the map. This too is being driven by ancient and powerful forces. Just what international events will occur before those ten horns are crowned is anybody's guess. What is sure is that the tiny little land and city over in the Middle East will continue to be that burdensome stone for all the governments of the world just as the Lord declared it would be. Peace in the Middle East will be the cry and concern of all nations. The emerging war on terror is inextricably tied to the Israeli issue and it is becoming ever more apparent that the world's destiny is linked to Israel's.

Let me engage, however, in a bit of prognostication based upon what we are to expect from the picture given in the Bible beyond the general trends of conflict that will continue to face Israel in the days ahead. If my understanding of Scripture is correct, then the pieces will need to be put in place for the future Assyrian state. The ancient power of Assyria has seemingly lost its distinct identity and land. The land is indeed there but the political and governmental identity is gone. It seems clear to me that ancient Assyria is to play a very prominent role in the time to come as is Egypt. The impact will be so great that Assyria is mentioned along with Egypt as being specially noticed in the kingdom. I predict that in accordance with the reemergence of Assyria we are going to see a separate regime emerge in Northern Iraq.

With that in mind, I would say that Turkey should be concerned with the southeastern portion of its country as well as Iran with its northwestern section. I believe those portions of the Middle East are destined to be brought together in governmental unity according to the ancient boundaries of Assyria. With that accomplished the political structure will be in place for the future kings of the north spoken of in Daniel 11 and the arrival of Daniel's fourth beast marked by the "Beginning of Sorrows." My understanding of this issue could, of course, be faulty and may turn out not to be a necessity at all. It may be that the Man of Sin will simply emerge from within the basic region of Northern Iraq. Only time will tell. However, it is interesting that Turkey, the surrounding northern regions and Iran, along with others, will come against that Antichrist at the time of the end in accordance with Ezekiel 38. Given what the modern situation has been in the Middle East concerning these nations, that is an easy scenario to foresee.

Nevertheless, what is certain is that Iraq and the land of Shinar are destined to once again return to center stage with Israel. Both are going to demand the world's attention as the end approaches. The Assyrian is going to emerge and put together a great and mighty Middle Eastern kingdom. The final king of the North will initially seemingly put an end to the ancient hatred, the Arab/Israeli conflict. Jerusalem will no doubt briefly enjoy a short stint as a truly international and interfaith city, providing a symbol for what is humanly possible with a platform and policy of peace. It will be one more grand achievement for mankind as he proves just what kind of society he can create with all his good intentions and "progress."

But alas, human nature remains the same. And beware, once I have your guns, you're mine! That amazing leader and peacemaker will be manifested for who he truly is. The infamous wicked woman, the harlot of Revelation, will return to her home in the re-established world city of Babylon. It is then that the serpent's long-sought-after dream will finally be realized. That great rulership and power that has been hindered since the days of Nimrod will be let loose on this world. He will believe that it is *his* day, but he will find that it is the Lord's Day after all.

"*That thou keep this commandment without spot, unrebukeable, until the appearing of our Lord Jesus Christ: Which in his times he shall shew, who is the blessed and only Potentate, the King of kings, and Lord of lords*" (1 Timothy 6:14,15).

In connection with this let me also make a brief comment on what I see as the utter lack of vision that exists on the part of many biblical commentators and prophecy buffs. Now, I mean no disrespect, but when I hear things like, "I can't imagine the United States not being involved" or "I can't envision Babylon becoming an important part of the coming global structure," I just have to wonder. You are, of course, free to differ as to just what you believe the Scriptures indicate for the coming times but that sort of reasoning is foolish. Just thinking of the United States' relatively recent history and emergence as a superpower ought to be enough to dispel that sort of thinking. Or what about the sun never setting on the British empire? The list could go and on but I would simply caution the student of Scripture that political structures can change in an instant, let alone over a generation or two. This is especially true when there is an economic crisis or major military conflict, and it is exactly that sort of turmoil that will pave the way for the coming world leader.

But this will all be on God's time, regardless of what we think we see happening around us. When WWI occurred many thought the tribulation was right on the doorstep. When WWII occurred many thought the tribulation was right on the doorstep. When the nation of Israel was formally recognized in 1948 many thought the tribulation was right on the doorstep. I do believe all of these events were significant in that they were crucial for setting the stage for the coming play. However, the play has not yet started. When it does you can then look back and see how various events, including September 11, worked to prepare the world for that time. But until then, the various props are being put into place and the actors are being groomed and readied. So, sure it's on the doorstep. But 1948 was more than 50 years ago. It is still extremely important for preparing for the time to come but don't forget how God sees and handles the passing hours of our domain.

The fact is that the Rapture could have occurred before 1948. It didn't, but hindsight is 20/20. In fact, most dispensational prophecy writers before 1948 thought that the Jews would be reconstituted in the land in accordance with the arrival of the Antichrist and his seven year agreement. Many more unexpected things may yet happen to the Jews and their control of the land, sovereignty, etc. before the arrival of the Antichrist, but the Rapture is dependent upon none of them.

We are not in the "end times." We are in the Dispensation of the grace of God to the Gentiles. As long as this period continues, the events of the "end times" are delayed. This administration of God, characterized as being the *longsuffering* of God, is literally extended day by day. The last days began with Pentecost but did not run to their expected end. God revealed that He was interrupting that prophetic program to do something new. We are described as those *"upon whom the ends of the world are come"* (1 Corinthians 10:11).

The only thing standing between this world and the prophetic "end times" is what God is currently doing among the Gentiles. Every day that goes by is quite literally the extension of God's grace and peace to a world that was, and is, ready to receive His wrath. But as long as His mercy and longsuffering continues to be offered, man's ungodliness will continue to increase. So once again, we may very well see things as they are moved into place for the coming time, but our departure is dependent upon none of them. Remember, the world will continue on after we leave. It picks up where this Dispensation ends. The trends of ungodliness are to continue and increase through this Dispensation right up into the Lord's Day.

*"Grace be to you and peace from God the Father, and from the Lord Jesus Christ, Who gave himself for our sins, that he might deliver us from **this present evil world**, according to **the will** of God and our Father"* (Galatians 1:3,4).

*"See then that ye walk circumspectly, not as fools, but as **wise**, **Redeeming the time**, because **the days are evil**. Wherefore be ye not unwise, but **understanding** what **the will** of the Lord is"* (Ephesians 5:15-17).

"*Walk in* **wisdom** *toward them that are without,* **redeeming the time**" (Colossians 4:5).

"*And now ye know what with-holdeth that he might be revealed in his time. For* **the mystery of iniquity doth already work:** *only he who now letteth will let, until he be taken out of the way*" (2 Thessalonians 6, 7).

"*This know also, that in the last days perilous times shall come...But evil men and seducers* **shall wax worse and worse,** *deceiving and being deceived*" (2 Timothy 3:1,13).

"*The Lord is not slack concerning his promise, as some men count slackness; but is longsuffering to us-ward, not willing that any should perish, but that all should come to repentance. But the day of the Lord will come...And account that* **the longsuffering of our Lord** *is salvation; even as our beloved brother Paul also* **according to the wisdom given unto him** *hath written unto you; As also in all his epistles, speaking in them of these things; in which are some things hard to be understood...*" (2 Peter 3:9,10,15,16).

Knowing what we do about this time we live in, it is quite natural therefore that we should see activity consistent with what is prophesied to come. However, God could just as easily bring certain pieces into place in an instant, weeks, months or years.

It is only a matter of time before that woman takes her seat as the lady of kingdoms, the golden city, to reign over the kings of the earth. Soon the call will be heard, "Intermission is over, the show is about to resume." And then the Lord will begin to perform "*his work, his* **strange** *work; and bring to pass his act, his* **strange** *act. Now therefore be ye not mockers, lest your bands be made strong: for I have heard from the Lord GOD of hosts a consumption, even determined upon* **the whole earth**...*This also cometh forth from the LORD of hosts, which is wonderful* **in counsel,** *and excellent in working*" (Isaiah 28:21,22,29).

"*I will therefore put you in remembrance, though ye once knew this, how that the Lord, having saved the people out of the land of Egypt, afterward destroyed them that believed not. And the angels which kept not* **their** *first* **estate,** *but* **left** *their own habitation, he* *hath reserved in everlasting chains under darkness unto the judgement of the great day. Even as Sodom and Gomorrah, and the cities about them in like manner, giving themselves over to fornication, and going after strange flesh, are set forth for an example, suffering the vengeance of eternal fire...And Enoch also, the seventh from Adam, prophesied of these, saying, Behold, the Lord cometh with ten thousands of his saints, To execute judgment upon all, and to convince all that are* **ungodly** *among them of all their* **ungodly** *deeds which they have* **ungodly** *committed, and of all their hard speeches which* **ungodly** *sinners have spoken against him. These are murmurers,* **complainers,** *walking after their own lusts; and their mouth speaketh* **great swelling words,** *having men's persons in admiration because of advantage...How that they told you there should be mockers in the last time, who should walk after their own ungodly lusts. These be they who separate themselves, sensual, having not the Spirit...And of some have compassion, making a difference: And others save with fear, pulling them out of the fire; hating even the garment spotted by the flesh"* (Jude 5-7,14-19,22,23)

— Chapter Twelve —

A Final Thought

First of all, if you are not a believer in the Lord Jesus Christ, I would encourage you to prayerfully consider the things you have read but, most importantly, turn your attention to Christ. He is the One I point you to, the One you should desire. The only words that really matter are the Lord's. I would never ask you to trust Christ so you could be "just like me." You need to trust Christ so you can be what *He* wants you to be, what you need to be. I fail. I disappoint. I am fallible and make far too many mistakes than I could recount here.

"*Not as though I had already attained, either were already perfect: but I follow after, if that I may apprehend that for which also I am apprehended of Christ Jesus. Brethren, I count not myself to have apprehended: but this one thing I do, forgetting those things which are behind, and reaching forth unto those things which are before, I press toward the mark for the prize of the high calling of God in Christ Jesus*" (Philippians 3:12-14). To be just like me is less than desirable. Ah, but to be like Christ, that is far better.

I cannot save you but I can tell you how you can be saved. I can communicate the message that God has committed to my trust through His word. And, believe me, I take the utmost care in doing so because I will have to answer to Him for how I have represented Him to you and presumed to speak on His behalf and in His stead. I will simply tell you that He is a truly awesome God, One with whom there is no equal or rival. He asks you to believe what He has said through His Word and promises that you can bank your soul on it. His word is sure and what He has said He will perform, it is guaranteed.

What He wants is to put His grace and wisdom on display in such an abundant way that there is nothing left to do but simply bow in utter amazement at the sheer marvel of it all. He has paid an extremely high and harsh price to be able to make this offer of grace to you. And so, "*I do not frustrate the grace of God: for if righteousness come by the law, then Christ is dead in vain.*" (Gal 2:21).

You need to be saved. You need to have a transformation take place whereby you can be acceptable to God and not have Him hold your prior offenses against you. You need a righteousness that you simply don't have. You cannot do this yourself. That is a debt you could never pay in a million years, regardless of how good you may think you are. The situation you are in is hopeless. You stand in the courtroom before the judge, justly accused, and all you can do is wait for the verdict to be read and shuffle off to the judgement you rightly deserve.

But then, a message is delivered to you. "*For Abraham believed God, and it was counted unto him for righteousness. Now to him that worketh is the reward not reckoned of grace, but of debt. But to him that worketh not, but believeth on him that justifieth the ungodly, his faith is counted for righteousness. Even as David also describeth the blessedness of the man, unto whom God imputeth righteousness without works. Saying, Blessed are they whose iniquities are forgiven, and whose sins are covered. Blessed is the man to whom the Lord will not impute sin*" (Romans 4:4-8).

But how can a holy and righteous judge let you go without offending justice? Someone must pay for the crimes you have committed. "*And therefore it was imputed to him for righteousness. Now it was not written for his sake alone, that it was imputed to him; But for us also, to whom it shall be imputed, if we believe on him that raised up Jesus our Lord from the dead; Who was delivered for our offences, and was raised again for our justification. Therefore being justified by faith, we have peace with God through our Lord Jesus Christ*" (Romans 4:22-25; 5:1).

It's not about you asking Jesus to do anything. It's about receiving what Christ has already done for you. He is the One who makes the invitation, not you. He offers you a free gift based on what He has already done. It is incumbent upon you to receive that gift knowing that there is nothing you could possibly do to earn or merit it. This is what God requires of every man and woman today. The requirement is faith. "*For by grace are ye saved through faith; and that not of yourselves: it is the gift of God: Not of works, lest any man should boast*" (Ephesians 2:8-10).

He came to save sinners. You must be a sinner to qualify for what He offers, so, admitting you're a sinner is a pretty good place to start. If in your pride you refuse, then good luck to you. The leaders in the divine religion didn't have the righteousness that God requires and I venture to say your righteousness doesn't even come close to theirs. You do share something in common with them, however. You refuse to acknowledge that you don't have the required righteousness and you are in need of it. So, you may join the religious crowd on the other side after all and spend eternity with the most religious of them—Satan.

If you are able to humble yourself and see yourself as God sees you, you then need to recognize that He came to *save* sinners. You are already under condemnation and Christ didn't need to come to give you more of that. Not only did He come for the purpose of saving sinners, but He is actually *able* to do it.

Do you have what most would consider to be a horrific background? Talk to the apostle Paul. "*Moreover the law entered, that the offence might abound. But where sin abounded, grace did much more abound: That as sin hath reigned unto death, even so might grace reign through righteousness unto eternal life by Jesus Christ our Lord"* (Romans 5:20,21). Not only was Paul involved in murder, he made it his job to persecute and kill God's people who dared to proclaim the name of Christ. Trust me, if the Lord could forgive Saul of Tarsus, He can most certainly forgive you.

However, this offer is for a limited time only. The current program with the Gentiles will come to a close and your prospects for winning the prize will greatly decrease. That is putting it very lightly. I encourage you to seek the Lord in prayer. Be honest with Him. If you question His existence, tell Him about it. Maybe yours is a cry of, "Lord I believe, help thou mine unbelief." That's fine. Just call on Him. If you sincerely come to Him for answers and are honest in your requests, He will open your heart and begin to perform a work that you cannot even understand. You might then find that you are able to see. Things might begin to seem a little less dark. He is waiting. If you ask Him to guide you in your blindness He will.

"Therefore seeing we have this ministry, as we have received mercy, we faint not; But have renounced the hidden things of dishonesty, not walking in craftiness, nor handling the word of God deceitfully; but by manifestation of the truth commending ourselves to every man's conscience in the sight of God. But if our gospel be hid, it is hid to them that are lost: In whom the god of this world hath blinded the minds of them which believe not, lest the light of the glorious gospel of Christ, who is the image of God, should shine unto them. For we preach not ourselves, but Christ Jesus the Lord; and ourselves your servants for Jesus' sake. For God, who commanded the light to shine out of darkness, hath shined in our hearts, to give the light of the knowledge of the glory of God in the face of Jesus Christ" (2 Corinthians 4:1-6).

I hope this book has contributed to giving you a better appreciation for the Word of God and His plans and purposes in the affairs of men. My objective in setting forth the material you have before you is not that you blindly agree with my understanding of Scripture. I do not desire that you simply are able to spout off by rote a particular set of doctrines or teachings. That does very little for the edification of your soul and has unfortunately contributed greatly to a neglect on the part of individual believers to seriously delve into the Scriptures themselves to discover what God actually teaches on the pages of His Word.

Simply believing in a pre-trib rapture or whatever because that is what you have been taught, or simply listing what can often be shallow reasons upon which to build doctrine is not taking advantage of the great reservoir you have been given from which to draw great understanding from the treasures of God's wisdom.

As a true believer in the Lord Jesus Christ, you have been given the precious Holy Spirit and the mind of Christ so you may know these things (1 Corinthians 2:1-16). God's desire is that you appreciate with Him all that He has accomplished, all that He is doing and all that He will yet do in the working out of the grand plans and purposes of His will. "*Now unto the King eternal, immortal, invisible, **the only wise God,** be honour and glory for ever and ever. Amen*" (1 TImothy 1:17).

What we have discussed in this book is only one small part of the many facets of the wisdom of God. But all of the many riches of God are connected in some marvelous ways and I hope that has been demonstrated in some small way by this work. God willing, there are yet many of His treasures of which I would like to speak, but if our plans should be interrupted then, "*...Having a desire to depart, and to be with Christ; which is far better*" (Philippians 1:23).

"*...And how ye turned to God from idols to serve the living and true God; And to wait for his Son from heaven, whom he raised from the dead, even Jesus, which delivered us from the wrath to come*" (1 Thessalonians 1:9,10).

TO GOD BE THE GLORY

To God be the glory—great things He hath done.
So loved He the world that He gave us His Son,
Who yielded His life an atonement for sin,
And opened the Lifegate that all may go in.

O perfect redemption, the purchase of blood,
To ev'ry believer the promise of God!
The vilest offender who truly believes,
That moment from Jesus a pardon receives.

Great things He hath taught us, great things He hath done,
And great our rejoicing through Jesus, the Son;
But purer, and higher, and greater will be
Our wonder, our transport, when Jesus we see.

Refrain:
Praise the Lord, praise the Lord,
Let the earth hear His voice!
Praise the Lord, praise the Lord,
Let the people rejoice!
O come to the Father, thro' Jesus, the Son,
And give Him the glory—great things He hath done.
                                        —Fanny J. Crosby

Shavuot

The Feast of Pentecost,
The Last Days
&

Repentance to Israel

I t should be clear by this point that in my understanding the biblical feasts are not a part of God's dealings in this mystery program. Therefore, they are not directly related to the Body of Christ but are wholly intended for Israel and the nations just as they are declared to be. In fact, of the feasts, only Succot is uniquely considered to be specially related to the nations. There is much Pauline truth concerning the mystery that is often read back into the Gospels and early chapters of Acts. But such should not be the case, and failure to rightly divide on this point will bring about error. We do have a relationship to the things in Israel's program, as we do Christ, but it is according to the mystery and is doctrinally different. Pentecost is wholly a part of the prophetic program. It is not the birthday of the Body of Christ or of any church, even in Israel's program.

God did not begin a new program at Pentecost, let alone the mystery. Here you supposedly have the beginning of this grand new entity about which God had said nothing before and yet it is a huge issue of prophecy in Israel's program. John the Baptist points to it as being significant to the nation as the climactic stage in the program has arrived. The Lord Himself all throughout the Gospels will speak of this event to come as the program moves on in His absence. I believe most of the confusion comes from a failure to recognize the distinction between the little flock in Israel's program—the Israel of God which constitutes the righteous remnant—versus the Body of Christ which is part of the mystery purpose of God.

In support of the contention that the Body of Christ began at Pentecost, some point to the conversion of Saul of Tarsus. "*And he fell to the earth, and heard a voice saying unto him, Saul, Saul, why persecutest thou me?*" (Acts 9:4). It is said that because the Lord says "me" that what Saul is persecuting is the Body of Christ. Let us briefly look at what the Lord said in connection with His judgement of the nations after His return.

"*And the king shall answer and say unto them, Verily I say unto you, Inasmuch as ye have done it unto the least of these my brethren, ye have done it unto me…Then shall he answer them, saying, Verily I say unto you, Inasmuch as ye did it not unto the least of these, ye did it not to me*" (Matthew 25:40,45).

The Lord had already spoken to His little flock about this.

"*He that receiveth you receiveth me, and he that receiveth me receiveth him that sent me. He that receiveth a prophet in the name of a prophet shall receive a prophet's reward; and he that receiveth a righteous man in the name of a righteous man shall receive a righteous man's reward. And whosoever shall give to drink unto one of these little ones a cup of cold water only in the name of a disciple, verily I say unto you, he shall in no wise lose his reward*" (Matthew 10:40-42).

Most people who understand the mystery nature of the Body of Christ, or consider themselves to be at least somewhat dispensational, do not believe that these references are to the Body of Christ but rather to the tribulation saints and those belonging to Israel's program. If you believe they refer to the Body of Christ, that is one thing and at least you are consistent. But if you don't—

and I count myself in that camp—then the fact is that what is said to Saul does not mean he was persecuting the Body of Christ. It means that the Lord is being sure to point out to you that Saul is persecuting the same group of saints the Lord had already spoken about. And if those verses in the Gospels, as well as other passages, refer to the Body of Christ then there is no need to raise up Paul as an apostle and be downright deceptive by having him say that he is revealing mystery truth and something that had never been revealed before. If what many commentators say is true, then there was absolutely no need to raise up Paul as that truth was already well spelled out before him.

Saul most certainly did persecute God's church which was in existence before Acts 9—or even Acts 2 for that matter. But the point is that he is raised up to declare that God is now doing something new. If you are a member of God's church today, you are not saved according to Israel's program like the twelve apostles, little flock, tribulation saints, etc. God has temporarily suspended His program with Israel and if you are saved today you are a member of the church *which is His Body*. You are saved in accordance with the mystery purpose of God and according to the program He has ushered in to accomplish it. It is because of what God is and is not doing today that you need to understand the ministry of the apostle Paul and rightly divide the word of truth.

According to the prophetic program, there was to be three baptisms for the cleansing of the nation Israel as it entered the climactic stage in the program. This was a *national* issue and was a part of the contract that they had entered into with God. At a particular time in the Fifth Course of Punishment, namely the fourth installment, the nation was going to be called on to offer a historical and national repentance in light of the kingdom of heaven and the promises of the Abrahamic Covenant being at hand. "*If they shall confess their iniquity, and the iniquity of their fathers, with their trespass which they trespassed against me, and that also they have walked contrary unto me; And that I also have walked contrary unto them, and have brought them into the land of their enemies; if then their uncircumcised hearts be humbled, and they then accept of the punishment of their iniquity"* (Leviticus 26:40,41).

A particular confession concerning the nation was going to be required of the nation. This issue then gets built upon throughout the rest of the Scriptures. This is why John the Baptist comes with his message preaching the baptism of repentance. This water baptism was not just some peripheral issue for the nation but John actually preaches the *baptism* of repentance and the Holy Spirit points to him in scripture as John *the Baptist*. Water baptisms were part of the ordinances of the Law and the idea that the water baptism of the Lord and the twelve is something different than that of John is simply not true.

It is the continuation of the prescription that had been laid out in Scripture for the nation as the Day of the Lord was approaching. *"And I knew him not: but that he should be manifest to Israel, therefore am I come baptizing with water"* (John 1:31).

This was the first step in the cleansing process for Israel as the separation out from the apostate nation took place and the Day of the Lord approached. *"And saying, Repent ye: for the kingdom of heaven is at hand...But when he saw many of the Pharisees and Sadducees come to his baptism, he said unto them, O generation of vipers, who hath warned you to flee from* **the wrath to come?** *And think not to say within yourselves, We have Abraham to our father: for I say unto you, that God is able of these stones to raise up children unto Abraham. And now also* **the axe is laid unto the root of the trees:** *therefore every tree which bringeth not forth good fruit is hewn down, and cast into the fire. I indeed baptize you with water unto repentance: but he that cometh after me is mightier than I, whose shoes I am not worthy to bear: he shall baptize you with* **the Holy Ghost, and with fire.** *Whose fan is in his hand, and he will thoroughly* **purge** *his floor, and gather his wheat into the garner; but he will burn up the chaff with unquenchable fire"* (Matthew 3:1,7-12).

The time had come when Messiah would begin to purge out the rebellious ones in the nation, and prepare His own to be able to endure the fiery trial to come upon the earth. The arrival of all this had come and the next baptism would prepare them in some unique ways. "*And behold, I send the promise of my Father upon you: but tarry ye in the city of Jerusalem, until ye be endued with power from on high*" (Luke 24:49).

Many of these powers can be found in Mark 16. Messiah is going to depart and the Holy Spirit will come and begin to testify with the twelve about some particular things. This is where it is crucial to understand that Israel and her program are not set aside at the cross. The cross was by no means an obstacle to receiving the promises but rather was the very thing that would bring about their fulfillment. That act of crucifixion was not going to be held against them.

The Lord had already said something significant concerning this subject. "*He that is not with me is against me; and he that gathereth not with me scattereth abroad. Wherefore I say unto you, All manner of sin and blasphemy **shall be forgiven** unto men: but **the blasphemy against the Holy Ghost** shall not be forgiven unto men. And whosoever speaketh a word against the Son of man, **it shall be forgiven** him: but whosoever speaketh **against the Holy Ghost**, it shall **not be forgiven** him, neither in this world, neither in the world to come*" (Matthew 12:30-32).

The Father had been testifying to them through His prophets all throughout the Old Testament. They had rejected Him and stoned His prophets. Now the Son was in their midst and they were going to reject and kill Him as well, but that would be forgiven them. They would still have an opportunity to repent, join the remnant, and be provided for in that Day of Wrath. In accordance with this the Lord declared from the cross, "*Father, forgive them; for **they know not** what they do*" (Luke 23:34). After Christ was raised and had gone back to the Father, the Holy Spirit would then come and testify to the nation.

"*...An evil and adulterous generation seeketh after a sign; and there shall no sign be given to it, but the sign of the prophet Jonas: For as Jonas was three days and three nights in the whale's belly; so* *shall the Son of man be three days and three nights in the heart of the earth"* (Matthew 12:39,40).

The resurrection was to be a sign to them and they were going to be given the opportunity to respond to it (see Acts 1–7). The Holy Spirit came and began to witness with the twelve about the resurrection. The signs of the coming kingdom are once again put on display as the remnant conducts themselves as the firstfruits of the coming harvest. The nation is handed an indictment and for those who had remained obstinate and rebellious, the hour of decision had come.

*"But ye denied the Holy One and the Just, and desired a murderer to be granted unto you; And killed the Prince of life, whom God hath raised from the dead; **whereof we are witnesses**…And now, brethren, I wot that **through ignorance** ye did it, as did also your rulers. **But** those things, which God before had shewed by the mouth of all his prophets, that Christ should suffer, he hath so fulfilled. **Repent ye therefore,** and be converted, that your sins may be blotted out, when the times of refreshing shall come from the Lord; And he shall send Jesus Christ, which before was preached unto you: Whom the heavens must receive until the times of restitution of all things, which God hath spoken by the mouth of all his holy prophets since the world began. For Moses truly said unto the fathers, A prophet shall the Lord your God raise up unto you of your brethren, like unto me; him shall ye hear in all things whatsoever he shall say unto you. And it shall come to pass, that every soul, which will not hear that prophet, shall be **destroyed from among the people**. Yea, and all the prophets from Samuel and those that follow after, as many as have spoken, have likewise foretold **of these days"*** (Acts 3:14,15,17-24).

*"The God of our Fathers raised up Jesus, whom ye slew and hanged on a tree. Him hath God exalted with his right hand to be a Prince and a Saviour, for **to give repentance to Israel,** and forgiveness of sins. And we are his witnesses of these things; and so is also the Holy Ghost, whom God hath given to them that obey him"* (Acts 5:30-32).

And in accordance with that prophetic program, they were called upon to respond positively to the indictment against them and believe a particular message. *"Now when they heard this, they were pricked in their heart, and said unto Peter and to the rest of the apostles, Men and brethren, what shall we do? Then Peter said unto them, **Repent**, and **be baptized** every one of you in the name of Jesus Christ for the remission of sins, and **ye shall receive** the gift of the Holy Ghost. For the promise is unto you, and to your children, and to all that are afar off, even as many as the Lord our God shall call. And with many other words did he testify and exhort, saying, **Save yourselves** from this untoward generation....And they continued steadfastly in the apostles' doctrine and fellowship"* (Acts 2:37-40, 42).

Again, we are not in view here as that promise had *not* been made to us. Also notice that water baptism was not an option, it was mandatory. Daniel puts this issue on display when he as a fore-type offers the national confession that would be required of Israel.

*"**We** have sinned, and have committed iniquity, and have done wickedly, and have rebelled, even by departing from thy precepts and from thy judgements: Neither have we hearkened unto thy servants the prophets, which spake in thy name to our kings, our princes, and our fathers, and to all the people of the land. O Lord, righteousness belongeth unto thee, but unto us confusion of faces, as at this day; to the men of Judah, and to the inhabitants of Jerusalem, and unto **all Israel**, that are near, and that are far off, through all the countries whither thou hast driven them, because of their trespass that they have trespassed against thee"* (Daniel 9:5-7).

I hope it is clear that the blasphemy against the Holy Ghost is what is recorded in Acts 1–7. It is an historical event dealing with the nation Israel and couldn't be committed by you today, no matter how hard you tried. Because they did it in ignorance there would still be an opportunity for them to escape the coming judgment. If what they had done was considered to be intentional, they would have had no remedy. (See Numbers 26:9-34 and the cities of refuge for more details on this.) They had been enlightened by the ministry of witness and signs in Acts 1–7 and, no longer being in ignorance, their continued rebelliousness would not be forgiven.

"*For it is **impossible** for those who were once **enlightened**, and have **tasted** of the heavenly gift, and were made partakers of the Holy Ghost, And have tasted the good word of God, and **the powers of the world to come**, If they shall fall away, to renew them again to repentance; seeing **they crucify** to themselves the Son of God **afresh**, and put him to an open shame…But that which beareth thorns and briers is rejected, and is nigh unto cursing: whose end is to be **burned**"* (Hebrews 6:4-6,8).

The water and the spirit are the first two baptisms and are required if one is to have any hope when the last baptism, the baptism of fire, begins to be applied to the nation. That is the end of the prophetic program and that is where Israel stood in the early chapters of Acts. Peter had officially declared to the nation that the last days had commenced.

Concerning the events of Pentecost the Scripture declares, "*And they were all amazed, and were in doubt, saying one to another, What meaneth this? Others **mocking** said, these are full of new wine. But Peter, standing up with the eleven, lifted up his voice, and said unto them, Ye men of Judaea, and all ye that dwell at Jerusalem, be this known unto you, and hearken to my words: For these are not drunken, as ye suppose, seeing it is but the third hour of the day. But **this is that** which was spoken by the prophet Joel; And it shall come to pass **in the last days**, saith God, I will pour out my Spirit upon all flesh…and on my servants and on my handmaids I will pour out **in those days** of my Spirit; and they shall prophesy: And I will shew wonders in heaven above, and signs in the earth beneath; blood, and fire, and vapour of smoke: The sun shall be turned to darkness, and the moon into blood, before that **great and notable** day of the Lord come. And it shall come to pass, that whosoever shall call on **the name** of the Lord shall be saved*" (Acts 2:12-21).

In the above verses Peter gives the scope of the last days from the very beginning with Pentecost to the very end with the return of the Lord at His great and terrible day on Rosh HaShanah. The message was that the baptism of fire is coming. If you want to be saved from the destruction that will come upon the apostate nation, submit to the water baptism of repentance, being converted in your thinking about what God has said and receive the baptism with the Holy Spirit. The message is one of fear in light of the coming Day of the Lord.

"Therefore being exalted, and having received of the Father the promise of the Holy Ghost, he hath shed forth this, which ye now see and hear. For David is not ascended into the heavens: but he saith himself, The LORD said unto my Lord, Sit thou on my right hand, until I make thy foes thy footstool. Therefore let all the house of Israel know assuredly, that God hath made that same Jesus, whom ye have crucified, both Lord and Christ" (Acts 2:33-36).

Now, if you are one of those foes, what might your response be? *"When they heard this, they were pricked in their heart, and said unto Peter and to the rest of the apostles, Men and brethren, what shall we do?"* (Acts 2:37).

Smart move. God might just be able to help you. *"Then Peter said unto them, Repent, and be baptized every one of you in the name of Jesus Christ for the remission of sins, and ye shall receive the gift of the Holy Ghost. For the promise is unto you..."* (Acts 2:38,39. See also Matthew 21:33-46.).

Let us briefly look at a few parables to further confirm this issue of repentance to Israel and substantiate that these are the last days of Israel's program, not the first days of God's mystery program with the Body of Christ. Remember, the issue is the coming Day of the Lord and the baptism of purging fire that will take place out there. When the Lord was on the earth He began to lay the axe to the root. He would call out and prepare His little flock and then have His Day during which He would swing His axe and the rebellious ones in Israel would be cut down and destroyed with the apostate nation.

"I tell you, Nay: but, except ye repent, ye shall all likewise perish. He spake also this parable; A certain man had a fig tree planted in

*his vineyard; and he came and sought fruit thereon, and found none. Then said he unto the dresser of his vineyard, Behold, **these three years I come** seeking fruit on this fig tree, and find none: cut it down; why cumbereth it the ground? And he answering said unto him, Lord, **let it alone this year also**, till I shall dig about it, and dung it: And if it bear fruit, well: and if not, **then after that** thou shalt cut it down"* (Luke 13:5-9).

The Lord sought fruit from that tree during the three years of His earthly ministry but found none. But, it was not to be cut down after the rejection of Him at the cross. They would be given another chance to respond in light of the crucifixion, and as we have seen, that is what is recorded in Acts 1–7. Only after that would He arise and begin to have His Day of Wrath.

*"And Jesus answered and spake unto them again by parables, and said, The kingdom of heaven is like unto a certain king, which made a marriage for his son. And sent forth his servants to call them that were bidden to the wedding: and **they would not come. Again**, he sent forth other servants, saying, Tell them which are bidden, Behold, **I have prepared** my dinner: my oxen and my fatlings **are killed**, and all things **are ready**: come unto the marriage. But they made light of it, and went their ways, one to his farm, another to his merchandise: And the remnant took his servants, and entreated them spitefully, and slew them. But when the king heard thereof, he was wroth: and he sent forth his armies, and destroyed those murderers, and burned up their city"* (Matthew 22:1-7).

This destruction is the same one spoken of in Matthew 24 that will take place in the Lord's Day. At that point the gospel of the kingdom will be preached unto all nations for a witness as described in the remaining verses of the parable. They will be bidden to the marriage and the great supper that will take place when the Lord returns. But please notice that it says "again" in verse 4 of the parable. First the Lord sends out His servants during his three years of earthly ministry. Then they get sent out *again*, only this time the message is that something has been killed and all things are now "ready." It is only after the cross that things are ready and only then that the kingdom can be "offered." (You also have this pre-cross bidding and post-cross bidding in Proverbs.)

Much can be gleaned from following the actions of this one named wisdom in Proverbs. Examine it and I think you will find that she parallels the conduct of Christ, the anointed One, when He began to testify to the nation in some very particular ways.

At a certain point in Proverbs we are told that "*Wisdom hath builded her house, she hath hewn out her seven pillars: She **hath killed** her beasts; she **hath mingled** her wine; she **hath** also **furnished** her table. She hath sent forth her maidens: she crieth upon the highest places of the city, Whoso is simple, let him turn in hither: as for understanding, she saith to him, Come, eat of **my bread**, and drink of the **wine which I have mingled**. **Forsake** the foolish, and live; and go in the way of understanding. He that reproveth a **scorner** getteth to himself shame: and he that rebuketh a wicked man getteth himself a blot...Give instruction to a wise man, and he will be yet wiser: teach a just man, and he will increase in learning*" (Proverbs 9:1-7,9).

As the Lord, wisdom sends out her maidens with an invitation, in light of the killing having been accomplished and all things having been prepared. I need not mention that the Lord also has *His* table consisting of *His* bread and the wine that He Himself mingled.

Let us look at one last parable that we have already examined in the discussion of rewards. "*And as they heard these things, he added and spake a parable, **because** he was nigh to Jerusalem, and **because** they thought that the kingdom of God should immediately appear. He said **therefore**, A certain nobleman went into a far country to receive for himself a kingdom, and to return. And he called his ten servants, and delivered them ten pounds, and said unto them, Occupy till I come. **But** his citizens hated him, and sent a message **after** him, saying, We will not have this man to reign over us...**But** those mine enemies, which would not that I should reign over them, bring hither, and slay them before me*" (Luke 19:11-14,27).

This message that they sent was the stoning of Stephen in Acts 7. It was the third opportunity given to them to repent. Stephen gives an official declaration to the leaders that Christ was standing at the right hand of God, signifying only one thing, the time for the fifth installment had arrived. Repentance would no longer be given to Israel and the Lord would begin to have His Day of Wrath.

But that day did not come. Rather, God would show forth all longsuffering and the vast extent of His grace by taking the number one persecutor of His people and raising him up as a chosen vessel to be the minister of a whole new program involving the mystery of Christ. With this man God would begin to form His one new man. Through the instrumentality of this Body *all* things will be under the headship of Christ and He will have the preeminence.

"*This is a faithful saying, and worthy of all acceptation, that Christ Jesus came into the world to save sinners; of whom I am chief. Howbeit for this cause I obtained mercy, that in me first Jesus Christ might shew forth all longsuffering, for a pattern to them which should hereafter believe on him to life everlasting. Now unto the King eternal, immortal, invisible, the only wise God, be honour and glory for ever and ever. Amen*" (1 Timothy 1:15-17).

Friends, this is all about the grace of God and Paul's apostleship. Over and over again the Holy Spirit will magnify Paul's office all throughout his epistles: "chief," "first," "pattern," "hereafter" and this is just in two verses. God began to do something with Paul. He was raised up to be the chief of a new administration that God was going to conduct, the one to which members of that new entity would look to be educated concerning their identity. Those instructions and that pattern are to be found in Paul's epistles, Romans through Philemon.

God would do something different with those who believed after Paul. There was a change in program. The pattern would be different. Nowhere are we instructed by Paul to be water baptized. As an ordinance of the law it has nothing to do with this program. Also, nowhere are we instructed that we need to do anything in order to receive a baptism from Christ with the Holy Spirit. We are told that having believed Paul's gospel, the gospel of the grace of God, we were baptized by the Holy Spirit into the Body of Christ. There is nothing but confusion to be had when one insists on laboring with God in something that He is simply not doing or engaged in.

Again, for Paul, simply preaching Jesus Christ was not enough. As chief, doctrinewise, Paul tells us exactly what we need for *godly* edifying which is in faith.

"*Now to him that is of power to stablish you **according to** my gospel, and the preaching of Jesus Christ, **according to** the revelation of the mystery, which was kept secret since the world began*" (Romans 16:25).

There is a wonderful unity when this truth is acknowledged and believers understand their identity as members of the Body of Christ.

"*I therefore, the prisoner of the Lord, beseech you that ye walk worthy of **the vocation** wherewith **ye are called**, With all lowliness and meekness, with longsuffering, forbearing one another in love; Endeavoring to keep **the unity of the Spirit** in the bond of peace. There is **one** body, and **one** Spirit, even as ye are called in **one** hope of your calling; **One** Lord, **one** faith, **one** baptism, **One** God and Father of all, who is above all, and through all, and in you all…that we henceforth be no more children, tossed to and fro, and carried about with every wind of doctrine, by the sleight of men, and cunning craftiness, whereby they lie in wait to deceive; But speaking the truth in love, may grow up into him in all things, which is the head, even Christ: From whom the whole body fitly joined together and compacted by that which every joint supplieth, according to the effectual working in the measure of every part, maketh increase of the body unto the edifying of itself in love*" (Ephesians 4:1-6,14-16).

It is interesting that the things the Holy Spirit addresses in the above passage are the very things that have caused so much division and confusion throughout the history of Christendom. He knew exactly what the tendencies of man would be in handling the Scriptures and has given us all the detailed instruction we need to be built up in the truth. In Israel's program there are many baptisms. In the mystery program there is only one.

And just so you don't think that perhaps "one" might mean a composite like the trinity, the Holy Spirit makes a point of listing each member of the godhead individually so you know that when He says "one" He means *one*. There is only one baptism today and it is the one performed by the Holy Spirit. When you believe that one message, you receive that one baptism whereby that one Spirit baptizes you into that one body. Having been baptized by the Spirit you belong to the only church that God has today, the church which is His body. If you are a member of that body, then there is only one denominational name that you are under or belong to—the name of Christ

"*For as the body is one, and hath many members, and all the members of that one body, being many, are one body: so also is Christ*" (1 Corinthians 12:12).

The Feast of Pentecost with its two wave loaves does not speak of Jews and Gentiles as the Body of Christ which is part of the fellowship of the mystery. As part of the prophetic program, Pentecost speaks of the remnant of Israel as the firstfruits of the harvest of the kingdom. The two wave loaves represent both houses of Israel.

After speaking of the ministry of the Spirit and the new covenant in Ezekiel 36, the Lord goes on in chapter 37 and declares, "*Moreover, thou son of man, take thee one stick, and write upon it, For Judah, and for the children of Israel his companions: then take another stick, and write upon it, For Joseph, the stick of Ephraim and for all the house of Israel his companions. And join them one to another into one stick; and they shall become one in thine hand. And when the children of thy people shall speak unto thee, saying, Wilt thou not shew us what thou meanest by these? Say unto them, Thus saith the Lord GOD; Behold, I will take the stick of Joseph, which is in the hand of Ephraim, and the tribes of Israel his fellows, and will put them with him, even with the stick of Judah, and make them one stick, and they shall be one in mine hand. And the sticks whereon thou writest shall be in thine hand before their eyes. And say unto them, Thus saith the Lord GOD; Behold, I will take the children of Israel from among the heathen, whither they be gone, and will gather them on every side, and bring them into their own land: And I will make them one nation in the land upon the mountains of Israel; and one king shall be king to them all: and they shall be no more two nations, neither shall they be divided into two kingdoms any more at all. Neither shall they defile themselves any more with their idols, nor with their detestable things, nor with any of their transgressions: but I will save them out of all their dwelling places, wherein they have sinned, and will cleanse them: so shall they be my people, and I will be their God"* (Ezekiel 37:16-23).

The Lord knew that this was going to be a major issue in the program when He gave Israel the feasts because the contract called for dividing the kingdom during the second course of punishment (Leviticus 26:19).

So, then, the Body of Christ by its very nature does not concern the Feasts and particularly Pentecost. Furthermore, the church that did exist at that time in accordance with the program did not begin at Pentecost. The little flock, the assembly of Psalm 22, was *added* to at Pentecost as those of the nation continued to separate themselves and respond positively to the repentance being given to the nation.

"And with many other words did he testify and exhort, saying, Save yourselves from this untoward generation. Then they that gladly received his word were baptized: and the same day there were **added** *unto them* **about three thousand** *souls. And they continued steadfastly in* **the apostles' doctrine** *and* **fellowship,** *and in breaking of bread, and in prayers"* (Acts 2:40-42).

As the firstfruits, they received the righteousness made available through the new covenant as ministered by the Spirit.

"Then Moses stood in the gate of the camp, and said, Who is on the LORD's side? Let him come unto me. And all the sons of Levi gathered themselves together unto him...And the children of Levi

did according to the word of Moses: and there fell of the people that day about three thousand men" (Exodus 32:26,28).

"Who also hath made us able ministers of the new testament; not of the letter, but of the spirit: for the letter killeth, but the spirit giveth life. But if the ministration of death, written and engraven in stones, was glorious, so that the children of Israel could not steadfastly behold the face of Moses for the glory of his countenance, which glory was to be done away: How shall not the ministration of the spirit be rather glorious? For if the ministration of condemnation be glory, much more doth the ministration of righteousness exceed in glory" (2 Corinthians 3:6-9).

So 3,000 die under the condemnation of the giving of the law, and 3,000 are given life at the giving of the Spirit. We, as members of the Body of Christ, have also been given the righteousness that is available through the New Testament. We have been given that righteousness, however, according to the mystery program. In order to be used by God for His plans and purposes He must first make us spiritually fit. That is true for the glory in Israel's program and that is true for the glory in God's program with the Body of Christ. That is why Paul in accordance with his apostleship was *separated* unto the gospel of God (Romans 1:1-7). That righteousness had been promised by God in Israel's program. The application of that righteousness in the mystery program was not.

If you want to look for the church in Scripture, you can find several and they are not hidden. If, however, you want to look for the Body of Christ, that is another matter. It is just what God has declared it to be, a mystery. Don't bother looking at the brides of the Old Testament which present a wonderful picture of the truths concerning the *prophetic* program. Don't bother looking at the Gentiles in the Old Testament which again present a marvelous display of the opportunity for Gentiles in Israel's program. Don't bother looking at codes, measurements and a host of other typological pictures and teaching tools which are all very relevant but are part and parcel of the prophetic program.

If you truly want to find the one new man in scripture, look for Christ. Wherever He is found in Scripture, that is where we may be located. We are not two loaves, or twelve loaves or any such thing. We are *one* new man. That means one loaf and one body.

"*For as the body is one, and hath many members, and all the members of that one body, being many, are one body: so also is Christ.*" You search for us in the prophetic scriptures but where do you look? "*And as they were eating, Jesus took bread, and blessed it, and brake it, and gave it to the disciples, and said, Take, eat; this is my body*" (Matthew 26:26). "*…The bread which we break, is it not the communion of the body of Christ? For we being many are one bread, and one body: for we are all partakers of that one bread*" (1 Corinthians 10:16,17).

Israel has twelve loaves, we have one. Christ most certainly loves with an everlasting love those who will be joined to Him whom He will dwell *with* in that earthly relationship of marriage. God has provided a relationship of union for this earth. But He also loves Himself, His *own* body, and between those two relationships He will fill all in all and *all* things will be under the *headship* of the Lord Jesus Christ (Ephesians 5:22-33).

There will be a great lack of appreciation for what God has recorded in His Word when we fail to rightly divide it and don't appreciate the revelation of the mystery committed unto the apostle Paul. There is nothing mysterious about what is going on in those early chapters of Acts and God had most certainly not set the nation aside and ushered in a whole new program. He is not dealing with the Gentiles there as he does today, and He is not forming His one new man there either. There is no need to run to Pentecost when you understand and appreciate all the glory and power that is available to us today.

"*Blessed be the God and Father of our Lord Jesus Christ, who hath blessed us with all spiritual blessings in heavenly places in Christ…And hath raised us up together, and made us sit together in heavenly places in Christ Jesus. That in the ages to come he might* *shew **the exceeding riches** of his grace in his kindness toward us through Christ Jesus...That he would grant you, **according to the riches** of his glory, to be strengthened with might by his Spirit **in the inner man;** That Christ may dwell in your hearts by faith; that ye, being rooted and grounded in love, May be **able to comprehend** with all saints what is the breadth, and length, and depth, and height; And **to know** the love of Christ, which passeth knowledge, that ye might be **filled with all the fulness of God.** Now unto him that is able to do exceeding abundantly above all that we ask or think, according to the power **that worketh in us,** Unto him be glory in the church by Jesus Christ throughout all ages, world without end. Amen"* (Ephesians 1:3; 2:6,7; 3:16-21).

Hallelujah, what a Saviour!

The Feast of Tabernacles

The Millennium,
The Second Sabbath after the First
&

The Lake of Fire

I f my understanding is correct, then there is also something else which is very special and significant concerning this "feast of the nations." The Feast of Tabernacles is not simply observed at the beginning of the Millennium. As we have seen, it marks the arrival of the long awaited joy and regeneration for earth that has been promised through the instrumentality of Israel finally fulfilling her role as that great blessing for the nations. At the heart of Tabernacles is the power over death and life that Christ has and its connection to the living waters that will issue out from the Lord's house. In furtherance of this concept read the Gospel of John.

However, this feast is also to be observed throughout the Millennium. While the kingdom *begins* at the start of the Millennium, it is to increase as Christ subdues all and the last enemy to be destroyed is death. (ICor 15:26). This victory over death is provided for the redeemed in God's program with earth at the first resurrection as we have already seen at the start of the Millennium. (Jn 11:25, 26).

However, there is still another resurrection to come where death and hell will be cast into the lake of fire along with all of the unbelieving and unredeemed dead of all ages. This is the second death, the resurrection of the unjust and will take place at the end of the Millennium when the absolute final house cleaning is accomplished.

It is my belief that the 8th day of the Feast of Tabernacles also looks forward to that event and is therefore specially identified in scripture as the *second* Sabbath after the *first*. The first resurrection took place on Daniel's 1,335th day, the 15th of Tishrei, the first day of the Feast of Tabernacles at the beginning of that glorious feast. The second resurrection will take place at the end of the Millennium on the second Sabbath after the first. It is at that time that Christ will deliver the fully accomplished and successful work that He was sent to do up to the Father. (ICor 15:28).

Amazingly, even after a thousand year demonstration of perfect, holy and righteous judgement and rule, there will still be those among the nations who harbor resentment towards Christ and His kingdom. They apparently learn little from their Millennial education under the instruction of Israel. The light and prosperity of that glorious city, the opened pit, the cemetery of Gog and the Babylonian prison of the damned were apparently not enough to change the hearts of these men as they traveled the Assyrian/Egyptian highway to worship the LORD of hosts.

Actually, this should not come as a big surprise. A perfect environment has never been enough to cause man to submit his will to the Creator. It was out of this ideal millennial state of affairs that Adam and Eve chose their will over God's. So, after a thousand years of this garden paradise, the serpent will once again make an appearance and offer that old familiar and ungodly temptation: "Ye shall be as gods."

If only they join the serpent in his rebellion, then they can overwhelm the city of the "oppressive" king, possess that mysterious tree and own eternal life for themselves. Rather than following the father of lies, they should have believed the words spoken by the one who is The Truth: "Ye shall surely die." If man refuses to humble himself and insists on hardening his heart, then God has absolutely no qualms about leaving him in his blindness to be carried away by every deception and temptation that desires to feed on his soul. I will say it again. If you aren't interested in humbling yourself before God, then He isn't interested in saving you. *"God resisteth the proud, and giveth grace to the humble. Humble yourselves therefore under the mighty hand of God, that he may exalt you in due time"* (1Peter 5:5,6).

God has no time for those that refuse the truth. If you are willing to sit at His feet and learn then He will gladly teach you. If you present yourself to Him as one in need of His grace and guidance, He is more than willing to meet you at your need. It's as simple as honestly recognizing who you are dealing with, the Creator Himself. He is truth and what He says therefore needs to be heeded.

The Lord positively hates pride. If you take refuge in your pride then you risk the danger of being left in your ignorance and vanity. The fact is that without God you don't know why you are here or what is going on in this universe. So you can either choose to believe what God says is the reality of the situation, or trust in your own imaginations. If you want to act like you are "big stuff" and "in charge," then that is how God will treat you, and hold you accountable accordingly. If you don't want to learn then He won't teach you. But that is a very dangerous predicament to be in because all is not well on planet earth. If that really is the Son of God hanging on that cross, then something is radically wrong in the universe.

There is a war on, folks, and without the blood of Christ atoning for his sin, a man is at enmity with God as long as He refuses to acknowledge his need for a substitute redeemer. The wages of sin is death. The cross of Christ speaks not only of mercy, but of God's judgement on sin. If you don't stand on the right side of that cross then beware! If your debt wasn't paid at Calvary, then you will have to pay it at the second death.

During the Millennium man has had his final opportunity to respond to God's graciousness. God will stand completely justified before all as man, even in those Edenic conditions, follows the path of rebelliousness. Only now, God has already repossessed this earth and there will be no long history of ungodliness following this rebellion. Christ had been commissioned to *subdue* all things and He will do exactly that.

"*And when the thousand years are expired, Satan shall be loosed out of his prison, And shall go out to deceive the nations which are in the four quarters of the earth, Gog and Magog, to gather them together to battle: the number of whom is as the sand of the sea. And they went up on the breadth of the earth, and compassed the camp of the saints about, and the beloved city: and fire came down from God out of heaven, and devoured them. And the devil that deceived them was cast into the lake of fire and brimstone, where the beast and false prophet are, and shall be tormented day and night for ever and ever*" (Revelation 20:7-10).

Never forget who is in charge. Don't these poor fools realize that Satan had to be *loosed* in order to do this? The only reason he is able to do anything is because God lets him. The serpent is truly the most pathetic creature in the universe because in all his attempts to thwart the plans of the Creator, he really does nothing but serve the purposes of God and bring about his own doom. This will be the hardest truth for Satan to swallow. In the end, the one who gloried in his own wisdom will be shown to be nothing but a fool. The Lord had given him one of the greatest privileges in the universe as the anointed cherub. Apparently that wasn't enough. His desire was to be like the Most High, but in all he does he could not be more *unlike* Him. Vanity and foolishness is the lot for all those who oppose the Creator and trust in their own wisdom. The fool fails to realize that anything he has was only made possible because of the Creator.

"*Behold, thou art wiser than Daniel; there is no secret that they can hide from thee...Thou sealest up the sum, full of wisdom, and perfect in beauty...Thine heart was lifted up because of thy beauty, thou hast corrupted thy wisdom by reason of thy brightness: I will cast thee to the ground*" (Ezekiel 28:3,12,17). "*To God only wise*"

(Romans 16:27). *"Professing themselves to be wise, they became fools"* (Romans 1:22). *"Be not wise in your own conceits"* (Romans 12:16). *"I will destroy the wisdom of the wise"* (1Corinthians 1:19). *"The wisdom of this world is foolishness with God. For it is written, He taketh the wise in their own craftiness. And again, The Lord knoweth the thoughts of the wise, that they are vain"* (1Corinthians 3:19,20). *"Now unto the king eternal, immortal, invisible, the only wise God, be honour and glory for ever and ever. Amen"* (1Timothy 1:17). *"To the only wise God our Saviour, be glory and majesty, dominion and power, both now and forever. Amen"* (Jude 25).

Man's probationary period has come to an end. God gives those on earth one more chance to take their rebellious stand and join their preferred leader. As the serpent slithers around God's kingdom to raise an army, he is doing nothing more than choosing his company for eternity. Sin and rebelliousness will be forever purged from this universe never to make an appearance again. With no more sin, there will be no more "wages" to pay (Romans 6:23). Death, therefore, will no longer be part of the human experience for any on earth.

Since the very beginning of Satan's rebellion in the angelic realm, this universe has been waiting for one particular event to take place. After the Millennium the time for that event finally arrives. Satan and his angels will be cast into the lake of fire that has been prepared for them and they will be accompanied by all those of the human race that have joined them in their rebellion against the Creator. God's gracious testimony to man has ended and after the second death there will never again be any question in this universe as to who is King of kings and Lord of lords.

With that event, we come to the end of the feasts and what God has revealed concerning His dealings with man. No doubt, there is much to be experienced and gloried in beyond this as we partake of the "dispensation of the fullness of times" (Ephesians 1:10). This is the privilege of all those that are counted among the redeemed in God's programs for this universe. Those of us who have humbled ourselves before Him and have been reconciled by the blood of Christ, will have the everlasting joy of serving Him in His reconciliation of all things. There will finally exist the harmony throughout creation that He had purposed for it from the beginning. The kingdom that had been established at the return of Christ will continue on throughout eternity and nothing will corrupt or defile God's creation ever again.

As wondrous as this will be for us, the greatest joy will be for the Lord Himself as He looks back upon the oceans of time and rests in the satisfaction of His strange, awesome and accomplished work. *"That in the ages to come he might shew the exceeding riches of his grace in his kindness toward us through Christ Jesus…For we are his workmanship, created in Christ Jesus unto good works"* (Ephesians 2:7). The glory that awaits us for that time is not revealed as those things are only to be known by His saints. The pleasures you have experienced here on earth do not even begin to compare with the unspeakable bliss that is the inheritance of all those that will enjoy the eternal fellowship of God through the Lord Jesus Christ.

"For after that in the wisdom of God the world by wisdom knew not God, it pleased God by the foolishness of preaching to save them that believe…But we preach Christ crucified, unto the Jews a stumblingblock, and unto the Greeks foolishness. But unto them which are called, both Jews and Greeks, Christ the power of God, and the wisdom of God. Because the foolishness of God is wiser than men; and the weakness of God is stronger than men. For ye see your calling brethren, how that not many wise men after the flesh, not many mighty, not many noble, are called: But God hath chosen the foolish things of the world to confound the things which are mighty; And base things of the world, and things which are despised, hath God chosen, yea, and things which are not, to bring to nought things that are: That no flesh should glory in his presence. But of him are ye in Christ Jesus, who of God is made unto us wisdom, and righteousness, and sanctification, and redemption: That, according as it is written, He that glorieth, let him glory in the Lord" (1 Corinthians 1:21-31). *"Who shall be punished with everlasting destruction from the*

*presence of the Lord, and from the glory of his power; When he shall come to be glorified in his saints, and to be **admired** in all them that believe (because our testimony among you was believed) in that day"* (2Thessalonians 1:8-10).

I pray that you do not find yourself at the second resurrection. There are no believers there. It is wholly for the unjust, the unbelieving, those who in their sinful hearts are at enmity with God. They have rejected His mercy and spurned His grace. They are cast into the lake of fire and never again will rebelliousness and sin plague this universe. If you have not been redeemed by the precious blood of Christ, the Lamb of God, the only worthy sacrifice, then that is where you will find yourself.

If you have not humbled yourself before Almighty God, acknowledged your sinfulness and helplessness, and trusted in Christ's cross work alone to deliver you, then that is the inescapable future you have to look forward to. The Lord Jesus Christ took the full punishment for your sinfulness so that you could stand justified before the HOLY God and not have to partake of the second death.

If you believe that, *"that Christ died for our sins according to the scriptures; And that he was buried, and that he rose again the third day according to the scriptures."* (ICor 15:3,4), then you can have peace with God. God's wrath has been pacified concerning you and your wickedness. As far as God is concerned, you already experienced that second death on the cross of Calvary some 2000 years ago (earth time). He no longer sees your sinfulness but only your Savior and *His* righteousness.

Your life therefore ought to be a sweet smelling sacrifice daily poured out to Him in thankfulness for this abundant mercy and grace that has been poured out for you. He gave His very Son for you! If you reject that then you had better fear. Because you know you are sinful and no matter how hard you try you will never measure up to God's holy standard. The only man who can claim acceptance with God based on his works is the God-Man, Jesus Christ. He *never* sinned, what about you?

Remember, the people at the second resurrection wanted to be judged by God based on their works. So they are. That is why they end up in the lake of fire with the other great religionists such as Satan. I thank God that the eternal life I possess is not based on my works and will never be judged so. I thank God that my sinfulness was judged on a wooden cross some 2000 years ago. Do you thank Him for that? Or are you trusting in your own righteousness to justify you before God? If so, then the lake of fire awaits.

My friend, Christ is not in the tomb. He is risen! And He's coming back! Are you ready? Praise God that you can be. Don't delay, trust Him today. Make sure today that your name is in the only book that will matter for eternity, the Book of Life. *"For what is a man profited, if he shall gain the whole world, and lose his own soul?"* (Mt 16:26). *"And fear not them which kill the body only, but are not able to kill the soul: but rather fear him which is able to destroy both soul and body in hell."* (Mt 10:15). *"For the wrath of God is revealed from heaven against all ungodliness and unright- eousness of men, who hold the truth in unrighteousness."* (Rom 1:18). *"And I saw the dead, small and great, stand before God; and the books were opened: and another book was opened, which is the book of life: and the dead were judged out of those things which were written in the books, according to their works...And death and hell were cast into the lake of fire. This is the second death. And whoso- ever was not found written in the book of life was cast into the lake of fire."* (Rev 20:12, 14, 15).

Appointed
Order Form

Postal orders: David W. Busch
P.O. Box 4266
Middletown, NY 10941

Please send *Appointed* to:

Name: _____

Address: _____

City: _____   State: _____

Zip: _____

Telephone: (_____) _____

Book Price: $19.95

Shipping: $3.00 for the first book and $1.00 for each additional book to
cover shipping and handling within US, Canada, and Mexico.
International orders add $6.00 for the first book and $2.00 for
each additional book.

Or order from:
ACW Press
85334 Lorane Hwy
Eugene, OR 97405

(800) 931-BOOK

or contact your local bookstore